THE ILLUSTRATED HISTORY ENCYCLOPEDIA

CIVILIZATIONS EXPLORATION & CONQUEST

D1296674

THE ILLUSTRATED HISTORY ENCYCLOPEDIA
CIVILIZATIONS EXPLORATION & CONQUEST

Charts the amazing progress of humankind, from the
Stone Age to the Space Age

PHILIP BROOKS • WILL FOWLER • SIMON ADAMS

southwater

CONTENTS

REACHING FOR THE FUTURE.....6–9

FIRST STEPS.....10

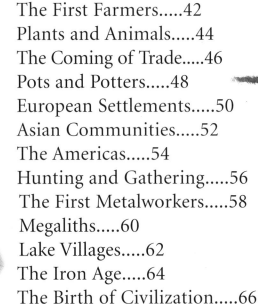

Introduction.....12
Finding the Evidence.....14
The Toolmakers.....16
The Coming of Fire.....18
The Spread of the Hominids.....20
Neanderthals.....22
Wise Man.....24
The First Europeans.....26
The Ice Age.....28
Images of the Ice Age.....30
The First Australians.....32
Early Americans.....34
The Thaw Begins.....36
A Better Food Supply.....38

Rock Paintings.....40
The First Farmers.....42
Plants and Animals.....44
The Coming of Trade.....46
Pots and Potters.....48
European Settlements.....50
Asian Communities.....52
The Americas.....54
Hunting and Gathering.....56
The First Metalworkers.....58
Megaliths.....60
Lake Villages.....62
The Iron Age.....64
The Birth of Civilization.....66

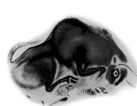

REALMS OF GOLD.....68

Introduction.....70
The Sumerians.....72
Ancient Babylon.....74
The Hittites.....76
The Assyrians.....77
The Persian Empire.....78
Parthians and Sassanians.....80
Islamic Empire.....82
Indus Valley Civilization.....84
Mauryan India.....86
Ancient Egypt.....88
African Civilizations.....92
Minoan Crete.....94
Mycenae.....96

The Etruscans.....98
Classical Greece.....100
Hellenistic Age.....104
Ancient Rome.....106
Early Dynastic China.....110
Qin China.....112
Han China.....114
Early Japan.....116
The Khmers.....118
North American
  Civilizations.....120
People of the Andes.....122
The Olmec.....123
The Maya.....124

CLASHING SHIELDS.....126

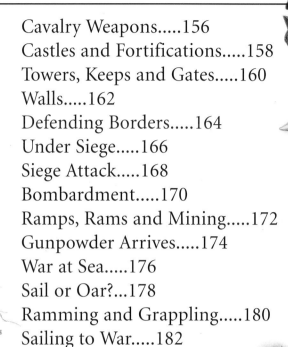

Introduction.....128

Clubs, Maces, Hammers and Flails....130

Axes and Throwing Weapons.....132

Slings, Bows and Crossbows.....134

Daggers and Knives.....136

Swords, Sabers and Scimitars.....138

Spears, Poles, Pikes and Halberds.....140

Ancient Firearms.....142

Armor.....144

Shields.....146

Helmets and War Hats.....148

Animals at War.....150

Horses in Battle.....152

Chariots and War Wagons.....154

Cavalry Weapons.....156

Castles and Fortifications.....158

Towers, Keeps and Gates.....160

Walls.....162

Defending Borders.....164

Under Siege.....166

Siege Attack.....168

Bombardment.....170

Ramps, Rams and Mining.....172

Gunpowder Arrives.....174

War at Sea.....176

Sail or Oar?...178

Ramming and Grappling.....180

Sailing to War.....182

JOURNEY WITHOUT END.....184

Introduction.....186

Egyptians, Phoenicians and Greeks.....188

Europe and Asia.....190

The Invasion of Europe.....192

The Vikings.....194

The Polynesians.....196

Crossing the Deserts.....198

The Chinese Empire.....200

Travelers in Europe.....202

The Portuguese.....204

Christopher Columbus.....206

Conquering the New World.....208

Around the World.....210

Into Canada.....212

The Northwest Passage.....214

The Northeast Passage.....216

Exploring Asia.....218

Advancing into America.....220

Across the Pacific.....222

Captain Cook.....224

Trekking across Australia.....226

The Amazon.....228

Deep inside Africa.....230

Livingstone and Stanley.....232

The North Pole.....234

Race to the South Pole.....236

Seas, Summits and Skies.....238

Blasting into Space.....240

GAZETTEER OF PEOPLE AND PLACES.....242

GLOSSARY.....248

INDEX.....252

Reaching for the Future

The study of history involves looking deep into ourselves and what made us. Our civilization today represents how far humankind has developed its ideas and abilities in a process that began with the first humans, or hominids, in prehistoric times. A look into humankind's development is a look into the processes that created the modern world.

The first people had to learn the skills that would allow them to survive, and then to make their lives more comfortable. By trial and error, they learned which plants and fruits were good for them, and how to make the weapons that allowed them to hunt animals.

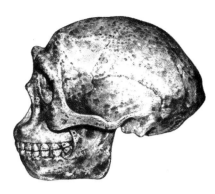

ERECTUS SKULL
One of the more recent ancestors of humans was *Homo erectus*. Its skull was wider and larger than that of its predecessor, *Homo habilis*, giving room for a larger brain. *Homo erectus* developed about two million years ago and was a skilled hunter.

A PLACE OF SHELTER
At Terra Amata, in southern France, there is evidence that hominids made a camp with simple shelters. These small huts were made out of tree branches, weighted down with stones.

Living in Groups

Family groups slowly grew, as larger numbers allowed people to live more safely. Cooperation allowed the development of special skills. For example, in return for weapons and other items, tool makers received a share of food gathered by other members of the clan and tribe.

Cooperation and experience led slowly to a better life. People began to make artistic efforts and spiritual searches. In time, roaming tribes of hunter-gatherers realized that they could plant seeds to provide better crops of vegetable foods. They also learned to herd animals that could later be slaughtered for food. This led to the first permanent settlements, which in turn encouraged social development.

UPRIGHT MAN
Homo erectus people looked very like modern humans, except for their ape-like faces. However, they were not as tall as most people today.

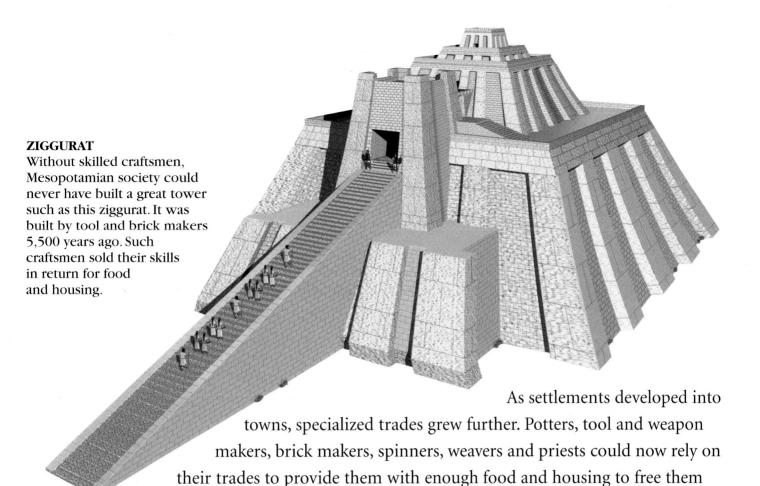

ZIGGURAT
Without skilled craftsmen, Mesopotamian society could never have built a great tower such as this ziggurat. It was built by tool and brick makers 5,500 years ago. Such craftsmen sold their skills in return for food and housing.

As settlements developed into towns, specialized trades grew further. Potters, tool and weapon makers, brick makers, spinners, weavers and priests could now rely on their trades to provide them with enough food and housing to free them from the need to hunt or farm. Trading between communities soon became more common and important.

Civilizations Develop

The process of civilization was gradually speeding up as villages developed into towns and then into cities. Rulers started to take over nearby regions and put them under their control. Civilization started at different times in various parts of the world. Some areas, such as the Great Plains of North America and some regions of the Middle East, Far East and Africa, did not develop civilizations because they could not be easily be farmed. The type of soil, the distance from water sources, whether the ground was high or low, and the climate, all affected the nature of the civilizations that emerged in any particular area.

In North Africa and the Middle East, great rivers such as the Nile in Egypt and the Tigris and Euphrates in Mesopotamia allowed the development of large and increasingly complex civilizations.

ATHENE
The Greeks believed in many gods and goddesses. Athene was the patron protector of Athens, and goddess of wisdom. The Athenians believed she brought the first olive tree to Greece.

ANCIENT GOD
Each civilization had its own spirits or gods, who ruled the spirit world. Neptune, shown here, was the ancient Roman god of the sea.

BATTERING RAM
Over the years, a vast array of weaponry has been developed. Rams were used to batter down fortress walls from c.500 B.C.

Natural barriers, such as mountains or deserts, limited the growth of some civilizations, such as the Greek city-states. By contrast, the landscapes of Central and South America were important in creating and defining the unique cultures that developed there.

Struggle and Conflict

A less welcome part of the spread of civilization was the growth of warfare. This grew out of the desire of rulers to take over a neighboring state or to gain control of a disputed area, a vital river or a region rich in agriculture or raw materials, such as timber or minerals. Ancient peoples did not generally think that war was reprehensible, and many civilizations gave their soldiers and generals a place of honor in their societies.

Warfare was one of the factors that spurred the development of technical skills such as metal-working. Soldiers saw the advantage of bronze weapons over copper and wooden weapons, and then the added strength of iron weapons over bronze weapons. As agriculture and trade led to major increases in the populations of the larger civilizations, the development of larger armies called for increased numbers of better weapons. This boosted technical skills and the race to find new sources of metals.

The Quest for New Horizons

Warfare, exploration and the constant search for raw materials developed as trade increased between countries. Progress continued even when the early civilizations disintegrated. The mighty Roman Empire was the last of these civilizations, and after its fall, there was a period during which a new world order took shape.

ROYAL NAVIGATOR
At the start of the age of exploration in the 1400s, Prince Henry of Portugal encouraged the study of navigation and supported many voyages of discovery.

Though many parts of the world lost some features of civilization, warfare and the urge to explore continued. New forms of warfare and weapons continued to develop as peoples such as the Vikings journeyed through and around Europe as well as west toward North America. The Chinese explored eastern Asia and the Polynesians roamed throughout the vast Pacific Ocean.

Exploration became a major force in increasing the wealth of many countries from the 1500s. The most important exploring nations were Portugal, Spain, England, France and Holland. These countries created trading networks that reached across the globe, all of which would have been impossible without the very strong tradition of sailing that they all shared. Within 100 years, explorers had created maps, sometimes accurate and sometimes not, of most of the world. After this time, explorers probed into the unknown territories of North and South America, Africa and Asia. The trader, the soldier and the priest followed in the footsteps of the first explorers. By the middle of the 1800s, most of the world had been mapped.

This was not the end of the exploration story, however, for there were many regions, such as the Amazon rainforest, about which people still knew very little. Scientists continue to discover more about the value of plants and to count the species of living creatures. Whatever the future brings, humans will continue to explore, as with the recent journeys to the moon.

IN A STRANGE LAND
The Spanish explorer Cabeza de Vaca lived for five years in the 1500s with Yaqui Native-Americans in what is now Texas.

TOP OF THE WORLD
Exploration has continued into modern times. Sir Edmund Hillary and Tenzing Norgay were the first to climb Mount Everest, the world's highest mountain, in May 1953.

FIRST STEPS

First Steps looks at the origins and development of humankind throughout prehistory. The first humans learned skills that allowed them to build shelter, hunt, grow food and eventually to establish settlements.

BY PHILIP BROOKS

Introduction

*F*IRST STEPS LOOKS BACK to the very beginnings of the human story. It starts at a time when people lived in caves and sheltered under cliffs, when the only tools were made of stone, when everyone had to hunt or forage for their own food, when clothes had to be made from animal skins. There were no cities, no large buildings, none of the comforts of modern life, and no one had worked out how to write. The term "prehistory" means the time before people were able to write their history down. Writing developed at different times in different parts of the world, so the date when the prehistoric period ended varies from one place to another. In Mesopotamia in South-west Asia, for example, writing came around 3000BC. In western Europe by contrast, widespread use of written scripts coincided with the Roman conquerors around 3,000 years later.

Prehistoric life can sound grim. Life was hard, travel must have been difficult, and many people died young without the benefits of effective medicine. Yet the period sees the beginnings of the very things that make humanity what it is today. Technology was simple, but it made possible amazing monuments like Stonehenge. Artists had only basic materials, yet they produced masterpieces on their cave walls. People cared for their

▲ HOMINIDS
The first human-apes appeared about four million years ago in Africa. They came down from the trees where they lived and began to walk on the ground on two legs. Scientists call them australopithecines.

▼ KEY DATES
How humans and human society developed in different parts of the world.

▼ CAVE ART
It seems that humans have always felt the urge for artistic self-expression. During the Ice Age, people lived in caves. Wall paintings from that time show people's skill in making their homes colorful and attractive.

	2–1 MILLION YEARS AGO	1 M.Y.A.–400,000 B.C.	400,000–30,000 B.C.	30,000–12,000 B.C.
AFRICA	Early hominids, the first human-apes, are alive in eastern Africa.	*Homo erectus,* a type of early human, use stone hand axes as a multi-purpose tool.	*Homo sapiens,* humans, appear in various places south of the Sahara.	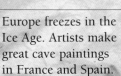
MIDDLE EAST & ASIA	*Homo erectus* is established in both Java and China, and has probably mastered the use of fire.		Neanderthals and "modern" humans are living side by side in Mesopotamia.	Rock painting
EUROPE		First known settlement of *Homo erectus* in Europe.	Neanderthals and "modern" humans are present, and may breed, but Neanderthals die out.	Europe freezes in the Ice Age. Artists make great cave paintings in France and Spain.
AMERICAS				The first settlement of North America begins as men and women cross the Bering land bridge from Siberia.

Skull of *Homo habilis*

Saber-toothed cat

M.Y.A.: Million years ago

▲ MAMMOTH SHELTER
Homes were built from whatever materials were available. Remains of mammoth bones suggest they were used to build massive shelters almost 10 feet high.

▶ FISH CARVING
After the Ice Age, food supplies were much better. Fish carvings found in Europe suggest that fish had become part of the staple diet.

sick, using medicines made from plants, and some illnesses were cured this way.

First Steps looks at prehistoric life all over the world. It begins with the origins of the human race in Africa and how people spread out around the world. It tells how people developed simple tools, survival skills such as hunting and food gathering, and the ability to make clothes and simple shelters. Gradually, human activities such as art, religion and ceremonies developed, signs that social groups were becoming more complex.

Next, *First Steps* shows the enormous progress made by early peoples, starting with the invention of pottery and the beginnings of farming, which helped men and women control their food supply. Trade then enabled more people to travel and new ideas to spread around the world. The next "revolution" was when people learnt how to use metals, by working copper, making bronze and smelting iron. Finally came the invention of writing, the development of large cities and societies, and the end of the prehistoric period. Throughout this period, people overcame tremendous obstacles, such as the huge climate changes of an Ice Age.

▼ WATCHTOWER
Eventually people began building permanent settlements. The walled city of Jericho dates from about 7000 B.C. and is one of the earliest cities discovered so far. It had watchtowers like this one, which were more than 30 feet high.

12,000–9000 B.C.	9000–6000 B.C.	6000–4000 B.C.	4000–2000 B.C.	2000 B.C.–A.D. 1
Japanese pot	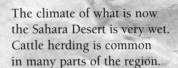 Auroch, an early bull	The climate of what is now the Sahara Desert is very wet. Cattle herding is common in many parts of the region.	Cuneiform writing from Mesopotamia	
The dog is domesticated in the Middle East. The first pottery is produced in Japan.	Farming is established in the Fertile Crescent.	Trading towns such as Çatal Hüyük, Turkey, begin to develop.	Potter's wheel invented; bronze-working begins; writing develops. Cities built in Mesopotamia.	
The great ice sheets begin to thaw as temperatures increase. Sea levels rise.	 Clovis points	Farming spreads to eastern Europe, probably from Turkey.	Stone circles and other megalithic monuments become common in western Europe.	First ironworking transforms tools and weapons.
People in Chile build houses from wood and skins—the first evidence of shelters in the Americas.	The Clovis culture: on the Great Plains people hunt using stone-pointed spears.	Cotton plant	The farmers of Mexico domesticate the maize plant. Other crops spread to North America.	The Olmec people of Mexico build the region's first large cities.

Finding the Evidence

▲ BURIAL URN
Some prehistoric peoples cremated their dead by burning the bodies on a funeral pyre. The ashes, and sometimes the bones, of the dead person might then be buried in a pottery urn like this one.

FINDING EVIDENCE ABOUT prehistory is like doing a gigantic jigsaw puzzle with most of the pieces missing. Often very little is now left of the prehistoric peoples who lived thousands of years ago. Archaeologists study every scrap of evidence they can find for clues as to how ancient peoples lived. Sometimes all that remain are a few bits of broken pottery, the foundations of some houses, or the occasional tool or weapon. Archaeologists have to learn what they can from fragments such as these.

Even when there is a big site—a stone circle, for example, or the remains of an ancient town—there are often more questions than answers. What were stone circles used for? Who ruled the first towns? How did people find out how to make bronze? Why did the cave artists paint their pictures? Questions like these still baffle archaeologists. The experts can suggest answers, but there are no certainties.

Graves can often give archaeologists some of the most fascinating clues about prehistory. They can be almost like time capsules. In many periods, it was the custom to bury a person with some of their possessions. Archaeologists call these items grave goods. These objects can tell us a great deal about the dead person's lifestyle, job, and wealth. They can also reveal something about the beliefs of the time. This is because grave goods were usually intended for use in the next world. Such finds suggest that people in prehistoric times believed in life after death. Some of the best evidence, though, comes from the bodies

◀ CHAMBERED TOMB
This type of tomb, common in prehistoric Europe, often contains several burials. These reveal a lot about ancient society. For example, the grave of a ruler or chief was usually treated differently than the others. It might be more carefully constructed or contain richer goods.

DEATH AND BURIAL
Archaeologists rarely know what they will find when they excavate a grave. There may be only a skeleton, or there may be lavish grave goods also. Whatever they find, it will probably be very fragile if it has been in the ground for thousands of years.

▶ GRAVE GOODS
Items in graves often reveal evidence about the spread of technology. For example, these grave goods from a cemetery at Varna in Bulgaria show that their owners had discovered how to work metal.

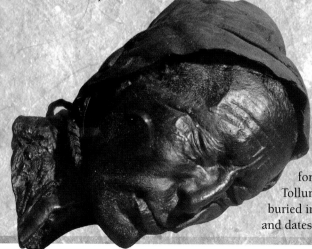

◀ TOLLUND MAN
Bodies buried in swamps and bogs are protected from the air. Skin, hair, and even clothing can be preserved for hundreds of years. Tollund Man was found buried in a bog in Denmark, and dates from about 251 B.C.

▲ PASSAGE-GRAVE BURIAL MOUND
Many passage graves, from around 3,000 B.C., have been found in northern Europe. A passage leads to the tomb at the mound's center.

themselves. By looking at a skeleton, for example, a trained observer can tell roughly how old the person was at their time of death and whether that person was male or female. It is also possible to measure how tall the dead person was and to determine quite a lot about build, physical development and strength. Often, archaeologists can find out about a person's diet by studying the teeth and doing chemical analyses of the bones. Sometimes they can even say why a person died, as some illnesses, such as arthritis, can be detected from the bones.

Studying the features and contents of an ancient grave can provide enough evidence to work out the approximate date when the person was buried. Factors such as the condition of the bones, the way the person was buried, and the type of grave goods that are found with the skeleton, can help to date the burial. How deep the body lies in the ground is also a clue. The deeper it is buried, the older it is likely to be. Archaeologists working in a vertical trench, for example, can often see layers of objects in historical order, from the oldest to the most recent, almost like a timeline.

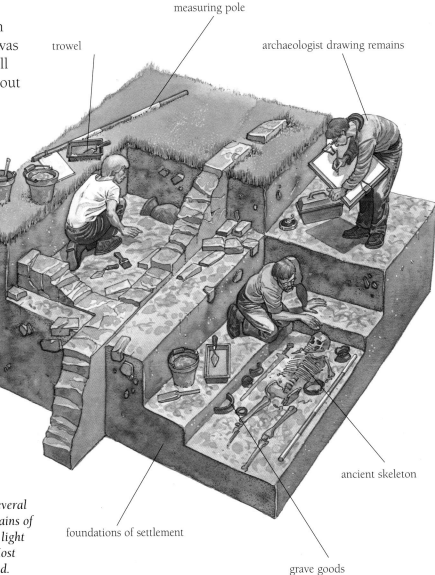

measuring pole

trowel

archaeologist drawing remains

ancient skeleton

foundations of settlement

grave goods

▶ ARCHAEOLOGICAL DIG
Archaeologists excavate an ancient site. They are working at several different levels. The skeleton is on an earlier level than the remains of the settlement above it. The archaeologists dig with care, using light tools, such as trowels and brushes, to avoid causing damage. Most importantly of all, they record in detail everything that they find.

▼ EXCAVATING GRAVES
Archaeologists have to be very careful when excavating dead bodies. This is not just because they are delicate. These are remains of real people, and they should be treated with respect. At this grave at Les Eyzies in France, archaeologists have worked slowly to remove the bones, which are at least 10,000 years old.

Dates and Dating

Prehistoric people lived thousands or even millions of years ago. However, because these people left no written records, archaeologists have to rely on other evidence to work out the dates of the remains they find. They have many ways of doing this, from studying the site of the find to using chemical analysis. Even so, nearly all the dates can only be approximate. The older the remains are, the less precise the dates are likely to be.

The abbreviations used with dates in this book are:

- M.Y.A. indicates "Million Years Ago." It is used for very ancient dates, a million or more years ago.

- B.C. indicates the number of years "Before Christ." Jesus lived 2,000 years ago, so you can work out a "number of years old" by adding 2,000 to a B.C. date.

The Toolmakers

▲ PEBBLE TOOL
Early hominids chipped away the sides of pebbles to make simple, sharp-edged tools.

PROBABLY THE BIGGEST prehistoric mystery of all is how the human race began. Many scientists think that modern humans evolved, millions of years ago, from creatures that looked rather like apes. They hoped to find a missing link, part-ape and part-human, between modern humans and our animal ancestors. No one has found this missing link. But palaeontologists (people who study fossils, the preserved remains of animals and plants) have discovered the remains of a group of creatures called early hominids. These are animals that share many features with humans. Hominids looked rather ape-like, and had smaller brains than modern humans, but they walked on two legs and could make simple stone tools. Our ancestors were probably rather like ancient hominids.

No one has ever found a complete skeleton of an early hominid. Often all that remains is a fragment of bone or a single tooth. Scientists have tried to find out all about the hominids from such meager evidence. However, they often disagree about which species of hominid a particular find belongs to, and how the various species relate to each other.

The earliest hominids, who lived in Africa between four million and 800,000 years ago, are called the australopithecines (southern apes). They stood and walked upright, but were shorter than modern humans, standing between 3 and 5 feet tall. Their bodies had a similar shape to humans', but their flat-nosed faces looked ape-like. Their brains were much smaller than human brains, but larger than those of today's chimpanzees and gorillas.

Australopithecines probably spent most of their time on the ground. Like modern gorillas

◀ *AUSTRALOPITHECUS ROBUSTUS*
Stocky and ape-like, this hominid probably spent much of its time living in trees, but it came down to the ground from time to time to search for food. Like the modern chimpanzee, it probably ate plants most of the time.

HOMO HABILIS

Since Louis Leakey discovered the first specimen of *Homo habilis* in 1964, many similar remains have been found in Africa—especially in the fossil-rich beds of Kenya and Tanzania. Although it is not certain whether these creatures are direct human ancestors, they are definitely our close relatives.

▼ PREDATOR
Early hominids had to guard against fearsome meat-eaters like this saber-toothed cat. Sometimes the best escape from dangerous animals such as this was to take to the trees.

▲ A LARGER SKULL—A LARGER BRAIN
Homo habilis had a much larger brain than the australopithecines, the southern apes. This was one reason why its discoverers decided that it should be included in the genus *Homo*, just like modern humans.

▼ A FIRM GRIP
Homo habilis had a hand that could grip objects firmly. This, together with its brain size, meant that the creature could make simple stone tools and may have been able to build basic shelters from tree branches and leaves.

pebble tool

simple brushwood shelter

and chimpanzees, they climbed trees to hide from enemies or to shelter from the rain. Remains of their teeth suggest that they ate mainly plants, plus a little meat. They probably also used the first simple tools.

In 1964, paleontologist Louis Leakey announced the discovery of the fossilized remains of a previously unknown hominid. It had a larger brain than the southern apes, so Leakey decided to place it in the genus *Homo*, the same as our own species. The fossil was 1.7 million years old, which makes it our oldest close relative. Stone tools were found near the remains, so Leakey named the fossil *Homo habilis* (handy man).

Like people today, the *Homo habilis* people probably ate quite a lot of meat, but no one knows whether they hunted animals for food or ate the remains left by other animals. Archaeologists have found remains of stone tools next to animal bones, such as simple choppers and hammers made from pebbles. They were probably semi-nomadic, staying in an area for a little while before moving on to a new area for food. When they moved, they left their tools behind.

Hominid uses its upright stance to gather berries.

▲ ROBUSTUS SKULL
The robust australopithecines had heavy skulls with massive jaws and strong ridges of bone across the brows. There were also flanges (areas of bone sticking out from the cheeks) on either side.

▲ AFRICANUS SKULL
Although Australopithecus africanus *had a more lightly built skull than* Australopithecus robustus, *it still had a heavy jawbone. No one is certain exactly how these two species were related.*

▶ "LUCY"
The most complete set of bones found belonged to a hominid that lived just over three million years ago. Archaeologists nicknamed it "Lucy." The bones show that it was a slim, possibly female, creature just over 3 feet tall. It weighed about 60 pounds and could walk upright. The slim build and upright stance suggest a more human-like creature than the other australopithecines.

▲ OLDUVAI GORGE
One of the most important hominid sites is Olduvai Gorge, on the Serengeti Plains in East Africa. Fossils of several hominids, including *Homo habilis*, have been found there, which makes this one of the great hunting grounds in the search for human origins. The gorge contains fossilized remains ranging from 100,000 to around 2 million years old, the older fossils embedded in the deepest rocks. Scatters of tools, from crude pebbles to stone axes, lie near the bones of their makers.

Key Dates

- 3.6M.Y.A. Southern apes are present in Laetoli, northern Tanzania.

- 3 to 3.75M.Y.A. Southern apes present in Hadar, northern Ethiopia. The most famous example is known to modern archaeologists as "Lucy," a member of the species *Australopithecus afarensis*.

- 1.8M.Y.A. Lake Turkana, Kenya, is home to various hominids, including australopithecines and creatures with larger skulls.

- 1.75M.Y.A. *Robustus* australopithecines live at Olduvai Gorge, northern Tanzania.

- 1.75M.Y.A. The toolmaker *Homo habilis*, the oldest known member of our genus, lives at Olduvai Gorge.

The Coming of Fire

AROUND 1.6 MILLION YEARS AGO, A GROUP OF hominids mastered a completely new skill. They learned how to use fire, which must have brought about a huge change in their lives. Suddenly, they were able to cook food instead of eating raw meat and plants. They could keep their drafty caves and rock shelters warm in winter. The heat and flames could even be used as weapons against enemies. Fire probably gave them a safer and more comfortable life than the earlier hominids had enjoyed. The hominids who mastered fire were about 5 feet tall. They had bigger brains and longer limbs than previous hominids, more like those of modern humans. Scientists called them *Homo erectus* (upright man). The *Homo*

◀ FIRE STICK
One way early people made fire was to put dry grass on a stick called a hearth. Then they rubbed another stick against the hearth to make a spark and set the grass alight.

FOOD AND RESOURCES

With their larger brains, *Homo erectus* people were probably better at hunting and finding new types of food than previous hominids. Their travels across Africa may have been to search for new sources of food. Besides hunting animals and gathering plants, they probably killed injured animals or scavenged meat left by other predators.

▲ HACKBERRIES
Gathering nuts and fruit, such as these hackberries, provided a large part of the diet of *Homo erectus*. They had to learn by trial and error which berries were good to eat and which were poisonous.

◀ WOOLLY RHINO
The *Homo erectus* people tried eating whatever meat they killed. They may have eaten large creatures like this woolly rhinoceros, hunting them in groups and sharing the meat.

▲ EAST TURKANA
Close to the mountains and lakes of Kenya, the site of East Turkana was one of the first homes of *Homo erectus* around 1.5 million years ago.

erectus people were more advanced in other ways. They made better tools than the earlier hominids and developed a hand ax, a pointed flint tool with two sharp cutting edges. Hand axes were useful for cutting meat, so the *Homo erectus* people could butcher animals more efficiently. As a result, they may have had more incentive to develop their technology—for example, creating smaller tools such as cutting blades.

Homo erectus people probably had more advanced social skills than earlier hominids. They may even have developed a simple language, which would have enabled them to talk to and cooperate with each other. This meant that they could perform tasks as a group, such as hunting large animals. They may have used fire in their hunting. Some archaeologists think that they lit bush fires to drive large animals into an ambush, where the creatures could be killed by a hunting group.

Fire also enabled them to survive in colder climates. This encouraged *Homo erectus* people to travel more widely than earlier hominids. Like *Homo habilis*, they were probably always on the move, making temporary camps as bases for hunting and gathering. Some of these homes may have been seasonal, occupied during the spring or summer when fruit, nuts, and leaves were plentiful. But *Homo erectus* people also traveled beyond their native Africa, and they were probably the first hominids to settle in Asia and Europe.

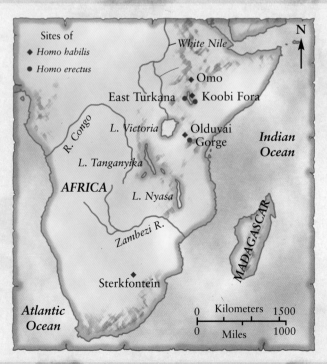

◀ *HOMO ERECTUS*
Cave-dwelling Homo erectus *people prepare to cook a meal in front of their cave. One member of the group makes stone tools, perhaps to cut up the dead animal; another tends the fire; and two children help an adult dismember the carcass before it is cooked on the hot fire.*

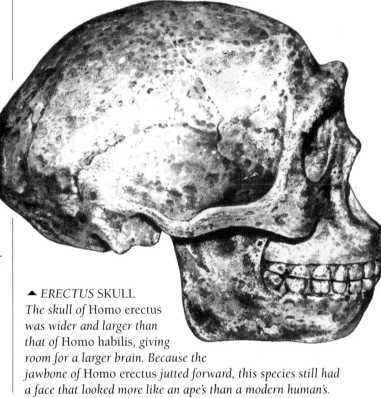

▲ *ERECTUS* SKULL
The skull of Homo erectus *was wider and larger than that of* Homo habilis, *giving room for a larger brain. Because the jawbone of* Homo erectus *jutted forward, this species still had a face that looked more like an ape's than a modern human's.*

Sites of
◆ Homo habilis
● Homo erectus

White Nile
N
Omo
East Turkana ● ◆ Koobi Fora
R. Congo
L. Victoria
Olduvai Gorge
Indian Ocean
L. Tanganyika
AFRICA
L. Nyasa
Zambezi R.
MADAGASCAR
Sterkfontein
Atlantic Ocean
Kilometers
0   1500
Miles
0   1000

◀ EARLY HOMINID SITES, EAST AFRICA
Most of the early remains of *Homo habilis* and *Homo erectus* have come from a cluster of sites in Kenya and Tanzania in East Africa. The structure of the rocks there has helped preserve these fossils. For example, at Olduvai Gorge, hominid bones and tools were left by the shores of a lake, later to be covered by mud and volcanic lava and preserved. Still later, geological faults caused the rocks to move, making the fossils visible.

Key Dates

- 1.6M.Y.A. The Pleistocene period begins. Animals such as horses, cattle, and elephants appear.

- 1.6M.Y.A. The earliest *Homo erectus* ever found comes from East Turkana, Kenya.

- 1.6M.Y.A. *Homo erectus* camp at Chesowanya in the Kenya Rift Valley. This shows possible evidence of the use of fire.

- 1M.Y.A. *Homo erectus* living in Olduvai Gorge.

- 500,000 years ago *Homo erectus* reaches northern Africa. Sites with evidence of *Homo erectus* have been found in Morocco and Algeria.

The Spread of Hominids

AROUND A MILLION years ago, the world's wildlife was on the move. Many tropical animals started to travel northward and eastward. Gradually, they moved away from the sweltering jungles toward cooler parts of the globe. Food was often difficult to find for the early hominids, so the *Homo erectus* people followed the tropical animals to places with more moderate climates. In doing so, they traveled great distances, from modern Africa as far as present-day Java, China, Italy, and Greece.

▲ A PLACE TO SHELTER
At Terra Amata, southern France, there is evidence that hominids made a camp with simple shelters. These small huts were made out of tree branches, weighted down with stones.

In Europe and Asia, *Homo erectus* people set up camps to which they returned year after year. One of the most famous of all is a series of caves at Zhoukoudien, China. Hominids stayed here for thousands of years (from about 600,000 to about 230,000 years ago), and archaeologists have found the remains of more than 40 *Homo erectus* people at the site. In the caves the archaeologists found a variety of tools, including choppers, scrapers, awls, points, and cutters, most of which were made from quartz. The more recent

in date the tools, the smaller and more finely worked they are. There is also evidence of fire in the Zhoukoudien caves. Similar remains have been found in *Homo erectus* sites in Europe and Southeast Asia. They reveal a people who gathered leaves and berries but were also cunning enough to hunt large mammals. The people moved around from one season to the next. If they could not find caves, they built simple shelters from branches and stones. They probably wrapped animal skins around themselves to keep warm in the winter.

One mystery is that many surviving *Homo erectus* skulls have had their bases removed. Some scientists think that this was done so that survivors could take out the brain. Perhaps these people were the first cannibals? There may be other reasons, such as to make containers to carry water.

Another puzzle is how *Homo erectus* died out. There are no *erectus* remains later than about 200,000 years ago. It is not known whether they perished because other hominids killed them, because their food supplies ran out, or because of ill health.

ANCIENT CULTURE

The *Homo erectus* people were able to produce a wider variety of tools, weapons, and other items than the earlier hominids, although the only objects to survive in large numbers are their stone tools. They were skilled flintworkers, creating implements with razor-sharp edges for butchering meat, cutting plant food, and scraping hides. They were probably also woodworkers, using wood to build simple shelters and make weapons such as spears and clubs.

◀ HAND AX
The double-edged stone tool was *Homo erectus*' most common and useful implement. It fitted comfortably into the hand and was easy to carry around. The two sharp edges could be used for cutting or chopping.

▶ PAINT
Stones marked with red ocher, a natural earth pigment, have been found at Becov in Bohemia, Europe. These finds date to 250,000 years ago and suggest that people may have decorated their bodies or items that they made. They may have mixed the ocher with fat to make a form of paint.

◀ UPRIGHT MAN
Homo erectus people looked much like modern humans, except for their ape-like faces. But they were not as tall as most people today.

▼ ON THE HUNT
A group of Homo erectus *people have worked together to trap three elephants in a swamp. They are now about to move in on one of the animals, to attack it with wooden spears and clubs.*

swampy ground

wooden spear

wooden club

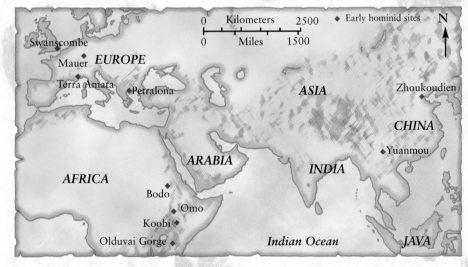

▲ *HOMO ERECTUS* SITES
This successful hominid spread from Africa to both Asia and Europe. In addition to sites in China, there are also many places in Europe with early hominid remains. In the case of most of the European sites, experts are uncertain whether the occupants were *Homo erectus* or an early form of our own species.

Swanscombe
Mauer **EUROPE**
Terra Amata
Petralona
ASIA
Zhoukoudien
CHINA
Yuanmou
ARABIA
INDIA
AFRICA
Bodo
Omo
Koobi
Olduvai Gorge
Indian Ocean
JAVA

0   Kilometers   2500
0   Miles   1500
♦ Early hominid sites
N

Key Dates

- 1M.Y.A. *Homo erectus* people are established in Olduvai Gorge.

- 1M.Y.A. *Homo erectus* invents the hand ax.

- 900,000B.C. *Homo erectus* is present in central Java. The hominids' long-distance movements show them adapting to different environments.

- 700,000B.C. *Homo erectus* reaches Ubeidiya, by the Jordan and Yarmuk rivers, Israel.

- 500,000B.C. *Homo erectus* settles in Europe.

- 400,000–230,000B.C. *Homo erectus* living at Zhoukoudien Cave, near Beijing, China.

Neanderthals

▲ CAVE WOMAN
Neanderthals like this female may have been the first hominids to care for the sick and disabled. This prolonged the lives of individuals who would otherwise have met painful early deaths.

A TYPICAL CAVE MAN IS usually portrayed as a stocky creature with heavy bones, a thick ridge across the brows, and a blank expression on his face. As far as we can tell, the Neanderthals, who lived in Europe and the Middle East 70,000 to 35,000 years ago, did look somewhat like this. They are our closest relatives among the hominids and were intelligent, with brains a similar size to our own. In fact, the Neanderthals were so similar to modern humans that some scientists place them in our own species, giving them a subspecies (*Homo sapiens neanderthalensis*). Others give them a species of their own (*Homo neanderthalensis*).

The Neanderthal people used their intelligence to develop tools and technology. Although their tools were still made of stone, they now had specialized items such as chisels and borers. They made these tools by chipping small flakes off carefully selected cores, or lumps, of flint. To chip off a flake of the right size and sharpness, a Neanderthal flintworker needed skill, patience, and a very great deal of practice.

Some of the most fascinating evidence about the Neanderthals comes from their burial sites. Several of these have been discovered, from the Dordogne, France, to the Zagros Mountains in Iran. They reveal the bodies placed carefully in their graves. Items such as animal horns or bones were deliberately placed around them, probably as part of a burial ritual. Sites like these have led modern archaeologists to believe that the Neanderthals were the first hominids to develop burial ceremonies. The burial sites also provided a great deal of evidence that enabled scientists to work out what these people looked like, from

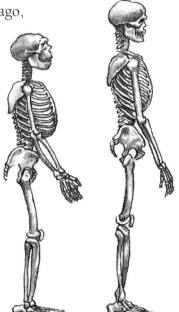

Neanderthal　　Modern human

◀ SKELETONS
Stockily built and with a large head, Neanderthals were strong hominids with brains about as big as our own. Modern humans were taller and more upright.

NEANDERTHAL LIFE

During much of the Neanderthals' lifetime, Europe and Asia were in the grip of an ice age. The Neanderthals had to adapt to the cold, making clothes from skins and finding whatever shelter they could. This necessity, together with their large brains, made them inventive and adaptable.

chopper

scraper

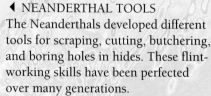
borer

◀ NEANDERTHAL TOOLS
The Neanderthals developed different tools for scraping, cutting, butchering, and boring holes in hides. These flint-working skills have been perfected over many generations.

◀ POLLEN GRAINS
By examining prehistoric pollen under a microscope, scientists have found that trees such as alder, birch, oak, and elm grew in areas in which the Neanderthals lived.

▲ NEANDERTHAL GRAVE
Skeletons from this grave at La Chapelle-aux-Saints in France, were found to be deformed and stooping. This could mean the people suffered from arthritis.

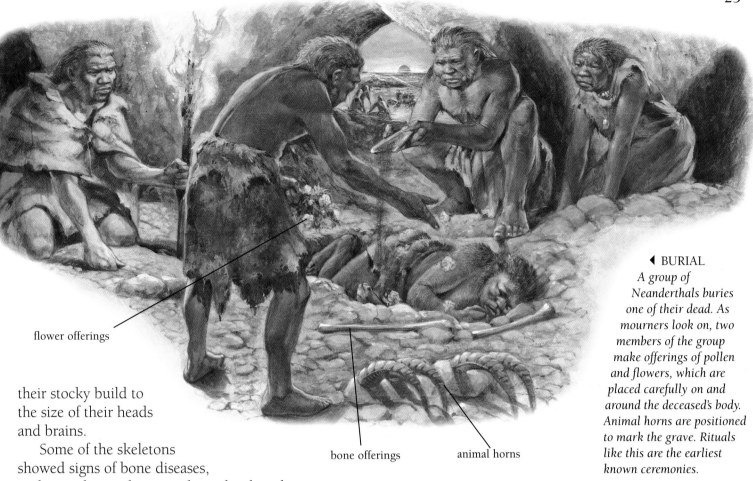

flower offerings

bone offerings

animal horns

◀ BURIAL
A group of Neanderthals buries one of their dead. As mourners look on, two members of the group make offerings of pollen and flowers, which are placed carefully on and around the deceased's body. Animal horns are positioned to mark the grave. Rituals like this are the earliest known ceremonies.

their stocky build to the size of their heads and brains.

Some of the skeletons showed signs of bone diseases, such as arthritis, that must have developed over many years. Any individual who developed such a disease would not have been able to hunt and gather food. Other members of their family group must have fed them and looked after them. So besides being intelligent, the Neanderthals may have been the first carers, helping relatives who were not able to fend for

themselves. The Neanderthals died out around 35,000 years ago, but it is not certain why. They may have perished through disease or have been killed by Cro-Magnons, *Homo sapiens* who lived at the same time. New evidence is now being found to suggest that Neanderthals interbred with Cro-Magnon people.

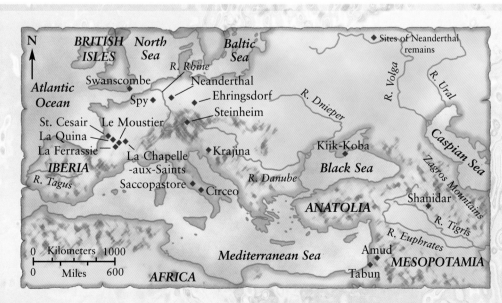

▲ NEANDERTHAL SITES
The homeland of the Neanderthals stretched from France and Germany to Mesopotamia in the east. The eastern and western populations were separated during ice ages, but both groups produced similar tools and buried their dead in a similar way.

Key Dates

- 120,000 B.C. Neanderthals living from Europe to Mesopotamia.

- 100,000–40,000 B.C. Neanderthals develop stone tools for several different purposes.

- 100,000 B.C. Neanderthals and *Homo sapiens* both living at Qafzeh, Israel.

- 50,000 B.C. Remains of a burial site of this date found at Shanidar Cave, northern Iraq.

- 40,000 B.C. Skull of this date found at Monte Circeo, Italy, had been smashed to remove the brain.

- 35,000 B.C. Neanderthals die out.

Wise Man

▲ FIRE
The discovery of fire by Homo erectus *was an enormous technological advance that* Homo sapiens *would have inherited.*

B Y THE TIME OF THE Neanderthals, members of our own species, *Homo sapiens*, or "wise man," were also living in many parts of the world. In some places, Neanderthals and humans lived close together, which suggests that Neanderthals could not have been our direct ancestors. If they lived together, we could not have evolved from both species. If this is correct, who were they?

Homo sapiens may have evolved from *Homo erectus*, or from another similar hominid that has not yet been discovered. Hominid bones, found in sites all over the world, seem to share features of *Homo erectus* and *Homo sapiens*. Although similar in size to ourselves, these hominids have bone ridges above the eyes and flattened skulls rather than dome-like heads. They date mostly from around 150,000 to 120,000 years ago and are classified by archaeologists as archaic *Homo sapiens*.

Some remains of *Homo sapiens* date from not long after these "archaic" bones.

◀ HUMAN FORM
The first members of Homo sapiens *were similar in appearance to modern people, except that they were generally somehat shorter. Their upright build made them well adapted to walking on two legs.*

▶ COUNTING STICK
Lengths of bone with small notches cut into them have been found at some Homo sapiens *sites. These may have been counting devices or an early form of writing. They may have been used to record a person's share of food.*

◀ EARLY HUMAN SKULL
Early humans had broad skulls that contained large brains. Their faces were flat, so they did not have the ape-like appearance of hominids like Homo habilis *or the Neanderthals.*

THE EARLY HUNTERS
The search for food was the most important part of life for early *Homo sapiens*. Some groups hunted herds of antelopes on the grasslands. Others went into the hills after wild sheep and goats or to the coast in search of seals and seafood.

◀ SEALS
For northern people who lived near the sea, animals such as seals were a valuable quarry. The animals provided a supply of meat, skins, bones (for tool-making), and blubber.

▲ BONE CARVING
Among the hominids, humans are the only artists. Early hunters liked to carve the creatures they chased, and animal bone was an ideal material—soft enough to carve but hard enough to last.

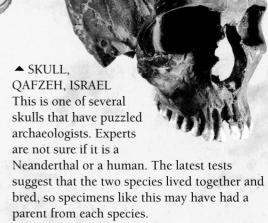

▲ SKULL, QAFZEH, ISRAEL
This is one of several skulls that have puzzled archaeologists. Experts are not sure if it is a Neanderthal or a human. The latest tests suggest that the two species lived together and bred, so specimens like this may have had a parent from each species.

Some experts think humans evolved in one area of Africa and then spread gradually across the world. This idea, which archaeologists refer to as the "Out of Africa" theory, is backed up by research based on DNA. This is the chemical in *Homo sapiens* bodies containing genes.

Other scientists believe that modern humans evolved separately in different parts of the world. For example, the population in Southeast Asia could have descended from *Homo erectus* people on Java. Europeans could have evolved from hominids from the Middle East that had interbred with Neanderthals.

By 100,000 to 90,000 years ago, modern humans had evolved in southern and eastern Africa. From here they traveled northward, crossing the Sahara and reaching the Middle East. For thousands of years the Sahara was wetter than it is today, and it was covered with grasslands cropped by grazing mammals. Hominids could cross this green Sahara with ease. By 75,000 years ago there were modern humans in eastern Asia. Later still, they would reach and settle in Europe.

As our ancestors spread across the globe, they settled in many different environments, from the warm African grasslands to the cold forests of northern Europe. They used their skills to adapt to each new place, using local materials to make clothes and huts, finding out about plants and animals, and learning how to fish. These early people were very advanced compared to many species.

▶ PREPARING SKINS
A hunted animal was not just a source of meat. The skins of larger creatures were removed, scraped clean, and trimmed. Then they were made into clothes, coverings for shelters, and simple bags and containers.

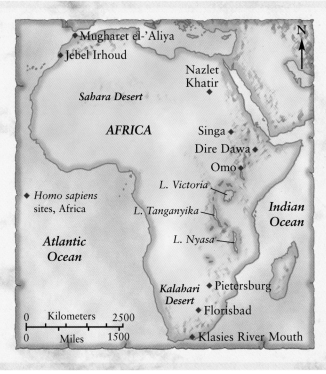

◀ EARLY HUMAN SITES
By 35,000 years ago, early humans had spread across most of Africa. They developed different lifestyles and tools to cope with the different conditions and materials that they found. The people of northern Africa, for example, produced quite finely worked flint scrapers and hand axes, similar to those made by the Neanderthals in Europe. In the south, however, many of the tools were much less finely chipped stone points and scrapers, but they were still sharp and effective.

Key Dates

- 150,000–120,000 B.C. Archaic *Homo sapiens*, the most ancient form of our own species, appears.

- 100,000 B.C. Modern humans begin to evolve in Africa.

- 100,000–70,000 B.C. African sites south of the Sahara show signs of modern human occupation. *Homo erectus* is still alive but is slowly replaced by *Homo sapiens*.

- 100,000–40,000 B.C. The Sahara is cooler than today. Hominids cross it to reach northern Africa.

- 75,000 B.C. Ice sheets in the northern hemisphere begin to get larger.

The First Europeans

▲ BISON CAVE PAINTING
When they discovered how to make colours out of earth and minerals, people began to paint pictures like this bison.

LIFE WAS HARD FOR THE first humans who lived in Europe. The climate was colder than it is today. Food could be difficult to find, and dangerous animals lurked in the forests. People survived by adapting and by becoming skilled at making things, such as tools and shelters. Slowly, over many thousands of years, they perfected the essential skills for survival.

The early Europeans are often called Cro-Magnons, after a site in the Dordogne, France. Cro-Magnon people kept themselves warm by making clothes from animal skins. They sheltered in caves when they could, but natural shelter was not always easy to find. They learned how to make simple homes, using whatever materials they could find. Tree branches provided a framework; this was covered with turf or animal skins to keep out the wind and rain. Another solution was to make a framework from the massive bones of woolly mammoths they had killed.

The Cro-Magnons were skilled toolmakers. Their best and sharpest tools were made from flint, which they could work into small points for spearheads and knives. They also used materials such as bone and deer antler to make tools. Small pieces of bone could be carved to make pointed needles, and antlers could be adapted to make tools such as hammers.

Wood was another useful material. Small flakes of flint could be wedged into a twig to make a knife with a handle. The shafts of spears were also made of wood. It is likely that wood was used in many other ways too, such as making simple containers, but all evidence of this has perished with time.

The greatest achievement of the early European people was in their art. It ranged from sculpture to cave painting and tells us a great deal about everyday life. Pictures of

◀ KALEMBA ROCK SHELTER
About 35,000 years ago, hunter-gatherers used this natural shelter at Kalemba in Zambia. Like other similar shelters all over Africa, it provided a good resting place for people out hunting animals or searching for plants to eat.

GROWING SKILLS

The remains and tools of early *Homo sapiens* seem primitive, but early humans were in fact very intelligent. They were using their abilities to adapt to all sorts of different environments. Human language must also have been developing during this period, but unfortunately no record of it exists.

◀ BEZOAR GOAT
This species of goat was a popular quarry for hunters in the rocky, mountainous regions of the Middle East. Groups of hunters would drive a herd into a canyon. Then they could kill as many as they needed and share out the meat among a large number of people.

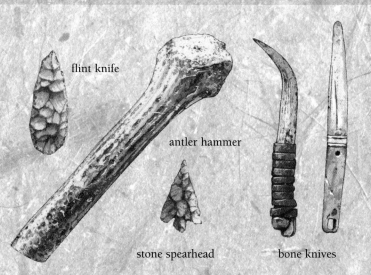

flint knife

antler hammer

stone spearhead

bone knives

▲ TOOLS
People learned to use several different materials to make tools. If no good stone was available, people used bone and antler for knives and points, as well as for tools like hammers.

◄ HUNTERS' CAMP
Early hunters traveled quite long distances looking for food but returned to regular camps at places where there was shelter and a water supply. A campsite could be used by members of the same tribe or group for thousands of years.

animals show the creatures they hunted, from wild oxen and deer to woolly mammoths and rhinoceroses. It is also possible to make out the skin clothing they wore. Female figurines suggest that the people worshiped a mother goddess or goddess of fertility. People who were intelligent enough to produce the art and tools of the early Europeans probably also had quite an advanced society. Although they lived in family-based bands, it is quite likely that these small groups may have come together at certain times. They probably joined together to hunt or for religious ceremonies celebrating important times of the year.

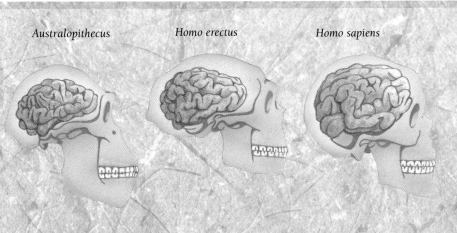

Australopithecus   Homo erectus   Homo sapiens

▲ THE GROWING BRAIN
Studies of early *Homo sapiens* show that their brains were similar in size to those of modern humans and much bigger than those of the earlier hominids. The australopithecines, which were the size of modern chimpanzees, had brains with an average cubic capacity just over half that of *Homo erectus*. Even the brain of *Homo erectus* was little over half the total volume of *Homo sapiens'* brain. Human inventiveness, creativity, language, and social skills are all the result of our bigger brains.

Key Dates

- 43,000B.C. *Homo sapiens* established in Bulgaria.

- 40,000B.C. Humans in western Europe living alongside Neanderthals.

- 35,000B.C. The Neanderthals die out. *Homo sapiens* is the only human form in Europe.

- 20,000B.C. French and Spanish flint-workers find out how to bake flints so they can be pressure flaked to make very fine shapes.

- 16,000–12,000B.C. Human settlement in Russia and Siberia. Mammoth-bone huts built at Mezhrich.

- 6000B.C. Europeans develop microliths, tools made of tiny fragments of flint.

The Ice Age

▲ CARVING
This head is carved from a piece of mammoth tusk, a favorite material for sculpture during the Ice Age.

THE EARTH'S WEATHER IS ALWAYS changing. For the last two million years, the temperature of the planet has seesawed up and down. This has produced a series of warm periods with cold ice ages in between. The last of these ice ages reached its peak about 18,000 B.C. The time around this peak (30,000 to 12,000 B.C.) is so important in human history that it is always known as the Ice Age.

Humans had spread over much of the world by the beginning of the most recent Ice Age. All that time, the ice sheets had pushed down from the north, covering huge areas of the globe. Places such as Scandinavia, Siberia, and northern Britain became unfit for humans.

During this period, much of northern Europe was covered with sparse tundra. Large parts of Spain, Greece, and the Balkans were in forests. The area north of the Black Sea in Russia was a vast grassland. These varied habitats were a challenge to early people, and they had to adapt to different conditions. Big-game hunters moved across the Russian plains. Hunter-fishers lived on the tundra and at the edge of the ice sheets. Hunters and food gatherers took shelter in the forests. People had to devise different tools, hunting techniques and social skills to suit these varied lifestyles.

Ice Age tools are more varied than those of previous peoples. People in the Ice Age still used stone for their knives and choppers. But they used more bone and

◀ MAMMOTH
This large Ice Age mammal ranged widely across Europe, Asia, and North America. It died out around 10,000 years ago.

ICE AGE LIFE
The Ice Age made life difficult in many places. The cold was not just uncomfortable, it meant that some food plants could not survive. In addition, many areas had few or no trees, so that people had no wood to make shelters. These difficulties forced people to find new ways of life. They had to experiment with new foods (such as fish) and new materials (such as, bones and antlers).

▼ MAKING FIRE
In a cold, damp climate, fire became even more important as a source of warmth. Making fire by rubbing sticks together to create a spark may have spread across Europe during the Ice Age.

◀ REINDEER
There are many surviving tools, harpoons, and carvings made from antler. This shows that reindeer-like animals were hunted across Europe during the Ice Age. Reindeer provided tasty, nutritious meat, as well as hides, bone, and antler.

▲ HARPOON POINTS
Ice Age hunters used harpoons for killing animals such as seals and for fishing in the rivers for salmon. The points took a long time to carve from deer antler and were prized possessions.

▶ MAMMOTH HUNTING

*Large, fierce, and with two powerful tusks, woolly mammoths were
an awesome sight for the people of the Ice Age. But these dangerous
creatures were such a good source of meat, skins, bones, and ivory
that the people risked injury or even death hunting and trapping them.*

antler than before. They discovered how
to use antler to make strong handles for
stone blades and ax heads. They carved
bone to make needles, which were
essential to sew together hides and furs for
warm clothes.

People still hunted large mammals such
as the woolly mammoth. They also learned
how to track and hunt animals that live in
herds, such as reindeer. This gave them a
rich source of hides, meat, and antlers.

Because resources were scarce, Ice
Age people probably became the first
traders, swapping food and materials.
Flints and furs, for example, could be
traded for food in times of shortage. People
traveled more, they met other groups, and
they probably found out about new
sources of food. Contact with other tribes
was an aid to survival. When different
groups met, it became necessary to have a
leader to act as spokesman. This was also a
time when personal adornment first
became important. A bone pendant or
bright body paint could mark out the
leader of a group.

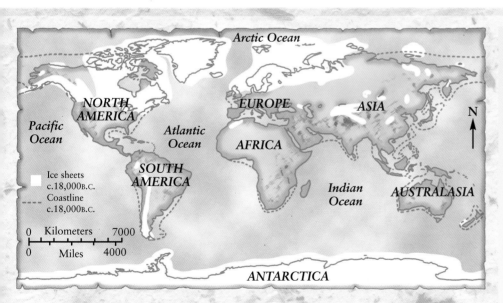

▲ ICE AGE WORLD
Lower sea levels made the world's continents larger during the Ice Age, and some
landmasses that are now separate were joined together. But the ice sheets in Europe,
Asia, and the Americas made vast areas of this land unfit for human life.

Key Dates

- 32,000–28,000 B.C. Aurignacian
  culture in western Europe produces
  flint scrapers and sharpened blades.

- 30,000–12,000 B.C. Main period of
  last Ice Age.

- 24,000 B.C. Hunter-gatherers in
  Europe build permanent dwellings.

- 20,000 B.C. Hunters in western
  Europe develop spears and spear-
  throwers. Hunters in Poland use
  mammoth-tusk boomerangs.

- 18,000 B.C. Peak of Ice Age.

- 18,000–12,500 B.C. People settled near
  Kebara Cave, Israel, make grinding
  stones. This suggests they were
  gathering and processing grains.

Images of the Ice Age

▲ MAMMOTH CARVING
Ice Age art was not always realistic, and carvers often made striking, stylized shapes. In the case of this mammoth, the shape of the animal reflects the shape of the bone from which it is carved.

THE PREHISTORIC CAVE paintings of Europe show a wide variety of creatures. These include groups of wild horses, herds of reindeer and wild oxen, wild cats, birds, and mammoths. The animals are shown in action, galloping and running across the cave walls as if they are being chased by human hunters. They are dramatic action pictures, yet they were produced in dark, damp conditions in chilly caves. Ice Age artists also made sculptures and modeled figures from clay. They engraved cave walls and carved antlers and mammoth tusks into models of animals.

The paintings and sculptures are often hidden so deep in underground caverns that many of them were not rediscovered until the 1900s. It is not known why the paintings were hidden away like this. In fact, no one really knows why the pictures were produced at all. Most experts agree that there was probably some religious reason for the paintings. They may have been used in magic ceremonies designed to help hunters or to promote fertility. Sometimes there are several different outlines in the same place, one drawn over another. This makes some cave paintings and engravings very difficult to see. Experts have spent many hours redrawing them in

▲ PAINTING TECHNIQUES
Artists used brushes or pads of animal hair when painting on cave walls. They sometimes put on the paint with their fingers or created a bold outline by drawing with charcoal.

ICE AGE ART

Because we do not know why Ice Age artists made their pictures and sculptures, it is difficult to decide what their work means. It does show how important animals and the natural world were to them. The cave paintings show the kind of animals these people ate and hunted and also which creatures they thought were the most powerful. These images, and the small carvings of the time, also provide some clues about Ice Age beliefs.

◀ ANTLER SPEAR-THROWER
A spear-thrower helped a hunter hurl his spear faster and farther than he otherwise could by acting as an extension of his arm. This made it easier to kill swift creatures such as deer. Hunters prized their spear-throwers, which were usually made of antler. This material lent itself to carving, and spear-throwers are often beautifully decorated. Swift-running animals like the horse shown here were favorite subjects.

◀ VENUS FIGURINE
Carvings of female figures, with their hips and bellies enlarged, have often been found at Ice Age sites. Archaeologists think they are fertility goddesses, and so have named them "Venus" figures, after the Roman goddess of love.

▶ IVORY HEAD
This female head from France, carved in ivory, shows a goddess. Goddess figures have been found in most areas of Europe, from France to Russia, so goddesses were probably the most important deities in Ice Age religion.

their notebooks to try to make the outlines clearer. For the prehistoric artist, the act of making the image seems to have been more important than the finished result. Perhaps the actual process of painting or engraving was part of a religious ceremony.

Ice Age painters used chalk to make white, charcoal for black, ocher (a kind of earth) for yellow, and iron oxide for red. Sometimes artists used minerals that they could heat to make other colors. The pigments were mixed with water and applied with fur pads, animal-hair brushes, or just with the artist's fingers.

Another technique involved spitting the paint out of the mouth or a reed to make a simple spray effect. The artists used oil lamps to light the caves and sometimes built crude wooden frameworks to gain extra height while working. With these simple techniques, Ice Age artists produced images that were surprisingly complex for such a simple society.

▲ CAVE PAINTING, LASCAUX
The caves at Lascaux, France, contain perhaps the most brilliant of all the known prehistoric paintings. Discovered in 1940, they show a variety of animals, including reindeer and horses. These finely drawn, brightly colored paintings began to show signs of damage in the 1960s because the atmosphere in the caves was affected by so many visitors. The caves were closed to the public, who now visit a replica called Lascaux II.

◀ ANTELOPE
This painting from a cave at Font de Gaume, France, shows the skill of the ancient artists. They caught the outline of the creature's head and horns, and cleverly shaded the animal's hide to create a sense of its bulk.

▶ MAKING PAINT
Artists found their colors in the earth and rocks. They mixed soils and minerals that they found with a medium such as water or animal fat. This produced a type of spreadable paint. They could also draw directly onto the rock surface with pieces of charcoal (burnt wood) or chalk.

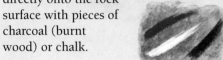

iron oxide

brushstrokes   chalk   charcoal

◀ LAMP
Many cave paintings are hidden in dark, underground caverns. The artists needed light to see what they were doing, so they used fires, flaming torches, or stone lamps like this one. The animal fat was burned in the lamps, to give a bright, but rather smelly, flame. Several hundred Ice Age lamps have been found by archaeologists.

Key Dates

- 30,000B.C. Earliest European cave art.

- 30,000B.C. European musicians make flutes from lengths of animal bone.

- 23,000B.C. First cave paintings made in the Dordogne, France.

- 23,000B.C. Venus figurines made in France and central Europe.

- 18,000–8000B.C. Main period of cave painting in caves at Lascaux, France, and Altamira, Spain.

- 16,000B.C. Antler and bone carving reaches its peak. Finely engraved and carved spear points and spear-throwers made.

- 11,000B.C. Cave painting ends.

The First Australians

▲ ENGRAVINGS
These patterns were cut into rocks at Panaramitee, Australia, thousands of years ago. They may be the world's oldest rock engravings.

DURING THE ICE AGE, the sea level was much lower than it is today. The channels separating Australia from islands such as Timor in Indonesia were far narrower. As a result, groups of islanders took to the sea in bamboo rafts or simple boats in search of fish and shellfish. Some time before 32,000 years ago some Indonesians found themselves on the coast of what is now Australia. No one knows whether they had deliberately looked for new land were blown off-course on one of their fishing trips. They moved inland and became the first humans to inhabit the Australian continent.

The remains of early settlement in Australia are quite

▶ DUGOUT CANOE
Early sailors, like the people who first crossed from Southeast Asia to Australia, may have hollowed out and smoothed wooden logs to make simple dugout canoes.

patchy. The people were spread over a wide area and must have covered vast distances both by sea and on foot. Stone tools, hearths, shell debris, fish bones, and other remnants point to a scattered population between 32,000 and 24,000 years ago. Important sites include Devil's Lair Cave near Perth, Western Australia, a rock shelter near the Cleland Hills in Northern Territory, and Koonalda Cave in South Australia.

At Devil's Lair, archaeologists found several items that were probably used in religious ceremonies. There were some stone plaques and a pit with human teeth that had been removed by sharp blows. At Koonalda Cave, the inhabitants engraved lines on the rock walls. Native Australians carried on making rock engravings into the 1900s. The finds dating from prehistoric times show how far back a rich native Australian culture goes.

Many early Australian sites were occupied for thousands of years. This can also make exact

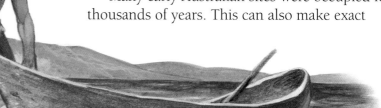

A SCATTERED PEOPLE
The first Australians traveled vast distances across their country to find food and good campsites. When they settled, they spread out thinly across the country. Sites in the south, which were well away from their original landing places, seem to have been most popular. The settlement process probably took place very slowly, spreading across the country over thousands of years.

◀ NECKLACE
People wore necklaces made of shells and animal teeth. Jewelry like this may have been a sign that the wearer was an important person. Such necklaces have been found in Asia as well as Australia. This indicates that the two regions were linked by a common people.

◀ HAND STENCILS
Stencils like this were probably made by spitting paint around and over the artist's hand. This type of art has been practiced in Australia since at least 22,000 B.C. The images, which are on the walls of rock shelters in southern and eastern Australia, show the importance of art to the island continent's earliest people.

dating of the art and artifacts difficult for archaeologists. One rock shelter, at Puritjarra, was used for nearly 7,000 years.

People had reached the island of Tasmania at the southeast tip of Australia by 32,000 years ago. They remained there even when the final Ice Age was at its coldest, when much of the island was covered by tundra and grassland. They lived in caves and rock shelters and survived by hunting the local animals, mainly the kangaroo and the wallaby. The new Tasmanians developed their own style of art. They painted hand stencils on cave walls and made tools

from a natural form of glass that they discovered in a crater formed by a meteorite from space.

The native people of Australia developed a lifestyle long ago that has lasted in some places to the present day. Over the millennia they adapted as their environment changed, from the chill Ice Age to the hot, dry climate of today.

▼ MAKING TOOLS
Early Australians became expert stoneworkers. They could chip away stones to make tools that were the right shape for the job and grind the edges of tools such as axes to make them sharp. Some of their tools were traded over long distances.

◄ EXPLORERS' MAP
Because the sea level was lower, larger pieces of land were above water, so the first people to travel to Australia had a shorter sea journey than travelers would have to make today. They probably crossed from places such as Java or the Celebes, sailing from island to island until they reached the northwestern coast of Australia. Even for such short trips, they needed to be good sailors and navigators. They probably built up their sailing skills over many years fishing off the Southeast Asian coasts.

Key Dates

- 30,000 B.C. Human settlement of Australia probably begins.

- 29,000 B.C. People are living in Tasmania, which is linked to the Australian mainland by a land bridge.

- 25,000 B.C. Puritjarra Rock Shelter, near the Cleland Hills, Northern Territory, is occupied.

- 24,000 B.C. Signs of human occupation near Lake Mungo, New South Wales.

- 22,000 B.C. Traces of human settlement at Koonalda Cave, on the Nullaboor Plain, South Australia.

- 10,000 B.C. The population of native Australians is about 300,000 people.

Early Americans

THE FIRST AMERICANS probably came from the extreme north tip of Asia, which is now Siberia. In the Ice Age the two continents were connected by a land bridge. The first peoples to cross this narrow neck of land found themselves in North America's bleakest, coldest spot. There would have been little vegetation. Most of their food came from hunting and fishing. They were well prepared for this, because the climate in Siberia was similar to that in North America. Many moved south in search of better weather and more plentiful food.

Archaeologists disagree about exactly when the first Americans arrived. The earliest firm evidence of

▲ THE JOURNEY FROM SIBERIA
It was a long, hard journey from Siberia across the land bridge to North America. We do not know what made people start this journey, but perhaps the harsh Ice Age conditions made them want to look for a place where food, warmth, and comfort were easier to find.

humans dates to between 15,000 and 12,000 years ago. However, in the same period, there is more widespread evidence for a hunting people who lived in central North America. Archaeologists called them the

THE GREAT MIGRATION
How do we know that the first Americans came from Siberia? One clue lies in the way the early Americans made tools and weapons. Many chipped tiny flint blades from bigger lumps of stone. They jammed these flints into grooves along the edge of a piece of bone to make a spearhead. Spearheads with this design have been found in both Siberia and North America.

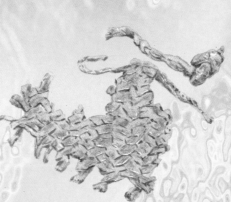

▼ MAMMOTH TUSKS
These fossilized tusks are among many mammoth remains preserved at the Hot Springs mammoth site, South Dakota. They show that the first American hunters were catching the same quarry as their ancestors in Asia.

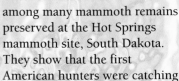

▲ CLOVIS POINTS
North American mammoth hunters fitted these finely worked sharp stone points to their spears. They made these points out of several different types of stone.

▲ WEAVING
A few fragments of twine have survived at Guitarrero Cave, Peru, to show that people could weave 10,000 years ago. These pieces may have been part of a bag or similar container.

Clovis people. They left behind finely worked flint spearheads, now called Clovis points after the town in New Mexico where the tools were found. These have been found at several places near the bones of large mammals such as mammoth and buffalo.. Clovis people probably hunted solitary animals, driving them into swamps where they could be killed.

As the ice melted, the mammoths became extinct, although no one really knows why. The Clovis people vanished as a variety of new environments, from vast woodlands to arid deserts, developed in North America. People learned to adapt to each environment, evolving into distinct societies, whose lifestyles changed little until recent centuries.

In South America there is also evidence for human settlement by 12,000 years ago. At Monte Verde, Chile, the cremated remains of humans have been found in a cave. This site also contains remains of two rows of huts with wooden frames that supported a covering of animal skins. The huts had clay-lined pits for cooking, and there were larger, communal hearths outside.

It is just possible that human life began in South America much earlier than the

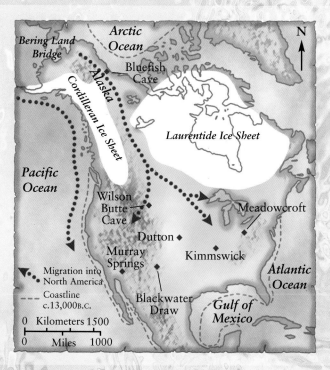

◀ SPEARHEAD
Spears, with notched bone spearheads bound tightly to wooden shafts with animal sinews, were used by early American hunters.

▶ MONTE VERDE
The huts at Monte Verde, Chile, made of wood covered with skins, provide the earliest evidence in America for manmade shelters. The remains were preserved in peaty soil; along with items such as a wooden bowl and digging sticks.

huts at Monte Verde. At Pedra Furada Rock Shelter, Brazil, there are areas of painted rock which some scientists date to around 32,000 years ago. Not all authorities agree with this dating, or with similar dates for some of the stone tools found at Monte Verde. If the early dates are correct, it is likely that settlement also began much earlier in North America but that the people left no surviving remains.

◀ NEW ARRIVALS
The first North Americans worked their way between the two main ice sheets. The Bering Land Bridge was created between Siberia and Alaska because the sea level was some 330 feet lower than it is today. Some people may also have come along the west coast on boats or rafts, stopping every so often along the edge of the Cordilleran Ice Sheet. When they finally reached beyond the ice, they found a vast empty land. Some people quickly moved east and west, while others pushed on further south.

Key Dates

- 13,000 B.C. Hunters from Siberia cross the Bering Land Bridge.

- 12,500 B.C. Humans at Meadowcroft Rock Shelter, Pittsburgh, Pennsylvania—the earliest known settlement in North America.

- 11,000 B.C. People living at Monte Verde in southern Chile.

- 9000 B.C. Clovis people hunting on the Great Plains.

- 8000 B.C. Human settlers are accompanied by dogs.

- 7500 B.C. The people of the Sloan site, Arkansas, bury their dead. This cemetery is the earliest discovered in North America.

The Thaw Begins

▲ FISH CARVING
Stone carvings of fishes, like this one, were found at Lepenski Vir on the river Danube. They may have portrayed a fish god.

AT THE END OF THE ICE AGE there was a great change in the world's climate. In much of Europe, Asia, and North America, the ice melted, making the sea level rise and causing floods in flat areas near the sea. The land bridge between Siberia and Alaska disappeared, cutting off North America from Asia. Britain, which had been joined to Europe, was now cut off by the North Sea. Large areas of land were lost around the coasts of Denmark and Sweden.

The change must have been terrifying at first. Many people fled the floods to settle in new areas. Their way of life changed. At the same time, the warmer weather transformed the landscape. In many places, ice and tundra were

▶ THATCHED TENTS
The Middle Stone Age settlement of Lepenski Vir was home to around 100 hunting and fishing people. They lived in tent-like houses made of wooden poles which were probably covered with thatch.

replaced by thick woods of birch and mixed forests in northern Europe, and deciduous woods in the south. People soon realized that these changes gave them new types of food. Among the woods lived animals such as wild pig and deer. Near the coast there were seals, waterfowl, and, in many places, shellfish. Food was more plentiful because the climate was warmer.

People developed new methods of hunting and fishing. These new techniques were more efficient than previous methods, so they did not have to move around so much to hunt for food. They set up special camps where food of a certain type was plentiful, or where they could mine flint to make their tools and weapons.

Most settlements in this period were by rivers or near the sea, where the people could usually rely on a good food supply. Rivers and coastal waters were the highways of the Stone Age. Rivers provided a way of traveling through the dense forests. People paddled along in their dugout canoes, perhaps exchanging valuable goods, such as furs or flint tools, with other travelers they met along the way.

LIFE DURING THE THAW
As the ice melted, some people moved inland, but for many the sea was too useful to leave behind. Such shellfish as oysters and whelks supplied tasty, nourishing food, so many people returned to the coast for at least part of the year.

scrapers, blades, and points from Star Carr

▲ FOREST FRUITS
The trees and shrubs of the new woodlands and forest edges yielded fruits such as blackberries to feed European gatherers.

▲ WILD BOAR
This woodland animal thrived in Europe after the thaw. It became a favorite target for many European hunters.

▲ TOOLS FROM STAR CARR
Hunter-gatherers camped regularly at Star Carr, near a lake in Yorkshire, England, at the end of the final Ice Age. They left behind many stone tools, such as scrapers, which they must have used to prepare animal skins, and smaller sharp cutting blades for butchering meat.

The new lifestyle meant that the people who lived in Europe after the Ice Age were on the whole better fed and more comfortable than their ancestors. They were more settled, so they had time to develop more advanced toolmaking skills. This made them more successful still. As a result, many more of their children began to survive to become adults. The total number of people began to rise, and the population began to spread, finding better places to settle and new sources of food.

▼ PINCEVANT

These round tents, held up with wooden poles, were the summer homes of people at Pincevant, France, at the end of the final Ice Age. All that was left to show modern archaeologists that tents had been pitched there were the rings of stones that had held the edges in place, together with hearths and some animal bones.

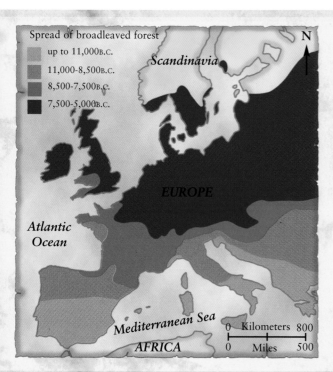

◄ SPREADING FORESTS

As the ice melted, forests spread slowly across Europe, covering the area in broadleaved trees. The spread of the forests began in the south, working its way north over a period of about 6,000 years toward Poland and Scandinavia, where mixed conifer and broadleaved forests grew. This new pattern of forests and woodland provided large areas of Europe with their typical landscape, one that survived for thousands of years. It still survives in some parts of Germany, central Europe, and Scandinavia.

Map legend:

Spread of broadleaved forest
- up to 11,000 B.C.
- 11,000–8,500 B.C.
- 8,500–7,500 B.C.
- 7,500–5,000 B.C.

Scandinavia

Atlantic Ocean

EUROPE

Mediterranean Sea

AFRICA

0 Kilometers 800
0 Miles 500

N

Key Dates

- 13,000 B.C. The ice thaws, sea levels rise, and lowland areas flood.

- 11,000 B.C. The dog is domesticated in the Middle East.

- 8000 B.C. Temperatures reach roughly their present levels in Europe.

- 8000 B.C. The Mesolithic period, or Middle Stone Age, begins in Europe.

- 7500 B.C. Red deer hunters settle at Star Carr, Yorkshire, England.

- 6500 B.C. Britain is cut off from Europe.

- 5500 B.C. Denmark is cut off from the rest of Scandinavia.

- 5000 B.C. Deciduous forests cover much of Europe.

A Better Food Supply

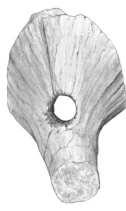

▲ MATTOCK HEAD
Deer antler was a good material to make a heavy tool such as a mattock. This was used by gatherers for loosening soil and cutting away plant roots for food.

MANY THINGS CHANGED IN North America at the end of the Ice Age. People were suddenly much freer to go where they wanted in search of food and raw materials. They found a range of different regions, from the grassy Great Plains to the drier areas of the southwest, all of which could be settled. At first they moved south, following the mammals and hunting them with their stone-pointed spears. They also spread out east and west across the continent, finding more and better sources of flint for tools and weapons. Archaeologists have traced many of the stone tools to where they were first made. Some of them were carried hundreds, or even thousands, of miles, which shows how far the hunters journeyed.

It took several thousand years for the climate and vegetation to settle down into the pattern that still exists today. As this happened, species such as mammoths became extinct, and people turned to smaller animals for food. The hunters also developed lighter, more

accurate spears, which enables them to bring down game without having to ambush it first. On the grasslands there were still large creatures, such as buffalo. These provided hunters with a number of different products, such as meat to eat and hides to make leather and bones for tools. From around 9000B.C., the people of the plains began to develop a lifestyle that would continue, with very little change, for many thousands of years.

The people of Asia, like the Europeans, took advantage of a better, more reliable food supply. They were healthier, and their population began to increase. However, they still relied on many of their old techniques for survival and shelter. In some places, people started to settle down and build permanent huts. Elsewhere, hunters still built temporary shelters from branches or mammoth bones and hides.

As the ice thawed in Africa and the Middle East, many areas

◀ ANTLER HEADDRESS
Archaeologists found this unusual antler headdress at the British Stone Age site of Star Carr, Yorkshire. It may have been used in a religious ceremony or as a disguise when hunting deer.

HUNTERS' WEAPONS
By the late Ice Age, weapons had improved. Although spearheads and harpoon points were still made of stone, antler, and bone, they were carefully carved so they worked well whenever they were used. When food was scarce, a hunter could not afford to lose his quarry because a blunt spear allowed an animal to escape.

▶ ANTLER POINTS
Hunters used deer antler to make deadly harpoon points. By carving away notches along one edge, then sharpening one or both ends, they made a barbed point. The advantage of this was that when a weapon was thrown at an animal it went in easily, but would not slip out as the creature ran away. Barbed points are still used by Arctic hunters.

◀ REPAIRING SPEARS
Stone spearheads such as North American Clovis points are virtually everlasting. But wooden spear shafts often break or split, so hunters had to fit their points to new ones. They fixed the points by splitting the shaft, jamming in the head, and binding animal sinew around the joint.

▼ HOME OF SKIN AND BONE
Like the people of the Ukraine, Siberian hunters built homes out of large animal bones and tusks, covered with skins and reinforced with timber if they could find it. Stones weighted down the skins on the ground. The people may have learned how to build these tents in the Ukraine before traveling eastward to their new homes.

that had been desert were covered with vegetation. Plants began to flourish in the Nile Valley and the eastern Mediterranean. This was a land of wild grasses, and people began to gather their seeds, grind them into flour, and make bread to eat. One group of people who we know did this were the Natufians, a people who lived near the Wadi en-Natuf, in what is now Israel.

These cereal gatherers were learning a lot of vital information about the various kinds of grain. For example, which provided the tastiest seeds, when best to harvest them, and the most effective tools to use. Later, they would put this knowledge to good use, changing to a settled way of life and becoming some of the world's first farmers.

Removing flakes from the flint.

Carefully shaping the edge. The hand is protected by animal skin.

Putting the point into the cleft stick.

◄ MAKING A POINT
A hunter hit a lump of flint with an antler hammer, removing bits from either side until the piece was the right thickness and shape. Then he took a pointed piece of antler and worked around the edge of the point, removing chips to produce a razor-sharp edge. Next he put the point in a cleft stick and wrapped it around with sinews to protect it. He then hit the base of the point with his hammer, to remove a flake and make a fluted shape to fit the shaft.

Key Dates

- 10,000B.C. The Natufian culture develops in western Asia. Its people build round stone huts, herd goats, and gather wild emmer wheat.

- 9000B.C. Population levels begin to rise in Asia, encouraging people to take up new lifestyles such as herding.

- 9000B.C. People in the Americas begin to hunt a wider range of smaller mammals. A more settled lifestyle begins to evolve.

- 5000B.C. Tools in America become more specialized, and grindstones are created for processing plant foods.

- 3500B.C. People in North America begin to live in permanent villages.

Rock Paintings

UNLIKE CAVE PAINTINGS, which were hidden deep underground, rock paintings were made on rocks and cliff faces out in the open air. Some of these drawings are engraved into the rock with a sharp stone tool. Others are painted with natural pigments in a similar way to that used for the cave paintings of the final Ice Age. Rock art occurs all over the world, from Africa to Australia. The drawings are usually easier to find than the cave paintings of western Europe, and in some places they are quite common. Some rock drawings date from 8000B.C., but others were made as recently as the 1800s. The more recent pictures are often similar in style to the ancient images. This makes them difficult to date, but it also shows how the art and lifestyles of many peoples altered little until the early 1900s. Rock art can tell us a great deal about the people who created it—especially the creatures they hunted and farmed, because animals appear in these paintings more than any other subject.

Some of the most interesting and best preserved rock art is found in Africa. In the Saharan region, the types of animals in the pictures show how different the area was compared with the desert of today. After the final Ice Age, when the Sahara was covered in grasslands and dotted with oases

▲ SAN HUNTERS
This modern rock painting by the San people, or bushmen, from the Kalahari Desert shows hunters chasing their quarry. It is one of many recent rock paintings done in a style similar to that used in prehistoric times.

◀ HAND PAINTING
One method used by rock artists was to take some paint into the mouth and spit it onto the rock to produce a stencil of the hand.

THE VARIETY OF ROCK ART

The most common subjects in rock art are animals, people, and patterns. Although the subjects are similar, the style of the pictures can vary greatly around the world. Some, like the paintings of the Sahara, are very realistic. Others, like the human figures of South America, are more like symbols than pictures of real people.

▶ GAZELLES
Artists from the Tassili Massif in the Sahara drew these gazelles. They were painted over 6,000 years ago. This was before the beginning of farming, when Saharan artists were still drawing the animals they hunted for food.

▲ BISON
The people of Bhimbetka, India, made rock drawings of animals for thousands of years. Bison, antelope, and deer, as well as people, were favorite subjects, and some, like this example, were filled in with delicate abstract patterns.

▲ HUMAN FIGURE
This rock engraving of a stylized person comes from Venezuela. No one knows what the circles and curves around it are, but they may be symbols of the Moon or Sun.

or shallow lakes, the area was home to wild oxen and gazelles. The local people hunted these animals and drew them on the walls of their shelters. After about 6000B.C., they began to draw domestic cattle, which shows that the change from hunting to farming near the oases happened around this time.

Other African paintings, such as those of the San people of what is now the Kalahari Desert, show hunters chasing their quarry. They are also shown fishing from their boats and gathering food. Pictures like these are almost certainly more than just decorations on shelter walls. The hunting pictures were probably produced as part of a ceremony performed before the hunt. The people hoped that drawing a successful hunt would make their own hunt turn out well. In a similar way, a picture of a group of men dancing around an antelope was probably intended to transfer some of the real animal's strength to the men of the tribe.

Paintings with a religious or ceremonial purpose are even more common in Australia. Stories of how the world was created have always been important to the native Australians. Each tribe has its own ancestor, usually an animal that is linked with some special part of the landscape. One Australian myth, which tells how the world was made, describes the way in which the rainbow serpent, who came from the sea, slithered onto the shore and created the landscape as he snaked his way inland. Rainbow serpents first begin to appear in rock paintings made by native Australians some 6,000 years ago.

▲ SPIRIT BEINGS
Australian rock painting represents spirits that were believed to be the ancestors of a particular tribe. They formed the center of the tribe's religious beliefs. The ancestors of different groups took different forms. Some were said to be animals; others were features of the landscape. They were all regarded with the deepest reverence by their people, as they are today.

◄ HUNTERS
Many rock drawings were made by hunting peoples, like these figures by the San people of the Kalahari Desert. The painted hunters seem to be moving with great agility, almost like dancers.

▶ LEAF
Depictions of plants are rarer in rock art than animals or people. They do occur occasionally, as in this Australian example from a site in the Northern Territory. Plant pictures may be linked to religion or the ancestors, or may have been done simply to create a decorative effect.

Key Dates

- 25,000B.C. Early inhabitants of Australia may be developing rock art.

- 20,000B.C. Rock artists may already be active in some parts of Africa.

- 11,000B.C. Rock art in central India shows hunters and prey.

- 8500B.C. The earliest rock paintings found in Saharan Africa portray wild animals.

- 8000B.C. The main period of cave painting ends in Europe. Rock art on cliffs and in shallower caves becomes common.

- 6000B.C. Saharan rock artists depict cattle, reflecting the change to the herding of livestock.

The First Farmers

▲ WHEAT
Finding a staple crop that provides basic energy needs is an important step in farming. Wheat is one of the most common. Others are millet, rice and maize.

HUNTERS AND GATHERERS were highly skilled at finding food. However, their success was dependent on the weather, local conditions and luck. If the weather turned bad or the local supplies ran out, people faced starvation. Around 11,000 years ago, a group of people in the Middle East changed this. They began to produce their own food by farming. It was one of the most important developments in the history of humankind.

Farming gave people control over their food supply. They did not have to wander through the countryside looking for food any longer. They could settle in one place, and as a result they began to build stronger, more comfortable houses than before. Farming also offered a more reliable supply of food, although in years when the harvest was bad, people had to return to gathering for a while.

The first farmers lived at the eastern end of the Mediterranean (now Israel, Palestine, and Syria) and in an upland region north of the river Tigris in what now forms parts of Iran and Iraq. This region has more rain than the surrounding plains, and grasses such as wheat and barley grow there naturally. Because of its climate and its shape on the map, the area is now known as the Fertile Crescent.

The people of the Fertile Crescent had gathered wheat seeds for thousands of years. They knew which types grew most vigorously and produced the best grain. By about 9000 B.C., they realized that they could plant these grasses and harvest them. At around the same time, they started to herd the wild sheep and goats. These animals provided milk and wool as well as meat. During the next 3,000 years, people also began to keep livestock, pigs, and cattle.

In good years, farming gave the people of the Fertile Crescent more food than they

◀ STONE TOWER
Jericho's tallest building was a stone tower. No one knows why the tower was built. It could have been a watchtower, or it might have had some religious purpose.

THE FARMERS' WORLD
Although farming created a lot of hard work, the people of the first agricultural villages did not spend all their time in the fields. In many places, they developed quite complex religious beliefs and ceremonies. They produced new styles of art, including sculptures modeled from plaster and pottery decorated with striking abstract designs of lines and rectangles. They also started to make larger baskets and clay containers for storing surplus grain.

◀ FIGURE SCULPTURE
The world's earliest large-scale human sculptures were produced in Ain Ghazal, Jordan. They were moulded in lime plaster over a skeleton of straw bundles. The eyes were outlined with dark paint. No one knows why they were made.

▶ SPOUTED BOWL
From the early farming site at Khirokitia, Cyprus, came this decorated pottery bowl. It was buried in the grave of an eight-year-old child, and was obviously a favorite object, as it had been repaired before the burial.

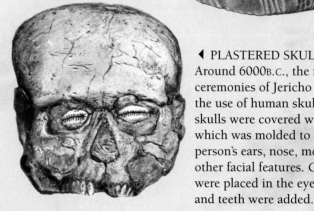

◀ PLASTERED SKULL
Around 6000 B.C., the religious ceremonies of Jericho involved the use of human skulls. The skulls were covered with plaster, which was molded to copy the person's ears, nose, mouth and other facial features. Cowrie shells were placed in the eye sockets, and teeth were added.

could eat. They stored the surplus in grain bins or baskets and traded it for materials, for tools, or for items such as pots and furniture.

Gradually, the farmers and craftworkers became rich. They built more and bigger houses clustered together. These groups of houses developed into small towns. The houses were made of mud bricks, providing warmth in winter while staying cool in summer. One of the first of these towns was Jericho, built near a spring north of the Dead Sea. The land around the town was good both for growing crops and for grazing herds and flocks of animals, and soon Jericho became a very prosperous town. It was not long before other towns were built in this area.

As farming spread farther afield, it was not very long before other regions began to produce their food in a similar way, and the pattern of human life had changed forever.

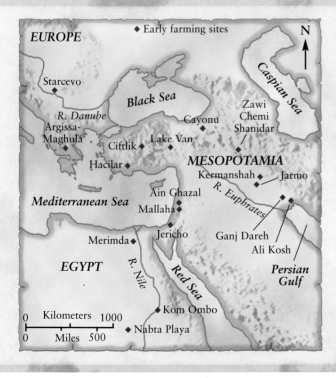

◀ EARLY FARMER
To begin with, farming was difficult, backbreaking work—even more so than the toil of hunting and gathering. There were only stone and wooden hand tools to work the soil. Seed had to be scattered by hand, and harvesting had to be done in the hot sun with a simple stone sickle.

◀ FARMING IN THE FERTILE CRESCENT
To begin with, farming was most successful where there were light soils. These could be easily worked with basic hand tools. There also had to be plants growing wild that were suitable for cultivating. From its beginnings near the Persian Gulf, the river Euphrates and the eastern Mediterranean, farming spread gradually outward. Egypt to the south and Turkey and Greece to the northwest were places where farming arrived early.

Key Dates

- 10,000 B.C. Cereal gathering begins in Palestine.

- 9000 B.C. Farming begins in the Fertile Crescent.

- 9000 B.C. The people of Syria and nearby regions sow wheat.

- 9000 B.C. Jericho develops as a small settlement around a spring.

- 8000 B.C. Animal herding is well established in the Zagros Mountains.

- 7000 B.C. Cereal farming is widespread from Turkey to the Fertile Crescent, in the Zagros Mountains, and in parts of Pakistan.

Plants and Animals

▲ DATE PALM
Early farmers in the Fertile Crescent used the date palm for its fruit, wood, leaves, and fibers.

THE FIRST FARMERS DID NOT simply take wild grasses and plant them in rows in their fields. They had to work hard to turn the wild species they found into true cereal crops. To begin with, they had to choose the plants that were the most suitable for food. In Europe and Asia, farmers chose grasses such as wheat and barley. Farmers in eastern Asia grew millet. Tropical African growers cultivated yams. The first farmers in North America selected corn, while those in South America chose potatoes and another root vegetable, manioc.

Farmers watched for the individual plants that were strongest or biggest. American corn farmers, for example, collected the seed from plants yielding the biggest cobs, and sowed these, to produce a crop with larger cobs next year.

Farmers in the Fertile Crescent had a different problem with their wheat. One species that grew well was wild einkorn wheat. But its seeds tended to break off and fall to the ground when they ripened, which made them difficult to harvest. Eventually the farmers noticed that a few plants had seeds that did not fall so quickly, so they bred their crops from these. Soon they

▼ CATTLE ROCK PAINTING
When the people of the Sahara began to farm, their artists started to paint pictures of cattle. This example shows a herd of cattle, of the type that were kept more than 4,000 years ago. The painting also includes some of the people who herded them. It comes from a site in the Tassili mountains, in the central Sahara.

ON EARLY FARMS
Early farms looked quite unlike modern ones. The animals and plants were different, and the farmer and his family usually shared their house with the animals. There were no machines, just simple tools and a lot of hard work. The whole family helped, especially at busy times such as harvest. Even young children lent a hand, which was good training for when they would be farmers themselves.

wild einkorn

domestic einkorn

◀ WILD AND DOMESTIC WHEAT
The main difference between wild and domestic einkorn wheat is the seeds. In the domestic variety these are much larger. The plant's stalk is also stronger, which stops the seeds from falling off before the harvest.

▶ WILD AND DOMESTIC CORN
Modern domestic corn has a larger seed cob than the ancient wild variety. Early farmers probably bred corn cobs that were larger than the wild varieties but not as big as today's giant cobs.

wild corn

domestic corn

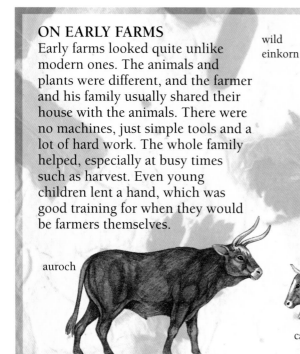

auroch

cattle

◀ WILD AND DOMESTIC CATTLE
The wild auroch was the ancestor of early farm cattle. Bones found by archaeologists show that early domesticated cattle were smaller than the wild ones. But early farmers probably tried different sizes to see which suited them best.

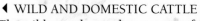

◀ A FARMING VILLAGE
The first farming villages in Turkey were small clusters of mud-brick houses, where people and animals lived close together for safety. In the hot, dry summers, the village streets were baked hard and dusty, but in the winter they became a mass of puddles and sticky mud. These farmers kept goats and cattle descended from the wild aurochs.

had developed a new species, domesticated einkorn wheat, with seeds that broke away only during threshing.

Early farmers bred their animals in a similar way, selecting the beasts with the features they wanted and breeding from them. But the changes to the animal species were less dramatic than with the crops. The pigs farmed in the Fertile Crescent, for example, were much smaller and more like wild boars than modern domestic pigs. Cattle, too, were smaller than modern cows, and sheep and goats looked like the wild species.

Most early domestic animals were smaller than their wild cousins. This is probably because farmers bred good-tempered, docile creatures that were less aggressive and easier to handle than wild animals. Instead of choosing large specimens, farmers would have selected animals that produced the best-tasting meat or the highest yield of milk. Gradually, the farmers built up knowledge and experience, and they must have discovered that the smaller animals often had the features they wanted.

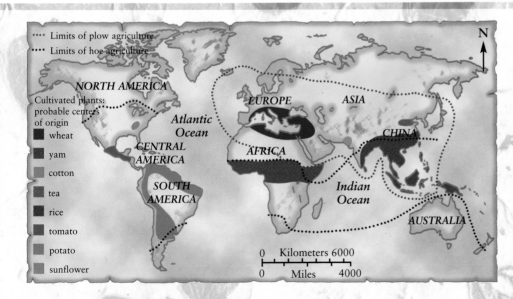

Limits of plow agriculture
Limits of hoe agriculture

Cultivated plants: probable centers of origin

- wheat
- yam
- cotton
- tea
- rice
- tomato
- potato
- sunflower

NORTH AMERICA
Atlantic Ocean
CENTRAL AMERICA
SOUTH AMERICA
EUROPE
ASIA
AFRICA
CHINA
Indian Ocean
AUSTRALIA
N

0   Kilometers 6000
0   Miles   4000

▲ PLANT DOMESTICATION
Farmers in different parts of the world grew different types of crops. In each area, one or two crops became the most commonly grown. They were varieties that were easy to grow in that particular area and provided a good basic crop.

Key Dates

- 9000 B.C. Sheep domesticated in northern Mesopotamia.

- 8000 B.C. First domesticated cereals grown around Jericho.

- 7000 B.C. Sheep and goats kept in the eastern Mediterranean.

- 7000 B.C. Barley grown in the Fertile Crescent. Emmer wheat in Palestine. Einkorn wheat in Turkey and Mesopotamia.

- 7000 B.C. Pigs are domesticated in southern Turkey.

- 6000 B.C. Cattle kept by farmers in north Africa and the eastern Mediterranean.

The Coming of Trade

▲ DAGGER
This dagger, with its long flint blade and its snake-shaped handle, was probably made for decorative effect rather than for use in battle.

FARMING MADE SOME PEOPLE well-fed, rich, and successful. They could trade the extra food they produced in exchange for luxury goods. Soon, this became a way of life for many farmers, and trading towns began to appear in the Fertile Cresecent and in Anatolia (Turkey). Most of these early towns disappeared long ago. As one set of mud-brick buildings fell into disrepair, they were knocked down. People built new houses on top of the old foundations. This happened many times over hundreds of years, and the town's ground level gradually rose as each group of houses was replaced. When a town was finally abandoned, the ruins, with their buildup of floor levels, was left in the form of a mound. In Syria and Palestine this type of ancient mound is called a tell. In Turkey it is known as a hüyük.

One of the most famous of these early town mounds is Çatal Hüyük in central Turkey. When archaeologists began to dig this mound, they found that it concealed an ancient town, occupied by a trading people who lived there between 7000 and

▶ BUILDING WORK
Clay was the main material for building in early trading towns of the Middle East. It could be molded into brick shapes while wet and left to dry in the sun. Surfaces were plastered to give a weatherproof finish outside and a smooth surface for decoration within.

6000 B.C. The countryside around the town was rich farming land. Charred remains from the town have shown that the people grew wheat, barley, lentils, and other vegetables, as well as eating such fruit as apples and wild nuts such as almonds.

The people of Çatal Hüyük probably traded in food products and raw materials for making tools. A favorite material was obsidian, a black glass formed naturally in volcanoes. Archaeologists have found a range of different tools and weapons made of flint and obsidian on the site.

The houses of Çatal Hüyük were built of mud brick. They were square or rectangular and built close together. One amazing feature of the town was that it had no streets. People entered their houses from the flat

MYSTERIES OF A TURKISH TOWN

There are still many mysteries surrounding the town of Çatal Hüyük in central Turkey, in spite of all the work of the archaeologists. No one knows for sure the meaning of the wall paintings in many of the rooms that have been excavated. The bulls, birds, leopards, and human figures were probably gods. However, it is not clear what the gods stood for, or how they were worshiped.

▲ BULL PAINTING
This mural is from a shrine at Çatal Hüyük. It shows a group of people baiting a gigantic bull. Bulls had religious significance because they were associated with a male god.

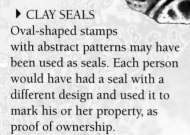

▶ CLAY SEALS
Oval-shaped stamps with abstract patterns may have been used as seals. Each person would have had a seal with a different design and used it to mark his or her property, as proof of ownership.

▶ BIRD WALL-PAINTING
These birds are probably vultures. People in some cultures left their dead out of doors until vultures had picked away the flesh.

roofs, stepping down wooden ladders to the floor below. Defending such places was easy.

Many houses contained at least one room set aside for religious ceremonies. These rooms, or shrines, are decorated with bulls' heads made of plaster and fitted with real bulls' horns. They also have wall paintings of animals and figures. Many of the figures are female, and archaeologists have also found more than 50 small statues of pregnant women, suggesting that the people worshiped a mother goddess.

In addition, the shrines contain platforms that may have been used as altars in some form of religious ceremony. When residents of Çatal Hüyük died, their bodies were left in the open air, where the flesh was removed by the vultures. Then their relatives brought the bones back into the town and buried them beneath these platforms.

Ladder gives access to roof.

Flat roof provides work space and route to neighboring houses.

Decorated room used as religious shrine.

Roof made of layers of timber, reeds, and mud.

◀ TOWN HOUSES
Houses at Çatal Hüyük were made mainly from mud brick. This material was even used for fixtures such as benches and hearths. The houses were packed closely together with only a few courtyards between them. This made the town compact and helped to make it easier to defend, with few corners where enemies or wild beasts could lurk.

◀ EXCAVATING A SITE
The most common way for archaeologists to dig is to make a trench, a rectangular hole across the site. They can find remains from different periods because these lie in bands like a layer cake, revealing small areas across a broad time span. When there are many remains of buildings and other structures, such as at Çatal Hüyük, archaeologists will sometimes excavate to a shallow depth, over a broader area to cover more of the site.

Key Dates

- 8000B.C. Trade begins to develops in the Fertile Crescent and Anatolia.

- 7000B.C. Çatal Hüyük becomes important as a town and trading center.

- 7000B.C. Jericho expands; religious rituals include decorating skulls with plaster and shells.

- 6800B.C. Pottery is widely used in the eastern Mediterranean.

- 6500B.C. More elaborate burials at settlements such as Çatal Hüyük and Jericho show that some people were more important than others.

- 5000B.C. Trade links established between Turkey and the eastern Mediterranean.

Pots and Potters

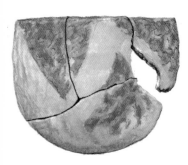

▲ PAINTED POTTERY
The earliest pottery was plain, but potters soon learned how to paint their wares to make them more attractive. This pot is from an early farming community in Europe.

WE TAKE POTTERY, SUCH as cups, bowls, mugs, and plates, for granted. Before pottery was invented, our earliest ancestors used hollowed-out stone containers and woven baskets. The first pottery was probably made around 10,500B.C. Pots are made from clay, which was dug from the ground, so they are cheap. They could be made in a variety of shapes and sizes, and held liquids as well as dry foods. Once people had discovered how to make pots, they never stopped finding new uses for them.

Pottery was probably discovered by accident. Early peoples baked bread and other foods in ovens which they made from earth. They piled up a mound of clay and made a hollow center in which they lit a fire. Inside, it became very hot. Eventually someone must have noticed that the sides of the clay oven had hardened with the heat.

It was probably some time before anyone had the idea of using this hardened clay to make containers. The earliest pots so far discovered come from Japan. From Japan, knowledge of pottery may have spread to China, where slightly more recent vessels have been found. However, in the rest of Asia, Europe, and Africa, pottery is much more recent. It is possible that it may have been discovered independently, as it was in America.

The first pots were made by the coiling process. The potter made a long, thin sausage of clay and looped it in a circle, spiraling upward to make the sides of the pot. Another ancient technique was to form pots by using a stone mold which was removed when the potter achieved the right shape. Much later, some time after 3000B.C., the potter's wheel was invented. This device is still used by potters all over

◀ TERRACOTTA FIGURE
Pottery can be molded into all sorts of shapes, not only containers. People soon realized that they could use it to make small, portable statues. These were common among early farming communities, and archaeologists have excavated shrines with large numbers of these figures.

POTS AND POTTERS

In hunter-gatherer societies, people generally collected food as they needed it. Farming produced a glut of food at harvest time. People now needed containers to store this food, so pottery and farming flourished at the same time. The earliest pottery is unglazed. This means that it absorbs moisture, so that it is best used for dry goods such as grain and other solid foods.

◀ UNGLAZED POTS
Simple unglazed storage jars are still made in many parts of the world. These jars, elegantly shaped and decorated with patterns made by the potters' fingertips, come from Ghana. Pots like this are sometimes given a colorful glaze.

▲ ROUND-BASED POT
This is one of the oldest pots so far discovered by archaeologists. It comes from Nasunahara, Japan, and dates to around 10,500BC. The pot has a beaded pattern in bands around the rim.

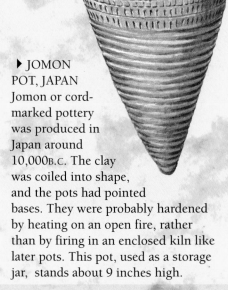

▶ JOMON POT, JAPAN
Jomon or cord-marked pottery was produced in Japan around 10,000B.C. The clay was coiled into shape, and the pots had pointed bases. They were probably hardened by heating on an open fire, rather than by firing in an enclosed kiln like later pots. This pot, used as a storage jar, stands about 9 inches high.

the world. The finished pots were fired and hardened in a kiln, which was similar to an ancient oven.

One advantage of pottery is that it is extremely long-lasting, and pots have survived to provide evidence for archaeologists. Each region and period has its own style of pottery. The color of the clay, the thickness of the pot, the style of decoration all vary from place to place and time to time. An archaeologist can often tell, even from a fragment of pottery, when and where it was made. They can therefore give a date to the sites where they find pots. Pots of foreign origin also provide clues as to trade and links between various countries.

▲ POTTERS AT WORK
The potter in the foreground is making a pot by coiling clay. She has prepared long, sausage-shaped pieces of clay and wound them around to build up the shape of the vessel. When she is happy with the overall shape, she will moisten her fingers and rub the surface of the pot to make it smooth. She may then make handles and stick them to the sides.

▲ EARLY POTTERY SITES
Archaeologists have discovered many remains of both early pottery and kilns in China and Japan. These areas continued to be at the forefront of developments in pottery until the 1800s. Kilns, glazing, and, much later, waterproof porcelain, were all discovered and first used in the Far East.

Key Dates

- 10,500 B.C. First Japanese pottery.

- 7000 B.C. Unbaked, sun-dried clay vessels made in Syria and Turkey.

- 7000 B.C. Hunter-fishers of southern Sahara are the first potters in Africa.

- 6500 B.C. First European pottery.

- 6000 B.C. Fishing communities in southern China make pottery.

- 3500 B.C. The tournette, a simple device for turning a pot, appears in Mesopotamia and Egypt.

- 3000 B.C. Potter's wheel invented in the Middle East.

- 1500 B.C. Glazed pottery which is resistant to water made in China.

European Settlements

▲ GREEK HOUSE
Early Greek farmers built small one-roomed houses with sloping thatched roofs. They often included a clay bin so that they could store their grain indoors. This house is from the village of Nea Nikomedeia in Greece.

FARMING SEEMS TO HAVE spread to Europe from the east, from around 7000B.C. It reached Europe from Turkey and then spread westward toward the Atlantic coast.

Then, as now, the European climate and landscape varied greatly. In the Balkans, where farming in Europe started, it was dry, and the land was suitable for sheep and goats, as well as for cereal growing. In northern Europe, early farmers led a very different life. The weather was colder, the soil heavier, and much of the ground was covered with forest. This was not good country for sheep and goats, so pig-rearing and cattle-herding were more popular. People could grow cereal crops, but the heavier soil was harder to cultivate than in the south. Gradually, over many centuries, the northerners developed strains of cereals that could grow in the heavy soil.

The woods of the north had many benefits. They were good foraging-grounds for pigs, and also provided a variety of food plants for people. They also sheltered animals, such as deer and wild boar, that could be hunted for both food and skins. The northern Europeans continued to hunt and gather to add variety to the food they produced on their farms.

The plentiful timber was also useful for building. The farmers of central and northern Europe cut down trees to make a stout framework for the walls and roofs

▲ FARMING SETTLEMENT
A small farming village in western Britain consisted of a few round thatched houses clustered together. Next to the houses were fields for animals and crops. A trackway gave access to the fields and connected this village with its neighbors.

CRAFTS OF THE FARMERS
With the settled way of life that came with farming, people began to develop their craft skills. Among the most important were building and pottery. These early farmers were skilled woodworkers. They made fences, tools, and containers.

▲ RAISED PATHWAY
People sometimes built farming villages in marshy land. They made wooden walkways raised on posts so that they could cross the swamps safely.

face pot, Hungary

Bandkeramik pot, Germany

▲ DECORATED POTS
Potters decorated pots by drawing patterns or simplified faces in the damp clay. Another design was made up of lines and dots in a style known by the German name *Bandkeramik*, meaning "banded pottery."

▲ SEATED FIGURE
This pottery statuette from a farming site in Hungary shows a man holding a sickle. He may be a grain god, or just an ordinary farmer.

of their homes. They used split logs to make the walls and plastered them over with daub, a mixture of mud and straw, to fill the gaps. This helped to keep out drafts. The roofs, which had a steep pitch to throw off snow and rain, were thatched. Some of these houses were up to 150 feet in length and are known as longhouses. They were Europe's first sizable, permanent dwellings. Besides a large room for the family, they usually also contained a storeroom for crops and an area for cattle. Sometimes humans and animals shared the same room. It was cramped and smelly, but people put up with this to make sure their animals were safe.

Farming villages became established in many river valleys. People used the rivers to travel between neighboring villages to trade. As they traveled, they also exchanged ideas about new discoveries and inventions. As a result, pottery techniques and styles improved and spread, and new ideas about crop and animal cultivation were shared. The people of Europe were developing skills that would stay in use for thousands of years.

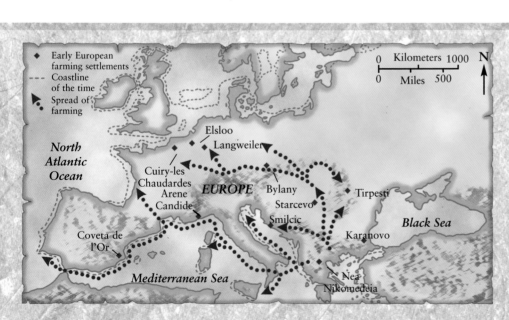

◀ EUROPEAN FARMERS
At Langweiler, Germany, farmers build a longhouse for their family and animals. They have constructed the walls and are now thatching the roof. To do this they have gathered reeds from a nearby river. Reeds make a longer-lasting thatch than grass or straw.

▲ FARMING REACHES EUROPE
From the Middle East and Turkey, farming spread gradually west along coasts and river valleys. The three main areas of farming in Europe were the Balkans, the Mediterranean coast, and north and west Europe, to which farming came last.

Key Dates

- 7000B.C. Farming reaches eastern Europe, probably from Turkey.

- 6200B.C. Farming begins in Sicily and southern Italy.

- 5400B.C. Farming spreads across northern Europe, from Hungary, through Germany, to the Netherlands.

- 5000B.C. Farming communities such as Langweiler are thriving.

- 5000B.C. Farming has spread across southern Europe and has reached the south of France.

- 4000B.C. Farming established in most of Europe.

Asian Communities

OOD SOIL AND USEFUL LOCAL crops encouraged Asian people to begin farming. This is how agriculture began in eastern Asia, in places such as the highlands of northwest and central India and areas around the banks of the Yellow River in China. Both regions had good natural resources and a climate suitable for farming. Archaeologists have found the remains of several early farming villages in both places.

▲ HARPOON HEADS, CHINA
Items like these bone harpoon points from the farming site at Banpo, China, show that hunting and river fishing were still key sources of food.

Central India had grassy uplands suitable for cattle grazing and river banks with rich soil for crops. Farming began early here, around 7000B.C. Barley was a popular crop, and farmers herded cattle, goats, and sheep on the hills. In some places, people gathered together to build villages. One of the first was called Mehrgarh, a cluster of houses by the river Bolan in northwest India. The houses were square or rectangular, and built of mud bricks plastered with mud. The flat roofs were made of reed thatch supported on long wooden poles. Inside, there were several rooms. Thick walls and small windows kept

▲ RICE FARMER
When the people had worked out how to cultivate the waterlogged fields of southern China and south-east Asia, rice became the staple crop of these areas.

the houses warm in winter and cool in summer. The style remained much the same for the next 1,000 years.

Communities like Mehrgarh grew. People built storehouses for grain to ensure a reserve when supplies became short. Some members of the community grew rich, perhaps by trading. Their graves contain favorite possessions, such as beads of shell or limestone.

Meanwhile, agriculture was developing in China. Here, millet was the favored crop, and the pig was the

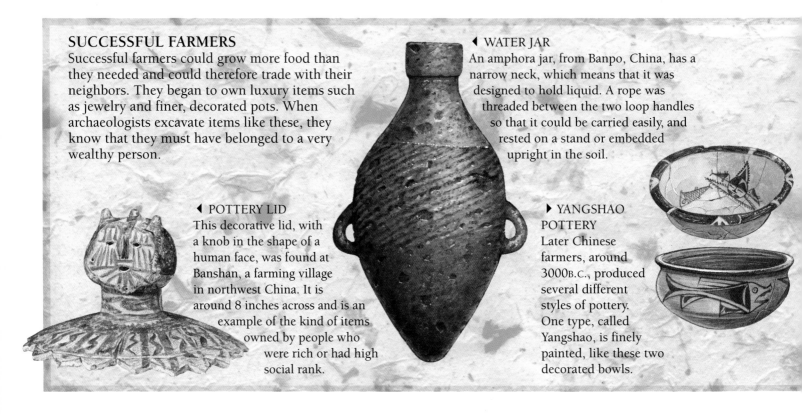

SUCCESSFUL FARMERS
Successful farmers could grow more food than they needed and could therefore trade with their neighbors. They began to own luxury items such as jewelry and finer, decorated pots. When archaeologists excavate items like these, they know that they must have belonged to a very wealthy person.

◀ WATER JAR
An amphora jar, from Banpo, China, has a narrow neck, which means that it was designed to hold liquid. A rope was threaded between the two loop handles so that it could be carried easily, and rested on a stand or embedded upright in the soil.

◀ POTTERY LID
This decorative lid, with a knob in the shape of a human face, was found at Banshan, a farming village in northwest China. It is around 8 inches across and is an example of the kind of items owned by people who were rich or had high social rank.

▶ YANGSHAO POTTERY
Later Chinese farmers, around 3000B.C., produced several different styles of pottery. One type, called Yangshao, is finely painted, like these two decorated bowls.

first creature to be domesticated. Farmers also grew vegetables, such as cabbages, and harvested fruit, such as plums. Later, they began to grow rice, which became the staple in most of eastern Asia. Rice was especially successful in southern China, where the ground was wetter.

Chinese farmers quickly learned that their soils needed a rest after a season of cultivation. They developed a method of farming that switched from one field to another. This allowed the land to have a fallow period, in which the land was not plowed or sown. They found that by leaving a long fallow period between periods of growing, the land could be restored. Much later, around 1100 B.C., they began to alternate crops of millet and soy beans. The bean plants brought goodness back to the soil, so that it was less important to have a fallow period.

Techniques of farming spread steadily across China. Wet farming techniques needed for rice were passed from south to north, along with strains of rice that grew more successfully in the north. China also had contact with Korea and Japan. These two areas had successful hunting and fishing communities. Agriculture did not become established there until much later.

straw thatch

plastered wall · supporting pole · central hearth

▲ FARMER'S HUT, BANPO
Chinese archaeologists found the remains of a cluster of houses belonging to the early farming community of Banpo in northern China, dating from about 6000 B.C. The buildings were oblong or round. They were built with a stout wooden framework filled in with a basketweave of thin branches. This was plastered over to make a smooth, weather-resistant wall. Thatch covered the roofs, but there was a central hole to let smoke escape from the fire in the floor below.

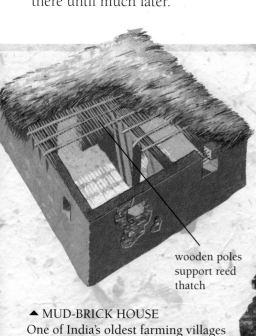

wooden poles support reed thatch

▲ MUD-BRICK HOUSE
One of India's oldest farming villages is Mehrgarh, by the river Bolan in northwest India. The houses are mostly square, have several rooms, and are made of plastered mud bricks.

▼ BURIAL
The dead at Mehrgarh in northwest India were buried in free areas in the village itself. The bodies were positioned on their sides, their knees bent. Grave goods were placed with them. Rich people's graves contained items such as stone and shell beads.

Key Dates

- 7000 B.C. Barley growing begins in India.

- 6000 B.C. Indian farmers build storehouses for their surplus food.

- 6000 B.C. Millet is the main crop of farmers in northern China.

- 5500 B.C. Date palms are cultivated in Mesopotamia.

- 5500 B.C. Indian farmers produce their own strains of wheat.

- 5000 B.C. Farmers of the Yangtze Delta area cultivate rice.

- 3500 B.C. Trade networks link the regions of China.

- 3000 B.C. Millet grown in Korea.

The Americas

▲ DEER FIGURE
People of southwestern North America made figures like this split-twig deer. These figures date to a period after 3500 B.C. and are often found near hunters' weapons and equipment.

W HETHER THEY WERE fishing or harpooning seals in the far north, hunting buffalo on the Great Plains, or gathering food in the south, the people of the Americas followed the food supply. Because crops grew in the least extreme weather conditions, they also had to move with the seasons. They became used to a restless life.

In Central America, environmental changes were often fast and unpredictable. Torrential rain was followed by baking sun. The people here longed for more control over their food supply, and they turned to agriculture before the rest of the Americas. However, they still needed good weather for their crops, which is perhaps why so many of them worshiped gods of rain and sun. The farmers hoped that worshiping these deities would bring them the most favorable conditions throughout the agricultural year.

One of the earliest crops in Central America was corn (maize), a plant that has been important in American farming ever since. It was developed from a

▲ HUT AND HUNTER
In eastern North America, hunters often built short-term shelters, like this hut. They made a framework of thin wooden poles, joined together at the top. This they covered with grass. Huts like this could catch fire easily, so the hearth was outside.

local wild grass called teosinte. Farmers tried different varieties, choosing the plants that grew best in local conditions. This proved a successful approach, and maize farming spread quite quickly.

Farther north, in what is now the southwestern United States, the first farmers experimented with various types of gourd and with plants such as sunflower and sumpweed. As the farmers of Central America began to trade more widely, they took their

AMERICAN FARMERS

The Americas contain a variety of different climates and environments, all with their own native plant species. For the early farmers, the challenge was to choose the best plants for their own region. Often this was simply a question of selecting from local species that were known to do well. But sometimes an imported crop, such as cotton in southern North America, was a success.

◀ POTATOES
Between 3000–2500 B.C., farmers in the hills of the Andes were growing the potato. For thousands of years, this useful root crop was grown only in South America, and many varieties of potato are still found only in the Andes.

▲ STONE WEIGHTS
Hunters in Kentucky attached these stone weights to the handles of their spear-throwers. This made their spears travel much farther and faster. As a result, when a spear hit an animal it was much more powerful.

◀ CLAY FIGURINE
Mysterious statuettes like this one have been found in numerous North American settlements. They have little in the way of modeling or facial features, so it is impossible to tell whether they represent male or female figures. They are made of clay and decorated with lines and dots. The clay was not fired, though; it simply became hard with age. No one knows what these figures were for.

domesticated maize, beans, and squash with them, and these joined the local plants to become staple crops in the north. For many people in the southwest, the plants were a welcome addition to foraged foods.

In South America people tried to cultivate a variety of crops, including gourds, squashes, manioc, potatoes, and various types of bean. In each area, they selected the best plants for local conditions and tried different growing methods over thousands of years. The region where farming caught on most quickly was Peru. In the Andes Mountains, hunter-gatherers began to grow crops such as gourds and beans to add to their existing

diet. They carried on using this mixed form of food supply for many thousands of years.

In the coastal areas, rivers had created narrow valleys as they flowed off the mountains to the sea. In the rich soil found in these valleys, people began to grow squashes and peppers, to which they later added maize. They also developed methods of irrigation to bring water from the rivers to their fields.

Animal farming was at first less popular in the Americas than in other parts of the world. There were few native species that were easy to farm. But in the Andes Mountains one species, the llama, was valued for its wool and milk, as well as being used as a beast of burden. The people of the Americas developed a variety of crops and farming techniques, but in many places wild foods were still widely available, and many groups carried on their lifestyle of hunting and gathering.

▼ RIVER TRANSPORTATION
Simple wooden canoes provided transportation along North America's rivers. There were various ways of making these. They could be "dug-outs," made by hollowing out a log. Another design was made of thin tree bark attached to a wooden frame.

▼ SUNFLOWERS
This giant member of the daisy family is found mainly in North America. Farmers prized it for its seeds, which can be eaten. Later they learned how to extract the oil from the seeds, using it for cooking. Some species also have edible roots.

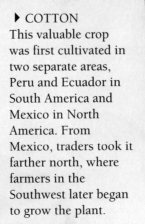

▶ COTTON
This valuable crop was first cultivated in two separate areas, Peru and Ecuador in South America and Mexico in North America. From Mexico, traders took it farther north, where farmers in the Southwest later began to grow the plant.

Key Dates

- 8500 B.C. Agriculture established in Peru. Crops grown include squash, beans, and grasses.

- 7000 B.C. In Central America people gather avocado, chillies, squash, and beans. These are plants farmers will begin to cultivate in the next 2,000 years.

- 6300 B.C. Farmers in Peru grow various root crops, such as oca and ulluco.

- 5400 B.C. The use of llamas for wool, milk and transportation is found in the Andes.

- 5000 B.C. Mexican farmers grow maize.

- 5000 B.C. Domesticated plants of Central America, such as the bottle gourd, begin to spread to North America.

Hunting and Gathering

FARMING WAS NOT FOR everyone. Hunting and gathering can provide a steady, reliable source of food as long as there are not too many people living in a small area. Africa is one part of the world where some peoples made the change to farming while others continued to hunt and gather for much longer.

After the final Ice Age, the Sahara was a much damper, greener environment than it is today. It became the scene for some of Africa's earliest experiments in farming. Rock paintings show how the people began to herd cattle, together with other local species such as giraffe.

▲ GIRAFFE
Artists painted both farm animals and the hunters' favorite quarry on the walls of rock shelters in the Sahara Desert. The giraffe was one of the creatures that people living in Africa both herded and hunted during prehistoric times.

When the Sahara dried out and gradually turned to desert, most agricultural activity was pushed to the south, between the Sahara and the Equator. This was where the climate allowed farmers to develop crops such as yam and sorghum, a cereal crop that was suited to warm places. This area became the heartland of African farming.

Still farther south, people carried on hunting and gathering. They ate a number of local plants, especially various palms and a shrub called bauhinia. In addition, they found out how to use other plants for more specialized purposes. A good example was the bottle gourd, which was suitable for making into containers.

The African hunter-gatherers also improved their tools. To make knives, they used tiny blades of sharp flint, which they glued into wooden handles using natural tree resin. They also carved hooks from bone for fishing. Such uses of the materials around them show how highly adapted they were to their environment.

Australia was another place where the traditional lifestyle of hunting and gathering continued. To begin with,

◀ ZULU HUNTER
Today, some African peoples still get some of their food by hunting, but now their spears are tipped with metal rather than the stone of earlier times.

USEFUL SPECIES
The early hunter-gatherers of Africa and Australia had a vast knowledge of plants. When they came across a new species they would try it out. This was a dangerous process, as many plants were poisonous. They gradually discovered plants that were good to eat and others that worked as medicines. Modern scientists are still investigating the plant medicines used by the world's hunter-gatherer peoples.

◀ ALMONDS
Nuts, such as almonds, that are native to North Africa and the Middle East, are a nutritious food. Gatherers made a point of going to the forest when they were in season. Nuts are easy to store and contain plenty of energy-building protein, useful to hunter-gatherers when meat is in short supply.

▶ JUNIPER BERRIES
Gatherers soon knew everything about the plants in their area. They discovered that some plants, though not good to eat, had other useful properties. Berries such as juniper, which grows all over the northern hemisphere, were valued for their perfume and their use in medicine.

◀ GOURD
Some species of gourd were very useful. When the flesh had been eaten, the outer shells made excellent containers. People made bowls with the larger fruit, while using smaller ones to make items such as dippers and cups.

people stayed near the coast, living on fish, eels, and, especially, shellfish. Remains of the shells, left in dumps that archaeologists call middens, have been found along both the north and southeast coasts. As time went on, the native Australians explored the river valleys, moving gradually inland. People discovered that cereal plants such as millet made good food. They developed hunting skills that enabled them to survive when they moved even farther inland toward Australia's hot and dry interior.

The early Australians traveled for miles, exchanging tools and shell jewelry, and creating the beautiful rock art, which can still be found all over the country. As they did this, they were also developing a complex series of myths about their ancestry that reflected their hunting and gathering lifestyle. Most important of all are the stories of Dreamtime, the period when the earth and the spirits of people were created. These myths held, and still hold, great religious significance for native Australians, and they reveal a people of profound beliefs.

▲ HUNTER-GATHERERS
This group of hunter-gatherers have found an area rich in food and have made a camp with a brushwood shelter that they will occupy for weeks or even months. While two men butcher the antelope they have killed, another group of people returns from gathering vegetables and wood for the fire on which they will cook the meat.

▶ ENGRAVED PEARL SHELL
In societies that did not use metals, all sorts of items were adapted for use as jewelry. This ornament, engraved with abstract designs, was made by native Australians from a piece of pearl shell.

◀ BARK PAINTING
A hunter throws his spear at a crane in this bark painting from Australia's Northern Territory. This style of painting is known as "x-ray," because the designs on the crane depict the bird's insides.

Key Dates

- 10,000B.C. Obsidian, a type of volcanic glass, used to make tools in the Rift Valley area of eastern Africa.

- 9000B.C. People move into the Sahara region; increased rainfall allows grasslands to grow along the edges of what is now desert.

- 7000B.C. African communities in the Sahara begin making pottery.

- 6000B.C. People start herding cattle in some parts of the Sahara region.

- 4000B.C. Sahara reaches its wettest, most temperate conditions, with Lake Chad at its largest.

- 3500B.C. Ostrich eggshell beads become popular as necklaces in eastern Africa.

The First Metalworkers

▲ GOLD BULL
The settlement of Varna, on the Black Sea, was one of Europe's first metal-working sites. Hundreds of gold ornaments, bracelets and beads have been discovered there.

As they created art on surfaces in caves, ancient peoples must have seen gold. They would also have seen copper, as it has a greenish tinge in the rock. Deposits of metal in rock are rare and difficult to extract. It was a long time before anyone worked out how to remove the material and then to work it into something useful. Eventually, someone found a place where there was enough metal to remove and found that it could be hammered into shape. Metal was beaten into ornamental objects such as beads, which were soon highly valued.

When craftworkers started to make pottery, they built kilns that could reach temperatures as high as 1,470°F. Before long, they found that heating certain rocks, or ores, in the kiln melted the metal they contained, so that it could be poured off and collected. They had discovered the process called smelting. This made it possible to extract much larger amounts of metal from the ore. People could make all kinds of items, such as jewelry and tools, out of copper instead

▲ BRONZE AGE SETTLEMENT
Most of the people of Bronze Age Europe lived in small villages with thatched houses, like those built by the first farmers. An area would be set aside for metalworking away from the houses, so that there was less risk of fire.

THE MAGIC OF METAL
The first metals must have seemed like magic. By heating the ore, the metalworker could make metal appear, apparently out of nowhere. It would first be seen in hot, liquid form, then it would miraculously set when it cooled. Copper and gold glittered beautifully in the light, so people found these metals very attractive.

▼ LONG-HORNED OXEN
Small, precious objects, such as pieces of jewelry, were among the first items to be made of metal, because they did not use too much of it. Early metalworkers could produce work of great skill, as these copper oxen found in Poland show.

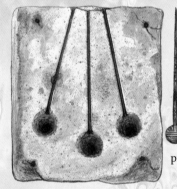
mold

pin

◀ MOLD AND PIN
A Bronze Age mold and matching pin show how the process of casting could be used to produce a number of items at speed—in this case three pins at the same time. The small holes at each corner would have matched with bumps in the other half of the mold, to ensure a perfect fit.

▶ COPPER AND TIN
The first important alloy was bronze, a mix of copper and tin. Tin is not common, so bronze developed slowly where there were good tin deposits—China, the Middle East, and parts of France, Germany, and Britain.

copper   tin

▶ CASTING

Metal items, such as tools and weapons, could be made by casting. The metalworker prepared a stone mold in two parts that fitted together exactly. When the halves were joined and secured with twine, the hollow inside the mold had the shape of the object to be cast. Hot molten metal was poured into the mold through a hole in the top. When the metal had cooled and set, the metalworker took the mold apart to reveal the object. The same mold could be used again and again.

of other materials. There was still a problem, however. Metals such as gold and copper were easy to work, but they were soft. They made good jewelry, but poor tools. The solution was to combine one metal with another to make an alloy that was hard-wearing. The best alloy discovered in the ancient world was bronze. This was made by mixing copper with a little tin. It was tough, quite easy to work, had a pleasant, gold-colored appearance, and could be sharpened.

Bronze became a popular material for jewelry, tools, and weapons. Sometimes, once a metalworker had smelted some copper and mixed in some tin, he would let the molten metal set into a bar and then hammer it into shape. Liquid metal can also be cast in a mold to produce all sorts of complex shapes. Casting was popular because it was easy to produce many identical

items using the same mould. However, since hammering hardened the metal, this method was still used to make objects such as weapons, which had to be very strong.

Metal technology probably began in the Middle East around 3000 B.C., and spread to other parts of the world during the next 2,000 years. The development of bronzeworking is so important that historians sometimes call this period the Bronze Age. Bronze did not reach all parts of the world. There was no Bronze Age in Australia, South America, or many parts of Africa. In such places, although people may have used gold or copper occasionally, they mostly made do with the stone technology they had developed. They had to wait until the coming of iron before they could take full advantage of metals.

▲ THE SPREAD OF COPPER IN EUROPE

In Europe, copper working began in two main centers, Iberia (southern Spain) and the Balkans, where plenty of the metal was available. From these centers, archaeologists have mapped and dated discoveries of bronze objects. This gives a rough idea of how knowledge of the craft spread across the European continent.

Key Dates

- 9000 B.C. Copper used in some parts of Asia for tools and weapons.

- 6000 B.C. Smelting and casting are developed in the Middle East and southeastern Europe.

- 4000 B.C. Knowledge of metalworking begins spreading to Europe, Asia, and North Africa.

- 3000 B.C. Bronze technology develops in the Middle East.

- 3000–1000 B.C. Better trade routes enable bronzeworking techniques to spread across much of Europe.

- 2000 B.C. Bronzeworking develops in China.

- 2000 B.C. Bronze is used widely in Asia for everyday tools and weapons.

Megaliths

▲ NIGHT SKY
People have always looked to the sky in their religion. Most stone circles and rows of standing stones are arranged to line up with the Sun, Moon, or stars.

TOWERING STANDING STONES, massive stone circles, and vast rows of stones are the most awesome of all prehistoric remains. Some of them are so huge that no one knows how Bronze Age people ever managed to build them. Because they are so big, they are known as megaliths, a term that comes from two Greek words meaning huge stones.

Another mystery is exactly what these vast monuments were for. Archaeologists think they may have been used for religious ceremonies. The stones are often lined up with yearly movements of the Sun and stars, so the ceremonies were almost certainly linked to the calendar and the seasons. They may have been fertility ceremonies, relating the crop-growing season to the annual movements of the stars.

There are two famous groups of megaliths in Europe, one on England's Salisbury Plain, the other in Brittany, France. Many of the British monuments are stone circles the most famous are at Stonehenge and Avebury. The main monument in Brittany is a series of rows, or alignments, of stones near the village of Carnac. In both cases there are many other prehistoric monuments nearby, such as smaller circles and alignments, earthworks, burial mounds, and single standing stones. Together these structures make up

▲ BUILDING STONEHENGE
Stonehenge in Wiltshire, England, the greatest of all the stone circles, was built with the simplest technology. The builders probably used sleds or rollers to move the stones, each weighing about 40 tons, about 15 miles to the site, before heaving them into place with a combination of ropes and levers.

THE CHANGING MONUMENTS

The megalithic monuments of Europe have stood for thousands of years, but they have not always looked the same. Archaeologists have found many holes in the ground where additional stones and wooden posts once stood, making these sites even more complex than they are today. The monuments were also altered throughout prehistory, with the removal of some stones and the addition of others.

◀ DOLMEN
Groups of stones like this are called dolmens. They started out covered with earth as the chambers of prehistoric burial mounds. When the mound was moved or eroded away, the roof and its supports were left.

▲ CALLANISH STONE CIRCLE
This is quite a small circle of 13 tall, thin stones. It is in the Hebrides islands, off Scotland, and is at the focal point of lines of standing stones. The stones, some of which are 15 feet high, were quarried only a short distance away from the site. Archaeologists have calculated that each of the stones could have been dragged along by about 20 people.

▶ FESTIVAL AT AVEBURY

Another British stone circle, at Avebury in Wiltshire, may been the scene of an annual harvest or farming festival like the one shown here. The form of the ritual is unknown, but there were probably processions, offerings, and observations of the stars or Moon.

entire regions that would have been known as holy places, landscapes devoted to religion.

The builders of the megalithic monuments had to move and lift huge stones, dig long ditches, and pile up enormous mounds of earth. Yet the people of the Bronze Age had no complex machinery, only rollers, levers, ropes, and simple hand tools. It must have taken the labor of hundreds of people over many years to move the stones. Clearly, a great deal of organization was needed, and probably a ruler with enough power to keep everyone at work on the task. Planning was also important, so that the builders could work out the precise positions for the stones. These vast temples suggest that Bronze Age societies were far more advanced than you would expect, considering the simple tools they had.

◀ MEGALITHIC SITES
Britain, Ireland and northern France are the main areas where megalithic monuments can be found. This probably shows that the people of these three areas were in regular contact, traveling across the English Channel and Irish Sea, when the megaliths were erected. They must have had similar religious beliefs and ceremonies, although we now know very little about these. There were once many more megaliths, but in the 1700s and 1800s farmers cleared away large numbers of these monuments from their fields.

Key Dates

- 4000B.C. Ditched enclosures common in many parts of Europe.

- 4000B.C. Long barrows and megalithic tombs become common for high-status burials in Europe.

- 3200B.C. People in Europe begin to build stone circles.

- 3000B.C. In Europe, much land is cleared for agriculture.

- 2100B.C. Stones added to a site originally made up of ditches and earth banks, make Stonehenge Britain's biggest megalithic site.

- 1500B.C. The age of stone circles and standing stones comes to an end.

Lake Villages

▲ POTTERY
The lake village people used lots of pottery vessels. Some were narrow-necked, like this jug, which was made for carrying water.

THE SHORES OF ALPINE LAKES in Europe are made up of bogs and marshland. They are difficult to cross and very hard to build on. Yet archaeologists have discovered the remains of several hundred Bronze Age villages in the European Alps. The small settlements, with their simple wooden houses, were in the middle of swamps by the shores of lakes such as Constance and Neuchâtel, on the borders of modern Switzerland, France, and Germany. Why did people put up with damp, boggy conditions?

The lakes themselves were rich in fish, which could be dried or smoked, to preserve them for times when food was less plentiful. Some way beyond the lake shores was grassland, which provided grazing for animals. The foothills of the Alps were thickly forested, offering a good supply of wood for building and fuel. Most important of all, the swampy conditions made it very easy to defend the villages against enemies.

Many villages sprang up by the lakes. People cut down trees from the alpine foothills to build their houses. Roofs were thatched with reeds from the lakesides. Each house was raised above the marsh with stout wooden poles rammed deep into the earth. Wood was also used to make pathways across the swamp and to build strong fences around each village. Most villages

TOOLS FOR THE JOB
In prehistoric times, most of the lakeside region of Europe was wooded right down to the lake shores. So, before they could start building homes, the villagers had to clear away some of the trees and prepare logs for building. For this, they needed heavy stone axes with long wooden handles. Once they were settled, they could use lighter metal tools for everyday work in the fields and around the village.

▶ AX HANDLE
Waterlogged soil near the Swiss lakes has preserved ancient wooden objects, such as this ax handle. This gives us knowledge of craft skills that we lack for most prehistoric peoples.

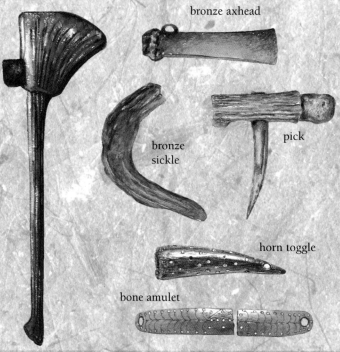

bronze axhead

bronze sickle

pick

horn toggle

bone amulet

◀ TOOL KIT
After about 2000B.C., the alpine lake people started to use bronze to make many of their tools. Axes for chopping and sickles for harvesting were two typical metal items. There were also picks with bone or antler handles.

◀ BONE AND HORN
Many items were made of these materials. Animal horn was a good material to make toggles to fasten coats and tunics. Bone could be carved into all sorts of shapes, including fastenings and pierced objects which may have been sacred charms.

were quite small, with up to 20 houses. Eventually, after 30 or 40 years, the wet ground made the poles supporting the houses rot. Either they were replaced or the people moved on to another site.

Trapped deep beneath the water, however, an amazing amount of evidence of these villages has been preserved. Archaeologists have brought to the surface some of the timbers from the houses and pathways, as well as bronze implements. In some cases even remains of the people's food and clothing have survived, preserved in the cold water.

Some of the settlements had at least one large house. This was probably the home of the village chief. Archaeologists have found decorated bronze weapons and jewelry in these houses, showing that these chiefs were rich and powerful.

▼ ON THE LAKESHORE
This view of a prehistoric lake village shows how close the inhabitants were to the resources they needed to live—reeds and fish in the lake itself, timber from the forests, and fertile fields nearby. For communities like this, easy access to these resources made it worthwhile to build in such a difficult, marshy area.

▲ REEDS
For thatched roofs, by far the best material is reed. It is strong and long-lasting and grows in abundance along the edges of lakes.

▼ LAKESIDE VILLAGE
Sites near lakes have always proved popular in places such as Austria, Switzerland, and their neighboring countries. Places such as Zurich, Neuchâtel, Lausanne, and Konstanz are all built by large lakes. Many of these modern towns and cities are built on the sites of prehistoric lake villages. The picture shows a lakeside village in the Austrian Alps. Today, many people like to visit lakeside sites because of the stunning scenery.

Key Dates

- 3000 B.C. Trading villages well established on the shores of the Black Sea; the inhabitants work copper and gold and trade along the local rivers.

- 3000 B.C. People settle along the shores of lakes in Europe's alpine region.

- 2000 B.C. Substantial wooden villages are built by the settlers in alpine areas. The people purposely select sites that are easy to defend and learn how to fortify their villages with boundary fences.

- 1600 B.C. The heyday of the lake villages comes to an end.

The Iron Age

▲ IRON DAGGER
Forged from iron and carried in a bronze sheath, this British dagger probably belonged to an important person such as a chief. It dates from the time when European society was led by warriors.

Bronze was a useful metal, but it was not as hard as stone. Neither was it always easy to find the copper and tin needed to make it. Many people carried on using flint tools and weapons. Then, in around 1300B.C., some metalworkers in the Middle East discovered iron.

Iron is a common metal in many parts of the world. It is easy to smelt, provided that the temperature in the furnace is high enough. It can be sharpened easily and can be strengthened by hammering. When metalworkers first began to smelt iron, they did not realize it was a common material. Because it was new and unusual, it was used for weapons carried by high-ranking men such as chiefs. Soon, however, they saw how common and useful iron was and began to make iron tools and weapons in large numbers.

Ironworking gradually spread throughout the Middle East and into southern Europe. Iron weapons helped empire-building peoples, such as the Hittites of Turkey, to conquer new territory. They helped the Greeks, who were building colonies around the Mediterranean, in much the same way. In India, where the people had found little copper, iron

▼ IRON AGE SETTLEMENT
When the people of Iron Age Europe built a fort, they defended it by building deep ditches. The earth from the ditches was thrown up to make massive banks, giving extra protection. Forts like this covered a huge area, with enough space for people, houses, and animals.

REMAINS FROM THE IRON AGE

Many of the most impressive remains from the Iron Age are actually made of bronze. Iron tools and weapons were made in large numbers, but most have rusted away. Bronze objects, on the other hand, are longer lasting, even if buried in the ground. As a result, many bronze items, buried in the graves of high-ranking chieftains, have survived.

◀ ▼ BROOCHES
Iron Age people fastened their clothes with brooches, which were usually made of bronze and could be very ornate. The fibula style had a long pin that worked like a modern safety pin.

fibula brooch   spectacle brooch

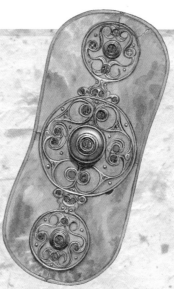

▲ BRONZE SHIELD
A shield, found in Battersea, London, was decorated by hammering the metal to make raised patterns. Colored glass and stones were added.

▶ LA TÈNE HORN
The curving, swirling lines of the decoration on the end of this horn are typical of the Celtic La Tène style, which developed during the late Iron Age in Europe. It is one of four horns made of bronze found in an Irish lake.

detail of trumpet end

made metal technology widely available for the very first time.

In Europe, iron transformed people's lives. It enabled the Celtic people, who lived in western Europe, to become warlike and powerful. They built large hill forts, protected by earthworks and fences, and fought off attackers with iron weapons. A whole village could fit into one hill fort, and these forts became bases for warrior chiefs.

The first phase of the European Iron Age is known as the Halstatt period, after a site in Austria where a number of iron swords were found. Halstatt chiefs grew rich, both from trading and from forcing neighbors to pay them tribute. Some chiefs even owned goods imported from as far away as Greece and Italy.

After about the 5th century B.C., the Celts began to produce metalwork beautifully decorated in a free, swirling style. This style is called La Tène, after the Swiss lakeside site where archaeologists have found many iron and bronze items.

By the time the Romans were building up their empire in Europe, the Celts were powerful enough to fight the Romans' armies and halt them for a while. The Celtic chiefs issued their own coinage, built strong forts, and traded with Rome in times of peace. For several centuries, these men of iron were Europe's strongest and most feared leaders.

▲ IRONWORKERS
In order to produce workable iron, the ore (the rock containing the metal) had to be heated to a high temperature. Early ironworkers made kilns of earth to contain the fire so that it could build up enough heat.

▲ IRON AGE SITES
Although Europe has perhaps the most famous of all Iron Age cultures, people in many other parts of the world discovered how to work iron. Eastern Asia and Africa were two areas that had notable Iron Age societies.

Key Dates

- 2000B.C. Middle Eastern people discover iron and make iron tools and weapons.

- 1000B.C. Ironworking established in central Europe.

- 800B.C. Beginning of Halstatt period.

- 600B.C. Iron discovered in China; hotter furnaces enable the Chinese to cast iron, something impossible in the west until much later.

- 500B.C. Ironworking begins in Africa.

- 500B.C. Ironworking well established in most of Europe.

- 450–100B.C. Fine metalwork of the La Tène period made in Europe.

The Birth of Civilization

▲ PAINTED POT
Pottery from the Mesopotamian cities is often of a very high quality: thin, well shaped, and with elegant decoration.

WHILE MANY OF THE EVENTS described in *First Steps* were happening, another development, more earth-shattering than all the rest, was beginning at different points on the globe. Small towns were growing into cities. Their inhabitants were putting up large temples and palaces, inventing written languages and creating complex societies in which there were many different jobs for people to do. There were farmers, craftworkers, priests, governors and kings. This new city-based way of life is what we now call civilization.

The place where civilization first began was Mesopotamia, the land between the Tigris and Euphrates rivers in what is now Iraq. This was part of the Fertile Crescent, where farming had started. It was the reliable food supply produced by farming that made the developments that followed possible.

As the farmers became more experienced, they worked out how to irrigate their fields so that they could bring water to the drier areas. This made the food supply more constant. The farmers could also increase

◀ WOMAN AND BABY
This figure of a mother holding a baby is made of clay. It dates from the 'Ubaid period, which lasted from 5500 to 4000B.C. At this time, towns were growing into cities, craftworkers were becoming more and more skilled, and local leaders were gaining in power.

the size of their fields by cultivating previously difficult areas.

At the same time, the people of Mesopotamia began to build large, comfortable mud brick houses. They created beautiful painted pottery, fine clay sculptures, intricate copper implements, and elegant jewelry with turquoise beads. People from other areas wanted these items, so the Mesopotamians traded with their neighbors, carrying their cargo by boat down the rivers and along the Persian Gulf. Gradually, the traders of Mesopotamia became rich, and their towns grew into cities. With cities came more power and more complex government. The priests, who were among the most powerful people, built bigger temples, another mark of civilization. Then came writing. At first, this was only a few simple symbols to show who

ARTS OF CIVILIZATION
One of the features of civilization was that society became more complex. In other words, it was divided into more social classes, with more powerful leaders and more difference between rich and poor. The rich people demanded better, more luxurious goods, from pots to jewelry, and in Mesopotamia this led to the growth of arts and crafts. Pottery, metalworking, building, and sculpture are all crafts that developed quickly at this time.

◀ POTTERY FRAGMENTS
Ancient rubbish heaps are treasure troves for archaeologists. Many pieces of broken pottery have been unearthed from the 'Ubaid period, from 5500B.C. to 4000B.C. They often have striking painted decoration.

◀ WRITING
The scribes of Mesopotamia wrote by making marks in clay tablets with a wedge-shaped reed. This writing is called cuneiform, from a Greek word meaning wedge.

◀ NECKLACES
Mesopotamian necklaces could have thousands of beads in several separate strings. The large one, found at a farming site called Choga Mami, has around 2,200 beads, crudely shaped from clay.

▶ HEAD FROM STATUETTE
Terracotta heads like these show the style of sculpture in Mesopotamia, with some features, such as the eyes, enlarged.

owned what. Later people developed more complicated writing systems that allowed them to record stories and religious texts.

The development of writing marks the end of prehistoric society. This happened at different times in different parts of the world. During the lifetimes of some of the prehistoric peoples, civilization was already present in Mesopotamia and other parts of the globe. Civilization came early to the Middle East, Egypt, the Indus Valley in India, and parts of China. Elsewhere, in Europe, North and South America and much of Africa, societies based on cities came much later.

In western Europe, for example, it was only with the arrival of the Romans that cities and writing appeared. The Romans took over the area they called Gaul (modern France) in the 1st century B.C., some 3,000 years after the first cities were built in Mesopotamia. Today, people in some parts of the world lead successful traditional lifestyles, adapted to their environment, just like their prehistoric ancestors. But even they are affected by the decisions of governments and businesses based in the world's cities.

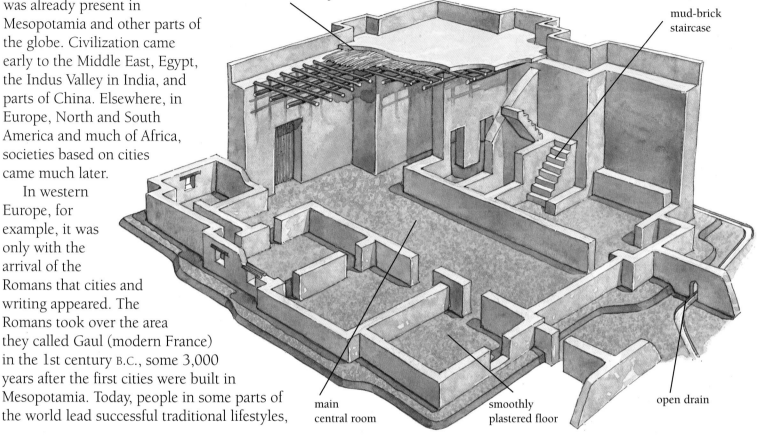

▼ 'UBAID HOUSE
Houses, like this one in modern Iraq, became larger and more complex in the 'Ubaid Period. They were still made of mud bricks, but had a large central hall, many smaller rooms, a staircase, and drainage into open gullies outside.

roof of plaster covering rushes on wooden poles

mud-brick staircase

main central room

smoothly plastered floor

open drain

▲ MARSH ARABS
These Marsh Arabs live in southeastern Iraq. They herd water buffalo and build houses out of reeds. This traditional lifestyle of the Marsh Arabs existed alongside the growing cities of Mesopotamia.

▼ ZIGGURAT
A Sumerian ziggurat consisted of a stepped platform made of sun-dried mud bricks. Only priests were allowed to climb to the top. An early example of a ziggurat is the White Temple of Uruk, made of whitewashed bricks, which dates back to the late 3000s B.C.

Key Dates

- 3500B.C. The first cities are built in Mesopotamia. Among the most important are Uruk and Ur on the banks of the Euphrates River.

- 3200B.C. Civilization spreads to Egypt.

- 3100B.C. Writing is developed in and around the city of Uruk; people write on clay tablets.

- 2500B.C. The first cities are built in the Indus Valley, Pakistan.

- 2300B.C. Several of the Mesopotamian cities unite as a single kingdom under Sargon of Agade.

- 1800B.C. Civilization develops separately in northern China.

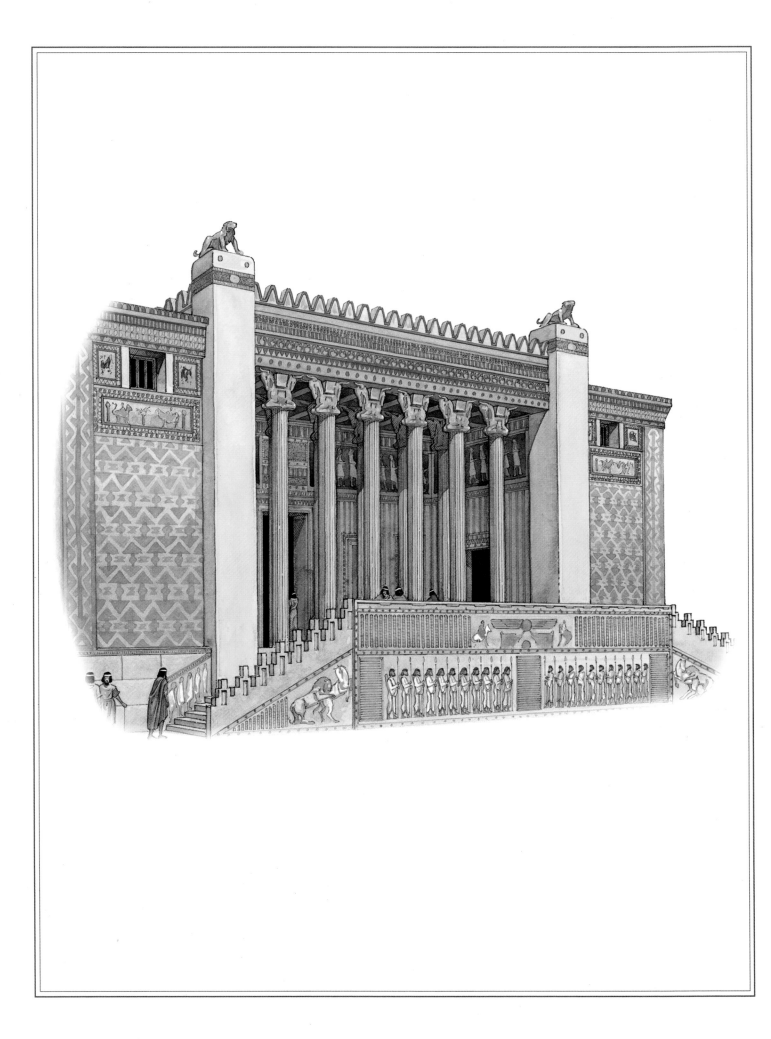

REALMS OF GOLD

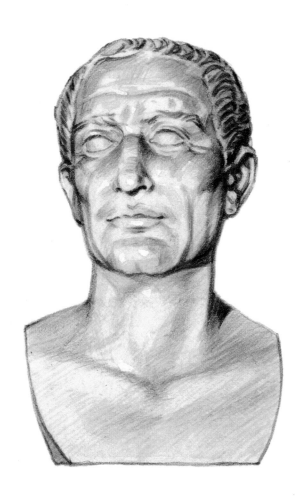

Realms of Gold looks at the great civilizations of the past—from Ancient Babylon to those of South and Central America. It explores the way people really lived, how they fought and how they organized their societies.

BY PHILIP BROOKS

70

Introduction

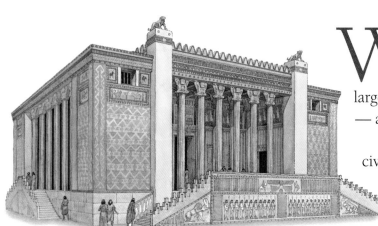

▲ BUILDINGS
The magnificent royal palace of Persepolis was built in ancient Persia's greatest city to reflect power and wealth.

▼ TIMELINE
The civilizations of the ancient world cover a vast time span of about 4500 years: from the first cities of Sumer to the later kingdoms based in Africa

WHAT IS A CIVILIZATION? The term comes from the Latin word, *civis*, which means "citizen of a city". So a civilization is a group of people living together in a large town or city, who have developed a culture — a way of life with its own special flavor. There are several key ingredients in a civilized culture. An early civilization may not have all of them, but it will certainly have some. They include writing, a system of government, organized religion and the ability to construct buildings and monuments on a grand scale. This book describes some ancient cultures that developed along these lines.

Most of the features of civilization began to develop thousands of years ago during the Stone Age. But it took a long time for people to bring all these ideas together and to build cities on a large scale. This happened at different times in different parts of the world, as is shown on the Timeline below.

No one knows why civilizations occurred in some parts of the world much earlier than others. But cities can only grow when the food supply is reliable enough to supply the town-dwellers, who have no way of growing their own food. People had to develop

▲ RELIGION
This stone carving from the Indus Valley civilization may have been a god or a king. As far as we know, all ancient civilizations had some form of organized religion.

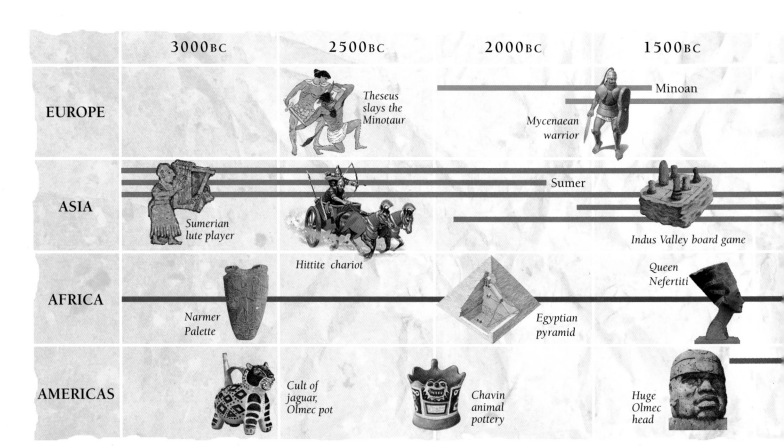

	3000BC	2500BC	2000BC	1500BC
EUROPE		*Theseus slays the Minotaur*	*Mycenaean warrior*	Minoan
ASIA	*Sumerian lute player*	*Hittite chariot*	Sumer	*Indus Valley board game*
AFRICA	*Narmer Palette*		*Egyptian pyramid*	*Queen Nefertiti*
AMERICAS	*Cult of jaguar, Olmec pot*	*Chavin animal pottery*		*Huge Olmec head*

efficient farming, and ways of storing and trading food, before they could build large cities. Trade in food also provided a network for trading the products of city workshops — items made of pottery, metal, and wood which city people sold.

Many ancient civilizations built up large empires, either by conquering their neighbors in battle or by building up trade networks which allowed them to dominate the surrounding peoples. This meant that many ancient cultures became rich, and their power spread over a large area of the globe. The Roman empire and the empire of Alexander the Great are two examples.

Civilizations such as these have left large amounts of evidence behind them. Archaeologists — people who study the remains of cultures — are still digging up artefacts made by craft workers thousands of years ago. Complex funeral customs, as in ancient Egypt, can tell us a great deal about the civilization. Together with ancient documents and the remains of ancient cities, these things provide a fascinating glimpse of how life was lived thousands of years ago.

▲ WRITING
The marks on this ancient bone are the earliest examples of Chinese script. Writing is a key feature of a civilization.

▶ TRADE
The Romans traded in ships such as this. As civilizations developed and produced a surplus of goods, they set up trading links with others.

▲ FARMING
A civilization can only develop when its food supply is secure and the growing of crops is not left to chance. Evidence shows that rice was cultivated in China around 5000BC. Rice farming arrived in Japan in about 200BC.

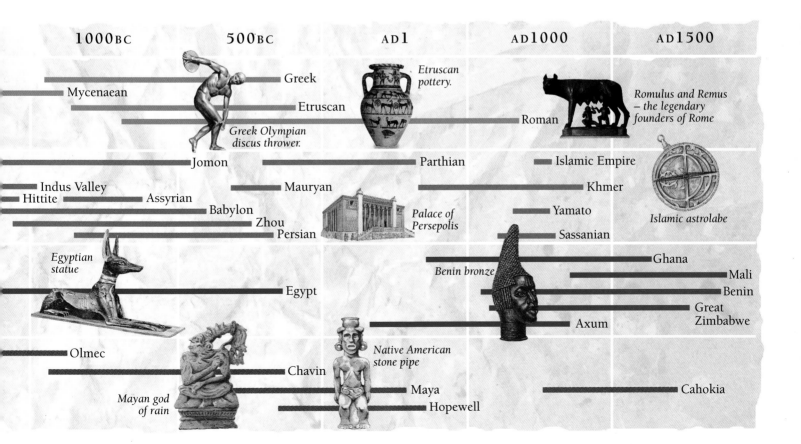

1000BC	500BC	AD1	AD1000	AD1500

Mycenaean

Greek

Greek Olympian discus thrower.

Etruscan

Etruscan pottery.

Roman

Romulus and Remus – the legendary founders of Rome

Jomon

Parthian

Islamic Empire

Indus Valley

Hittite

Assyrian

Mauryan

Khmer

Islamic astrolabe

Babylon

Zhou

Persian

Palace of Persepolis

Yamato

Sassanian

Egyptian statue

Benin bronze

Ghana

Mali

Egypt

Benin

Axum

Great Zimbabwe

Olmec

Native American stone pipe

Chavin

Mayan god of rain

Maya

Hopewell

Cahokia

The Sumerians

HOME TO THOUSANDS of people and bustling with activity, the world's first cities were built in Mesopotamia, the land between the Tigris and Euphrates rivers in what is now Iraq. The narrow streets and whitewashed mud-brick houses of cities such as Uruk and Ur were home to craftworkers who made pottery and metalwork that were traded as far afield as Arabia and India. People from the region made the world's first wheeled carts and chariots, and invented the world's first known writing system, called "cuneiform" script. For these reasons, Mesopotamia became known as "the cradle of civilization".

One group of people to settle in Mesopotamia were the Sumerians. They arrived in Sumer, the southern part of the area, in about 5000BC. The climate was hot and dry but farmers learned to use water from the rivers to irrigate their fields and grow plentiful crops of wheat, barley, dates and vegetables.

The Sumerians' first city was Uruk, which they built by the River Euphrates. By 3500BC, some 10,000 people lived there. The winding streets of the city surrounded its biggest building, the temple of Anu, the greatest of the Sumerians' many gods. Here the priests worshipped Anu in the hope that he would bring good weather and rich harvests. The people, who knew that they would starve if the harvests were poor, brought generous offerings to the temple. This made the priests some of the richest, most powerful people in the city.

Soon, other cities were founded all over Mesopotamia. They were similar to Uruk, with large temples, called ziggurats, and mud-brick houses. Each city was independent, with its own ruler, priests and merchants. As the cities grew rich from their trade, they competed with each other for power over the whole region.

The Sumerian cities remained independent until about 2350BC. Then the Akkadians, from an area north of Sumer, conquered the area and made it part of their large Mesopotamian empire.

▶ PLOW
Sumerian farmers developed the ox-drawn plow in about 4000BC. It was much more efficient than a hand-held plow and meant that they could grow a great deal more food.

◀ LUTE PLAYER
Musicians playing lutes, pipes and tambourines, provided entertainment while people banqueted, drank beer, and watched celebrations. The people of Ur enjoyed music at home and at great festivals such as New Year.

FERTILE LAND
Separate city states made up the Sumerian civilization but there were similarities between them. Each used the Tigris and Euphrates for trade and transportation and all had mud-brick buildings. Also, they relied on fertile farmland to produce food. The region was so fertile, it is often called the Fertile Crescent.

▶ GRAVE GOODS
Gold items, such as jewelry, were placed in the tombs of the early kings and queens of Ur. Servants followed their king or queen to the grave. After a royal death, the servants walked into the huge tomb, drank poison, and lay down to die next to the body of their royal master or mistress.

▲ STANDARD OF UR
Pictures made from shells and precious stones show a row of Sumerian farmers herding cattle and sheep. Below them, workers carry heavy loads. These pictures, known as the Standard of Ur, may once have decorated a Sumerian musical instrument.

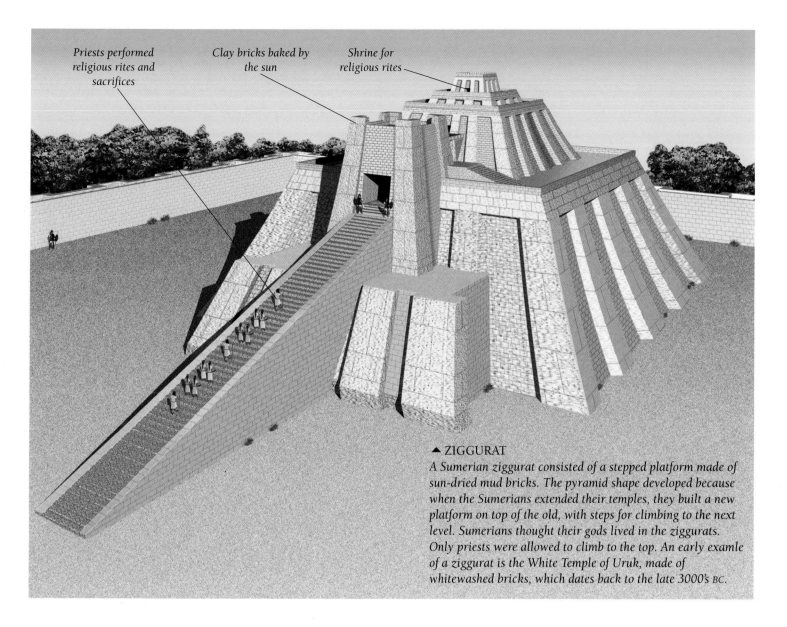

Priests performed religious rites and sacrifices

Clay bricks baked by the sun

Shrine for religious rites

▲ ZIGGURAT
A Sumerian ziggurat consisted of a stepped platform made of sun-dried mud bricks. The pyramid shape developed because when the Sumerians extended their temples, they built a new platform on top of the old, with steps for climbing to the next level. Sumerians thought their gods lived in the ziggurats. Only priests were allowed to climb to the top. An early examle of a ziggurat is the White Temple of Uruk, made of whitewashed bricks, which dates back to the late 3000's BC.

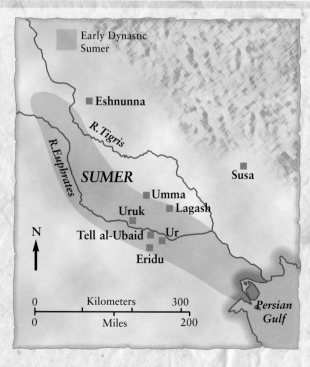

◄ SUMER
The Sumerian civilization consisted of independent, walled city states such as Ur, Lagash, Umma and Uruk. It arose in the area known as Mesopotamia, or "the land between two rivers", which covered much of what is now present-day Iraq.

Key Dates

- 5000BC The Sumerians, a farming people, settle in southern Mesopotamia.

- 4000BC Ox-drawn plow introduced.

- 3100BC Uruk becomes one of the world's first cities. Sumerians develop the potter's wheel and wheeled transport.

- 2900BC Earliest known writing.

- 2500BC Ur becomes a major city.

- 2350BC King Sargon from Akkad conquers the area of Sumer.

- 2100BC Ur is the most important Mesopotamian city, under King Ur-Nammu.

- 1700BC Ur declines, and the city of Babylon gains in strength.

Ancient Babylon

A ROUND 1900BC, the Amorites, a people from Syria, moved into Mesopotamia, the land between the Tigris and Euphrates rivers. They farmed barley, herded sheep and goats and were skilled in all sorts of crafts, from metal working to perfumery and from leather making to beekeeping.

The Amorites made their capital at the city of Babylon, by the Euphrates. During the late 1700s BC, their king Hammurabi conquered the whole of southern Mesopotamia, which became known as Babylonia. The conquered land contained peoples of many different cultures and laws, so Hammurabi decided to unify the laws. They were inscribed on a stone stela, or tablet, for all to see.

Under Hammurabi, Babylon became a great center of science and learning. Babylonian scholars developed a numbering system, based on groups of 60, which is how we get our 60-minute hour and 360-degree circle. The scientists of Babylon were also renowned astronomers, recording the movements of the moon and stars across the night sky.

Many neighboring rulers were jealous of Babylon's power and the wealth the Babylonians earned from trade and the city was attacked many times. Hittites, from the area that is now Turkey, raided Babylon, then Kassites, from mountains to the east, invaded and took over the city. They turned Babylon into an important religious center, with a large temple to the supreme god, Marduk.

▲ CLAY LION
A clay lion which stood guard outside one of the Babylonian temples. Its intricate detail shows that the Babylonians were skilled sculptors. The lion was a popular symbol of royal power.

▶ ISHTAR GATE
The Ishtar Gate, decorated with spectacular blue stone, straddled the Processional Way which led into the city of Babylon. Three walls ringed the city, each so thick that two chariots could drive side by side along the top.

SCIENCE AND LAW
Babylon was a sophisticated city and a center for science, literature and learning. Scholars studied mathematics and astronomy, the science of the stars. Their ideas continue to influence us today.

◀ THE LAWS OF HAMMURABI
Hammurabi's laws were carved into a stela of black basalt rock. They include laws about money, property, the family and the rights of slaves. According to the law, a wrongdoer had to be punished in a way that suited the crime. The phrase "an eye for an eye and a tooth for a tooth" originates from Hammurabi's laws.

▲ MAP OF THE WORLD
A stone map showing the known land masses surrounded by a ring of ocean. The map was made by Babylonian scholars more than 3000 years ago. They labeled it with wedge-shaped cuneiform writing.

◀ HANGING GARDENS
King Nebuchadnezzar built fabulous hanging, or terraced, gardens for his wife Amytis to remind her of the green hill country of her home in Media. One of the ancient world's great wonders, no one today really knows what the gardens looked like.

▼ DRAGON OF MARDUK
The dragon symbolized Marduk, supreme god of the Babylonians. The Babylonians worshipped many gods. They included the sun god, Shamash, and Ishtar, goddess of war and love.

In around 900BC, the Chaldeans, horsemen from the Gulf coast, invaded Babylon. Their greatest king, Nebuchadnezzar II, rebuilt the city more magnificently than before. He gave it massive mud-brick walls, strong gates and a seven-story ziggurat. He also built a palace for himself and the Hanging Gardens, which was one of the Seven Wonders of the ancient world.

Babylon became the largest city in western Asia. Trade along the rivers, and via the caravan routes leading eastward to Iran, also made it wealthy once more. Its magnificence survived until it was again invaded, this time by the Persians.

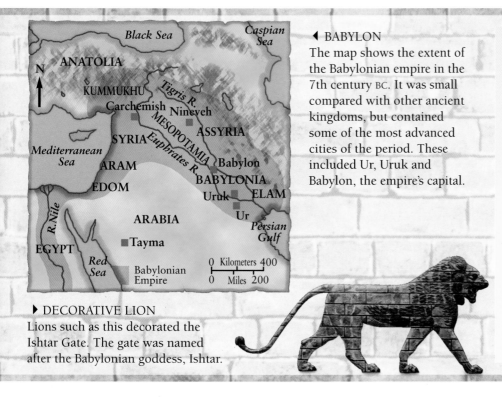

◀ BABYLON
The map shows the extent of the Babylonian empire in the 7th century BC. It was small compared with other ancient kingdoms, but contained some of the most advanced cities of the period. These included Ur, Uruk and Babylon, the empire's capital.

▶ DECORATIVE LION
Lions such as this decorated the Ishtar Gate. The gate was named after the Babylonian goddess, Ishtar.

Key Dates

- 1900BC Babylon becomes the chief city of the Amorites.

- 1792–1750BC Reign of King Hammurabi, law-giver and conqueror of Mesopotamia.

- 1595–1155BC The Kassites rule the city of Babylon.

- 900BC The Chaldeans take over Babylon and begin to rebuild it.

- 605–562BC Reign of King Nebuchadnezzar. He builds the fabulous Hanging Gardens. Babylon is the most sophisticated city in the Middle East.

The Hittites

ROM THE COLD, mountainous region of central Anatolia (modern Turkey) came the Hittites, powerful peoples who flourished between about 1600 and 1200BC. A warlike group, they battled constantly with their neighbors for control over Mediterranean trade.

The Hittites had to master a harsh homeland, finding lands to farm wheat and barley and raise sheep and cattle. They built a huge stronghold at Hattusas, in the center of their kingdom. From here, they recruited and trained a powerful army. They were among the first to use horses in warfare and developed the chariot as one of the most feared weapons of battle.

They attacked the Mitanni, from northern Mesopotamia, and took over Syria. Their charioteers even threatened the power of the great Egyptian empire. The Hittites also used peaceful means to increase their power. They made treaties with the Egyptian pharaohs, which have been found in clay tablets in the massive royal archives at Hattusas. These show that the Hittites sometimes bought off their rivals with gold.

The Hittites had a strong land army but found it hard to defend their coasts. Invaders from the sea, known as the "Sea Peoples", attacked them constantly. This, together with bad harvests and pressure from Egypt, led to their downfall in around 1200BC.

▲ PRISONER
Egyptian mosaic tile, dating from c.1170BC, shows a Hittite prisoner.

◀ SOLDIER OR GOD?
No one knows for sure whether this armed man is a soldier or a Hittite god. He seems to be flexing his muscles. Placed at the gate of the city, he would have put fear into the hearts of any attacker.

▼ LION GATE
Fearsome-looking lions decorated the stone gateways of Hattusas, the Hittite capital and one of the strongest cities of its time. Set among cliffs and mountains, the city was well protected from enemies.

ARMIES

Both the Hittites and Assyrians had powerful armies but the Assyrian army was the most feared and efficient of its time. Consisting of foot soldiers and heavily armed cavalry, Assyrian armies were huge, several thousand strong. Many of the soldiers were captured people from lands that the Assyrians had conquered.

◀ CHARIOTEERS
Much of the Hittite military success came from their skill as charioteers. Their chariots, which could hold up to three people, one to drive the horses, and two to fight, were feared by all.

Boghazkoy

Tarsus

Caspian Sea

Nineveh
Ashur

N

Mediterranean Sea

Hittite Empire

Assyrian Empire

Persian Gulf

0   Kilometers   400
0   Miles   250

▲ HITTITES AND ASSYRIANS
The Hittites controlled much of modern Turkey and parts of northern Mesopotamia and Syria. Their real center of power was around Hattusas and the cities of Alaca and Alisar. The Assyrian empire stretched from the Mediterranean to the Persian Gulf.

The Assyrians

THEY WERE THE MOST FEARED people of the ancient world. The armies of the Assyrians attacked swiftly, ransacking villages, battering down city walls, and killing anyone in the way. They carried away precious metals, timber, building stone — anything they could use. They took prisoners to work as slaves on building projects in their cities along the upper Tigris river — building luxurious palaces, towering temples, and massive city walls.

The Assyrians seemed unstoppable. They conquered an empire that stretched from the Nile Delta to the ancient cities of Babylon and Ur. They built beautiful cities, such as Nineveh, Nimrud and Khorsabad, which were among the most magnificent the world had ever seen. Their royal palaces were decorated with stone reliefs that portrayed the success and glory of their kings. The reliefs survive today and show us much about the Assyrian kings and their lives — their war triumphs, use of chariots and battering rams, victory celebrations, conquered people bringing them lavish tribute, and hunting scenes.

The main strength of the Assyrians was their army but as Assyria grew in size, the soldiers could not defend the whole empire at once. One conquered city could not defeat the Assyrians but when the people of Babylonia and Media joined forces they could win, and the vast Assyrian empire quickly crumbled.

▲ WINGED SPHINX
Massive carved stone sphinxes guarded city gates and palaces. Winged beasts, they had bull or lion bodies and human heads with long beards, like those worn by Assyrian kings. The Assyrians believed the monsters gave heavenly protection and warded off evil wrongdoers.

▼ THE ROYAL HUNT
Assyrian kings enjoyed hunting, particularly for lions, wildest of all creatures. They wanted their people to think their strength was god-like and often had themselves portrayed performing feats of incredible strength and bravery.

▲ COURT LIFE
A stone relief shows musicians with harps and flutes playing at the palace of Assurbanipal in Nineveh. Reliefs such as this tell us much about court life.

▼ BATTERING RAMS
Assyrian soldiers used a fearsome fighting machine, part battering ram, part tower, to attack and break through the walls of enemy cities. While the metal-tipped battering ram was driven against the walls, soldiers on the tower used picks to break them down.

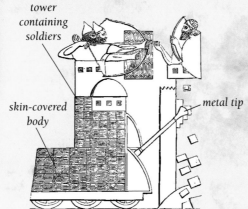

tower containing soldiers

skin-covered body

metal tip

Key Dates

- c.2000BC Hittite farmers settle in Turkey.
- 1550BC Hattusas becomes Hittite capital.
- 1380–1346BC Hittites flourish.
- 1250BC Assyrians and Sea People attack Hittite empire.
- 1200BC Hittite empire declines.
- 883–859BC Nineveh built.
- 744–727BC Assyria reaches greatest power.
- 721–705BC King Sargon builds Assyrian capital, Khorsabad.
- 664BC Assyrians conquer Egypt.
- 612BC Nineveh destroyed.
- 609BC Babylonians defeat Assyrian army.

The Persian Empire

▲ PERSIAN SOLDIER
Mosaics of Persian soldiers decorated the palace of Susa. They were the keepers of law and order. An elite force of 10,000 warriors were called "immortals" because when one died, he was replaced immediately.

THEY BEGAN AS A SMALL nation from the region near Babylon. Suddenly, in around 549BC, the Persians seemed to be everywhere. Led by Cyrus the Great (r. 559–530BC), the Persian army pushed west and east, conquering a vast area that stretched from modern Turkey to the borders of India. Cyrus, and the emperors that followed him, gained enormous wealth from their conquests. They built cities with huge palaces, drank from gold and silver vessels, and surrounded themselves with luxury.

The Persian Empire was vast and mountainous and contained many different peoples, who often rebelled against Persian control. To keep order, the Persian rulers had a very effective army. Known as "the immortals", these 10,000 specially trained men were feared wherever they went and moved quickly to put down rebellions.

The emperors did not only rely on brute force. They also organized the empire so it could be controlled easily. They divided it into 20 provinces, each governed by a satrap, an official who ruled on behalf of the emperor. Each province raised taxes and tributes. The satraps were extremely powerful in their own right, so the emperor sent spies, known as "the king's ears", to each province to listen out for treachery and to check that the satraps were sending all the taxes to the emperor, not keeping some for themselves. The Persians also built a network of roads to link the corners of their empire. Spies, tax collectors and traders could travel easily around the countryside.

▲ TRIBUTES
Once a year representatives from the provinces came to the royal palace at Persepolis. Everyone brought gifts for the emperor — gold from India, horses from Assyria, two-humped camels from Bactria.

KING OF KINGS
Cyrus the Great belonged to the Achaemenid dynasty. He, and the Persian emperors who followed him, gave themselves the title King of Kings. They lived in great splendor and had absolute power. Below them, and their nobles, most of the population were farmers, craftworkers, serfs and slaves.

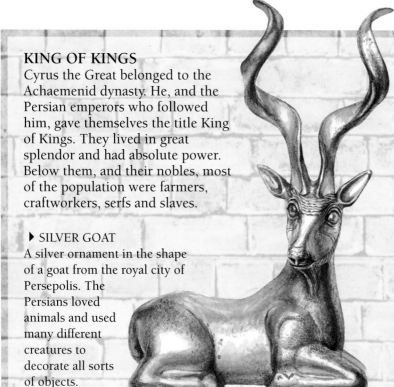

▶ SILVER GOAT
A silver ornament in the shape of a goat from the royal city of Persepolis. The Persians loved animals and used many different creatures to decorate all sorts of objects.

▲ DARIUS THE GREAT
Emperor Darius I ruled the Persian Empire from 522 to 486BC. He was head of the army and a wise ruler. He also founded Persepolis. During his reign, the empire reached its greatest extent.

▼ PERSIAN NOBLES
A Persian nobleman stands between two soldiers. Nobles were wealthy and educated. Darius appointed his satraps, or provincial governors, from noble-born families.

Bulls, facing in opposite directions, topped the columns

▼ PERSEPOLIS
The massive audience hall in the palace of Persepolis. The emperors, Darius I and Xerxes built a magnificent palace at the city of Persepolis. The huge staircase leading up to the audience hall was so wide that 8 horses could ride up it side by side. People came from all over the empire to pay tribute to the emperor who sat on his throne at the far side of the hall.

Carved reliefs show people bringing tributes

Doorway into royal audience hall

The Persians' wealth grew and the emperors brought skilled workers from all over the empire to build cities and palaces. Stone masons came from Greece, brickmakers from Babylon and goldsmiths from Egypt. The Persians also imported raw materials such as cedar wood from the Lebanon and ivory from Ethiopia.

Some people did fight off Persian invasions. The Scythians, fearless horsemen from the north, held back Persia's army, and the Greeks fought off two invasion attempts. The Greeks hated the Persians and eventually Alexander the Great, the famous conqueror from the Greek world, destroyed the Persian empire in 333BC.

▲ THE PERSIAN EMPIRE
The map shows the Persian Empire at its greatest extent in about 518BC. By then, Persia was the largest empire that the world had seen. It stretched from India to the Mediterranean. Susa was the capital. The empire included areas that had previously produced great civilizations: Egypt, Sumer, the Indus Valley and Anatolia.

Key Dates

- 835BC The Medes, from Media, southwest of the Caspian Sea, rule much of Iran.

- 549BC Cyrus becomes leader of the Persians. He conquers Media, Ionia and Lydia, so creating the first Persian empire.

- 522–486BC Reign of Darius I.

- 518BC Darius conquers parts of Egypt.

- 513BC Darius takes over the Indus Valley area.

- 490BC Persians invade Greece but are defeated at the Battle of Marathon.

- 480BC Xerxes leads another attempted invasion of Greece.

- 330BC Persia becomes part of the empire of Alexander the Great.

Parthians and Sassanians

CONQUERED BY THE GREAT Macedonian leader, Alexander the Great, the Persian empire ceased to exist. But after Alexander's death in 332BC, Persian leaders began again to take control of their native land. Once more they created a large empire, uniting diverse people, from sheep-herders in Iran to Mesopotamian farmers, under all-powerful emperors, whom they called the King of Kings.

Alexander, and the Achaemenid emperors before him, had shown the Persians that they needed a strong army to create a great empire. But the new Persian leaders, under two dynasties, the Parthians (240BC–AD226) and the more successful Sassanians (AD226–646), who replaced them, went further. They rebuilt society as a system of rigid social classes: nobles, priests, warriors, high and low officials, and peasants.

◀ PARTHIAN SHOT
Parthian cavalry pretended to retreat, then, unexpectedly, fired arrows backwards with deadly accuracy.

Everyone knew their place. People's whole lives, from the type of job they did to their choice of marriage partner, from how much tax they paid to the type of food they ate, all depended on the class to which they belonged.

This rigid class system kept the country united. At the top of the social tree, and sovereign ruler, was the emperor, the King of Kings himself. The people were reminded of his greatness, because the Sassanian emperors put their own images on everything they created. Their palaces and cites were decorated with stone reliefs and sculptures showing them in battle or enjoying sports such as hunting and horseback riding.

▶ ROCK RELIEFS
Sassanian rulers recorded their achievements in stunning reliefs carved on the cliff faces of their native province of Fars. These show subjects such as Persian knights and Sassanian troops.

ZOROASTRIANISM
The Persians adopted Zoroastrianism as their religion. Zoroaster, or Zarathustra as he was also called, lived in about 1000BC. He taught that life was a fight between good and evil. Zoroastrians believed that the source of good in the world was the Wise Lord, a god of light and truth called Ahura Mazda. A sacred fire burned in every Persian temple as a symbol of his light and eternal goodness.

▶ AHURA MAZDA
The chief god of the Persians was Ahura Mazda, source of all goodness. A winged figure, he was the symbol of Zoroastrianism. Priests tended his sacred fire. They were called Magi, from which comes the word "magic".

▲ SACRED BULL
In ancient Persia, the bull was a symbol of power. The Persians also believed it was the first animal to be created and that, after the first bull was killed, all the other animals of the world were born from its soul.

▶ PARTHIAN AND SASSANIAN EMPIRES
The map shows the Parthian and Sassanian empires. They were not as vast as the first Persian empire but these later empires were still large. Parthian lands stretched from the farming area of Mesopotamia, north of the Persian Gulf, to the homelands of herders and nomads in central Iran. The domains of the later Sassians stretched still further east to the Indus River.

◀ CTESIPHON
The capital city, Ctesiphon, stood on the Tigris River, near to present-day Baghdad in Iraq. It grew dramatically in size during the Sassanian period, possibly containing several hundred thousand people. The Sassanians divided the city into two large suburbs. One part was for captives from the Roman empire, and the other was for the emperor and his family. The royal family lived in this large stone-built palace with its great vaulted central hall.

One of the most important classes was the priests. They were the leaders of the Zoroastrian religion. This faith had been developed in about 1000BC but the Sassanians made it the state religion, although contemporary eastern religions and other cults exerted an influence.

Under these later Persians, trade, industry and the arts flourished. They made developments in farming and improved irrigation systems. The local population rose but farmers worked the land too hard. Crops failed and the region became poor once more. Eventually, the Muslim Arabs invaded, finally ending the later Persian empires.

▲ STUCCO PANEL
Part of a decorative border from a Sassanian house. The upper classes loved luxury and their homes were decorated with ornate plasterwork, called stucco. This plasterwork was decorated with guinea fowl.

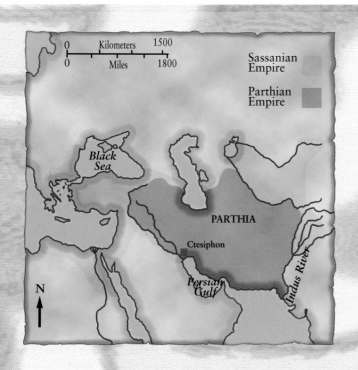

Key Dates

- c. 240BC–AD226 Parthian dynasty rules lands in Persia.

- AD109 Silk trade links China and Parthia.

- AD224 Ardashir, son of high priest Sasan destroys Parthian power. He founds Persian Sassian dynasty.

- AD226–642 Sassanian dynasty rules Persia.

- AD531–578 Reign of Khusrau Anushirvan. He reforms tax system and improves irrigation in Mesopotamia.

- AD614–628 Reign of Khusrau Parviz, conqueror of Egypt and Syria, the last of the great Sassanian kings.

- AD637 Muslim Arabs invade and destroy Sassanian Empire.

Islamic Empire

▲ MUSLIM WOMEN
Traditionally, Muslim women cover their heads out of doors and wear clothes that cover them completely.

I N THE 7TH CENTURY AD, a new faith appeared that has become one of the world's greatest religions. It emerged in the Arabian peninsula, where the Arab people lived by farming and trading. They had worshipped many gods but in about AD610, the prophet Mohammed, a merchant from Mecca, announced that a new religion had been revealed to him. It was based on belief in a single god, Allah, and he called it Islam, meaning "submission to God's will".

Mohammed and his followers, who are called Muslims, spread the new faith throughout Arabia and beyond. Soon it became the basis of a new and growing empire, which brought learning, art and science to peoples as far afield as Morocco and Persia.

The early Muslims sent out missionaries to convert people. They were followed by Arab merchants, who traveled across the desert with processions of camels, known as caravans, trading in

◀ DOME OF THE ROCK
The Dome of the Rock in Jerusalem is the oldest surviving mosque, or place of Muslim worship. It was built at a place where Mohammed was said to have stopped on his journey to heaven.

luxuries such as precious stones, metals and incense.

Next followed armies, led by the caliph, ruler of the Islamic world. Within 30 years of Mohammed's death, they had conquered a huge area, stretching from Tunisia in the west to Persia in the east. Later, Islamic armies pushed even farther afield, conquering Spain and reaching the borders of India.

Islam was based on the Koran, the Muslim sacred book. Muslims were expected to learn how to read Arabic so that they could read the Koran. This meant that the Islamic empire became highly educated. Schools were attached to every mosque and universities were founded in major cities such as Baghdad. Muslim scholars also collected information from all the conquered countries. Soon the Islamic

SCHOLARSHIP
Baghdad was a center of culture and learning and Muslim scientists were famous worldwide. Arab scholars studied the stars, mathematics, medicine, engineering, history, geography and philosophy. Islam tolerated other religions so Christian and Jewish scholars were also welcome.

▲ ASTROLABE
Islamic scientists developed the astrolabe. A flat disc with a rod that could be pointed to the sun or stars, it helped Arab sailors find their way.

◀ CALLIGRAPHY
The art of calligraphy, or beautiful handwriting, was one of the many arts that flourished in the Islamic world.

▼ HOUSE OF LEARNING
Islamic scholars study in a mosque, a Muslim place of worship. Arabic textbooks, particularly in medicine, were used in Europe for centuries.

▲ BAGHDAD
Through the centuries, Baghdad has survived repeated damage by wars, floods and fire. Today it is home to millions of Muslims.

▶ SPREADING ISLAM
Arabian merchants blazed new trails across the deserts to spread the new faith. They crossed western Asia and northern Africa.

empire contained the world's finest scientists, doctors and most able writers. The arts also flourished and houses and mosques were decorated with beautiful tiles and stonework.

Religious faith, learning and a powerful army made the Islamic empire successful and long lasting. It survived until the 13th century.

▲ ISLAMIC EMPIRE
The Islamic empire reached its height in AD750, as shown in the map. In some areas, such as Spain, Muslim rule lasted for hundreds of years. In other areas, such as North Africa and much of western Asia, large Muslim communities continue to exist to this day and Muslims can now be found all over the world.

Key Dates

- AD632 Death of Mohammed.

- AD634 The first caliph, Abu Bakr, conquers Arabia.

- AD635–642 Muslims conquer Syria, Egypt, and Persia.

- AD661 The beginning of the Omayyad dynasty.

- AD698 Muslim soldiers capture Carthage.

- AD711 Muslims begin to invade Spain. The empire expands to include northeastern India.

- AD750 Abbasid dynasty founded.

- AD762 Baghdad becomes the Abbasid capital.

Indus Valley Civilization

I N AROUND 2500BC, a mysterious civilization grew up on the plain of the Indus River, in what is now Pakistan. Archeologists have so far been unable to read their writing, find out what their religion was, or work out why their civilization collapsed. But we do know that the Indus Valley people were very successful. They farmed the fertile soil by the Indus and used clay from the river banks to make bricks. With these they built several huge cities.

Most of what we know about the Indus Valley Civilization comes from the remains of their great cities Mohenjo-Daro and Harappa. They built them on the flood plain of the river. Because the river flooded regularly, they constructed massive mud-brick platforms to raise the buildings above the level of the flood waters.

▲ GODDESS
Small clay figures showing a woman with a decorative head-dress, have been found at Mohenjo-Daro. These were most likely representations of a fertility or mother-goddess.

Each city was divided into two areas. One was where the people lived. Flat-roofed, mud-brick houses were arranged in neat rows along straight streets and alleyways. Most houses had a courtyard, a well for water, and even built-in toilets with drains to take the waste to sewers beneath the streets.

The other half of each city was a walled area containing the larger buildings — a public bath, a great hall, and a massive granary, or grain store, the size of an Olympic swimming pool. Priests and worshippers may have used the baths for ritual washing before religious ceremonies. Near the granaries were large threshing floors where farmers brought their grain to be threshed before selling it to the people of the city.

The Indus civilization continued for about 800 years but then began to decline. Houses fell into ruin and many people left. No one knows for certain why this happened. Bad floods and a rising population may have forced farmers to grow too much food, exhausting the land and causing poor harvests and famine.

◀ GOD-KING
A stone bust showing a man dressed in a patterned shawl. The quality of the carving and the thoughtful expression may mean that the man was an Indus god or perhaps a king.

DAILY LIFE
From the evidence, it seems that Indus Valley cities were full of life and activity. Archeologists have found weights and measuring sticks, which suggests that they were trade centers. Merchants and traders probably thronged the streets, which also contained skilled craftworkers. Farmers too brought their crops into the cities to sell.

◀ CLAY SEALS
Stone seals, such as this, probably belonged to merchants who used them to "sign" documents and property. Seals featured an animal, such as bull, antelope, water buffalo, or tiger, each of which was found in the region.

▲ GAME PLAYING
Archeologists have found board games and toy animals showing that Indus people enjoyed playing games.

▶ CART MODEL
Small clay models, such as this one, pulled by a pair of bullocks, prove that the Indus people used the wheel. They would have used full-size carts to carry grain and other produce.

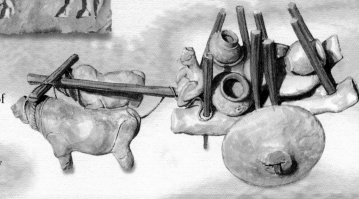

▼ MOHENJO-DARO
The streets of Mohenjo-Daro ran straight and crossed at right-angles, just like the streets of a modern American city. The city seems to have been carefully planned, which was unusual at the time.

Houses of mud bricks, baked in a kiln

Houses with bathrooms and toilets

Straight streets organized on a grid pattern

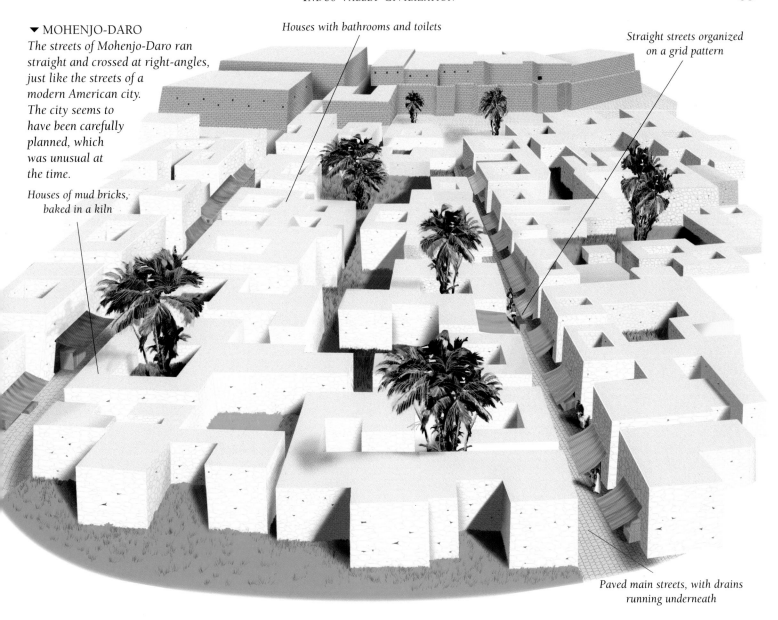

Paved main streets, with drains running underneath

▶ INDUS VALLEY
The map shows the extent of the Indus Valley Civilization. It was centered on its great cities, such as Mohenjo-Daro and Harappa, but many people lived in the country in small towns and villages, making their living on the land. They became rich growing corn to trade in the cities, adding to their diet by hunting wild animals. They were also probably the first people to grow cotton as fabric for clothes.

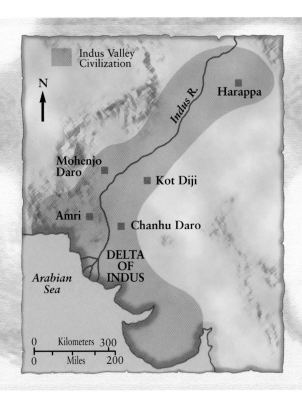

Indus Valley Civilization

N

Harappa

Indus R.

Mohenjo Daro

Kot Diji

Amri

Chanhu Daro

DELTA OF INDUS

Arabian Sea

0   Kilometers   300
0   Miles   200

Key Dates

- 3500BC Groups of farmers settle in scattered communities in the Indus Valley.

- 2500BC First Indus cities built.

- 1800BC Decline of Indus Cities begins. Population falls and cities are poorly maintained.

- 1000BC Much of population has shifted to Ganges Valley.

- c.1500BC Aryan peoples from the northwest invade Indus Valley. Invasions may have been a cause of cities' destruction.

Mauryan India

▲ BATTLE OF KALINGA
A noble Indian warrior. In 261BC, Asoka conquered the kingdom of Kalinga. Hundreds of thousands of people were killed. The cruelty of the battle changed Asoka for ever.

MORE THAN ONE thousand years after the decline of the Indus Valley Civilization, a new and glorious empire emerged in the Indian subcontinent. It was known as the Mauryan empire, after the Mauryan dynasty, or ruling family. Between 322BC and 185BC, the Mauryan emperors brought peace and Buddhism into war-torn India and united that vast area for the first time.

India's huge subcontinent has always been home to a huge variety of peoples with different languages, beliefs and customs. By the 6th century BC, there were 16 separate states in northern India alone. Most were centered on mud-brick cities along the Ganges River. The Ganges cities were often at war with each other, competing for fertile land. In the 4th century BC, one kingdom in the northwest, Magadha, emerged as a major power and began to defeat its neighbors. Its leader was Chandragupta Maurya, a nobleman and warrior.

Chandragupta drove out Greek invaders and built an empire that included the whole of northern India from the Hindu Kush to Bengal. His son continued the expansion but it was under his grandson, Asoka, that the Mauryan empire reached its greatest glory.

Asoka began with further conquests, including the kingdom of Kalinga, but he was shocked by the destruction of war. He decided to become a Buddhist and determined that others should follow his new faith of peace and non-violence.

Asoka sent out missionaries and ordered messages about his beliefs to be put up all over his empire. Buddhist texts and sayings were carved on pillars and specially smoothed cliff faces. They explained his belief that everyone is responsible for the welfare of others. They also instructed people to tolerate the beliefs of others and always to avoid violence.

Inspired by his new faith, Asoka built hospitals and introduced new laws. A network of roads was built that connected towns throughout the empire. Farming improved and trade expanded. The Mauryan empire brought peace and prosperity to many parts of India. However, it needed Asoka's leadership to hold it together. After his death, the empire fell apart when Brihadnatha, the last Mauryan emperor, was killed.

RELIGION
Two of the world's great religions — Hinduism and Buddhism — came from India. Hinduism dates back some 4000 years. Asoka introduced Buddhism. By the end of the Mauryan period it was the most widespread faith in northern India. Asoka also sent Buddhist teachers to neighboring countries, such as Burma, to spread the faith.

◄ COLUMN
Asoka's columns were usually topped with one or more lions. Sayings on the column written in local script told people to avoid violence, eat vegetarian food and respect the beliefs of others. They also reminded everyone of how Asoka's rule helped ordinary people, by building roads, rest houses and wells.

◄ BUDDHA
The founder of Buddhism was Siddhartha Gautama, an Indian prince who was born in 563BC.

▲ RAMAYANA
An Indian miniature shows a scene from one of India's great epic poems, the *Ramayana*. Its hero, Rama, was identified with the Hindu god, Vishnu.

◀ HOLY RIVER
Indians have bathed in the River Ganges for centuries although the temples may not have been there during the time of the Mauryans. To Hindus, the Ganges is sacred. It is believed that bathing in its waters washes away sins.

▲ STUPA
The Mauryans built Buddhist shrines, called stupas, in the form of dome-shaped massive mounds, sometimes known as "temple mountains". Asoka built many stupas. One of the oldest to survive is at Sanchi, in central India.

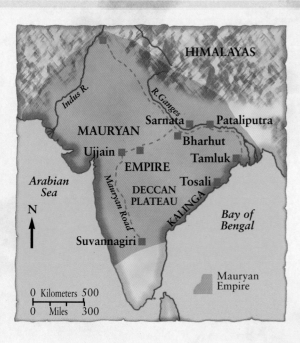

◀ MAURYAN EMPIRE
The map shows the Mauryan Empire at the time of Asoka. His grandfather, Chandragupta, took control of much of northern India, and also made conquests in Pakistan and Afghanistan. Chandragupta's son, Bindusara, conquered large areas of central and southern India, although the southern tip remained unconquered.

Key Dates

- 327–325BC The Macedonian leader, Alexander the Great, conquers the Indus Valley and the Punjab.

- 322BC Chandragupta Maurya takes over the Punjab and founds Mauryan empire.

- 303BC Chandragupta conquers the Indus Valley and part of Afghanistan.

- 301BC Bindusara, Chandragupta's son, comes to the throne and extends the Mauryan empire.

- 269–232BC Reign of Asoka. Buddhism becomes state religion and Mauryan empire flourishes.

- 184BC The death of Brihadnatha, the last Mauryan emperor.

Ancient Egypt

▲ THE NARMER PALETTE *The slate shows Narmer. He was also called Menes, meaning "the founder".*

FIVE THOUSAND YEARS AGO, a great civilization — that of Egypt — emerged in northern Africa. Ruled by powerful pharaohs, ancient Egypt dominated the region for three thousand years and was one of the most successful of the ancient civilizations.

The Egyptian civilization began with Narmer. In about 3100BC, he unified two kingdoms — Upper and Lower Egypt — and became the first king or pharaoh. The pharaoh was the most powerful and important person in the kingdom and was believed to have the same status as a god. Under Narmer, and the pharaohs who followed, Egypt prospered. To help them wield their power, the pharaohs trained a civil service of scribes or writers. The scribes recorded and collected taxes and carried out the day-to-day running of the kingdom, which was divided into a number of districts. Merchants traveled to neighboring areas such as Palestine, Syria and Nubia, and the Egyptian army followed, occupying some of these areas for a while.

The land of ancient Egypt was dry and inhospitable and the Egyptians relied on the great River Nile for survival. It was the life blood of the region and provided everything — fertilizer for the land, water for farming and irrigation, and a highway for Egyptian boats, called "feluccas", which were some of the world's earliest sailing craft.

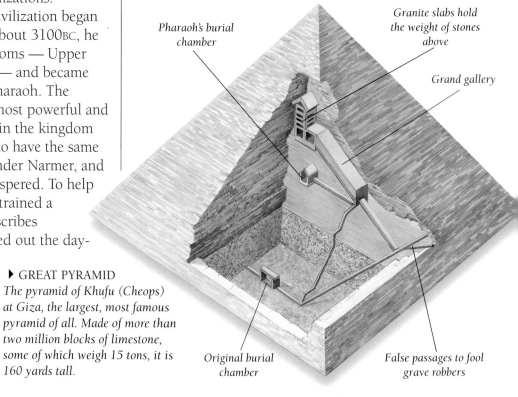

Pharaoh's burial chamber

Granite slabs hold the weight of stones above

Grand gallery

Original burial chamber

False passages to fool grave robbers

▶ GREAT PYRAMID
The pyramid of Khufu (Cheops) at Giza, the largest, most famous pyramid of all. Made of more than two million blocks of limestone, some of which weigh 15 tons, it is 160 yards tall.

AFTERLIFE
The Egyptians believed in life after death. They also believed that their pharaohs were gods, who would continue living after their bodies had died. For this reason they built the pyramids to safeguard their bodies.

▶ THE SPHINX
Half pharaoh, half lion, the great Sphinx at Giza symbolized royal power. Some 20 yards high and 60 yards long, it was carved out of limestone rock in about 2620BC.

▲ THE GREAT PYRAMIDS
The pyramid of Chephren, pictured above, dates from 2560BC. The top of the original flat casing still survives. Many pyramids had steps on the outside. Literally tens of thousands of workers labored to build the great pyramids.

Once a year the Nile flooded, its rich silt nourishing the land on either side. All the land watered by the river was needed for cultivation, but during the floods, no one could work the land. This was when all the able-bodied men of the kingdom went to labor on large-scale building projects, such as cities and temples to the many gods of Egypt. They also built the great pyramids, the tombs and last resting places of the pharaohs and some of the biggest stone structures ever built. The desert lands were where these burial tombs were built.

Body wrapped in bandages   Decorated mummy case

◀ MUMMIFICATION
When a pharaoh died, his body was preserved. The inner organs were removed and the body was treated with a chemical and then wrapped in linen bandages. The "mummy" was then put in a decorated coffin and left in the pyramid tomb.

▶ CLOTHING
Egyptian clothes were usually made of linen, woven from flax. The richer the person, the finer the cloth.

▼ PAPYRUS
The Egyptians invented a kind of paper, called papyrus. They made it from the stems of papyrus reeds that grew beside the Nile. The English word "paper" comes from the word papyrus.

◀ BRICK MAKING
Tomb paintings tell us much about Egyptian daily life. Here Egyptian crafts-people make building bricks using soft clay from the Nile, combined with straw.

▲ HIEROGLYPHICS
The Egyptians invented a form of picture writing, now known as hieroglyphics. There were more than 700 different picture signs, each one corresponding to one sound or word.

Ancient Egypt

▲ RAMESES II
This huge statue of Rameses II, who reigned from 1304 to 1237BC, stands in front of the great temple of Abu Simbel. It was one of many monuments that he had built to remind Egyptians of his power.

PHARAOHS RULED ancient Egypt for the whole of its long 3000-year history. The later pharaohs, from the period known as the New Kingdom, were the most powerful. They extended the empire, and sent ambassadors all over western Asia. They built huge temples and erected colossal statues of themselves. For about 500 years, New Kingdom Egypt was the world's most magnificent civilization.

The Egyptians believed their pharaohs were gods. To them the pharaoh was both Horus, the falcon-headed sky god, and Amun-Re, the sun god. This god-like status gave the pharaohs absolute power. They appointed the priests, as well as all civil servants and chief ministers. They also controlled the army, which grew large with recruits from conquered regions all the way from Sudan to Syria.

Everywhere they went ordinary Egyptians were reminded of the pharaoh's power. In front of the temples were massive stone statues of the king in the guise of the sun god. Carved inscriptions told anyone who could read of the pharaoh's godly rank. People also read of the pharaohs' victories in Palestine and Nubia and of their peace treaties with the Hittites of Turkey.

▶ TUTANKHAMUN
Pharaoh Tutankhamun was only 18 when he died. However, he is the most famous pharaoh because when archeologists found his tomb in the 1920s, its contents, including his golden death mask, were still complete.

◀ TOMB TREASURES
Most ancient Egyptian tombs were robbed hundreds of years ago but when it was opened up, Tutankhamun's tomb contained everything that had been buried with him, including food, furniture, jewelry and his glittering gold coffin.

EGYPTIAN WOMEN
Women of all classes in ancient Egypt had many rights, compared to women later in history. They ran the household and controlled their own property. They followed skilled professions; such as midwifery, served as priestesses, and could hold important positions at court.

◀ NEFERTITI
The wife of the New Kingdom pharaoh Akhenaten was Queen Nefertiti. She ruled with her husband, assisted in religious ceremonies, and had a strong political influence.

▲ HUNTING
Egyptians enjoyed hunting. The pharaoh and nobles hunted in the desert, where they caught antelopes, gazelles and wild oxen. They also hunted geese and other waterfowl on the banks of the Nile.

◀ TOMB
WORKERS
The workers who built the royal tombs lived in Deir el-Medineh, a village specially built for them in the desert. When they died they were buried in tombs in the cliffs above the village. At work, the laborers were divided into gangs of 60 craftsmen for each tomb. They were supervised by a foreman and worked an eight-hour day, eight or nine days at a stretch but they were well rewarded. Once, they went on strike when rations failed to arrive. It may have been the first recorded strike.

The most famous of the Egyptian pharaohs came from the New Kingdom. They included Rameses II and Seti I, who were renowned military leaders, Akhenaten, who briefly abolished all the gods except for the sun god, the boy-king Tutankhamun, and Hatshepsut, a powerful queen who ruled with all the might of her male relatives.

After the glory of the New Kingdom, Egypt survived numerous invasions and changes of pharaoh. The last ruler of an independent ancient Egypt was Queen Cleopatra VII, famous for her love for the Roman leader Mark Antony. Much Egyptian culture, from its gods to its funeral customs, survived, but after Cleopatra's death in 30BC, Egypt became part of the huge Roman empire.

◀ ANCIENT
EGYPT
The map shows the extent of ancient Egypt. Lower Egypt was in the north. The kingdom of Upper Egypt was in the south. Farther south still was Nubia, a source of precious materials such as gold and ivory, which the Egyptians later conquered.

Key Dates

- 3100–2686BC Upper and Lower Egypt are united.

- 2686–2181BC Old Kingdom. The pharaohs build up their power and are buried in pyramids.

- 2182–2040BC The pharaohs' power breaks down and two rulers govern Egypt from separate capital cities, Heracleopolis and Thebes.

- 2040–1786BC Middle Kingdom.

- 1786–1567BC Invasion forces sent to Egypt from Syria and Palestine.

- 1570–1085BC New Kingdom. Egyptian pharaohs rule once more and the civilization flourishes.

- 1083–333BC The empire collapses. Egypt divides into separate states.

- 333–323BC Egypt becomes part of Alexander the Great's empire.

African Civilizations

AFRICA IS A HUGE and ancient continent. Its northern region produced the great Egyptian civilization. But further south, below the Sahara desert that divides the continent, other civilizations and kingdoms also appeared. Many were skilled metalworking cultures that produced tools, beautiful jewelry and sculpture. They sent merchants on long trading journeys. Some merchants crossed the vast Sahara desert with their camels, braving heat and drought to reach the ports of the Red Sea coast and the trading posts of North Africa.

African civilizations were scattered far and wide across the continent. But there were several main centers. Ghana, Benin, Mali and Songhai were small kingdoms that flourished, at different times, in West Africa. The people were Bantu-speakers, descendants of the Bantus, farmers and herders who originated in West Africa about 4000 years ago. They opened up trade links with the Muslim rulers of North Africa, sending ivory, ebony, gold, copper and slaves northwards and bringing back manufactured goods such as pottery and glassware. They learned how to work iron, perhaps from people in North African cities such as Carthage. As demand for their goods increased, their kingdoms flourished.

There were also numerous trading kingdoms in East Africa. The most famous was on the Zimbabwe plateau. Here the Shona people had fertile land and rich sources of copper and gold. Their merchants traveled to the east coast of Africa, where they traded with ships coming from

▲ BENIN BRONZES
Craft workers from Benin, in what is now Nigeria, made beautiful cast bronze figures — such as this head of a royal woman.

▶ AXUM
The Ethiopian kingdom of Axum traded with India and the Islamic world. Its rulers built a palace at Takaji Mariam and many stone obelisks, some over 30 yards high. Most people lived in small thatched huts.

EARLIEST CIVILIZATIONS
South of Egypt, the first civilization to emerge in Africa was the kingdom of Kush, which flourished on the Nile from about 500BC to AD350. Its capital was Meroe, an important iron-working center. From about 500BC, metal working spread south to other parts of Africa.

◀ GOLD
Skilled gold workers from the ancient kingdom of Kush made this gold papyrus holder in about 590BC. Much later, African gold workers, especially from Ghana and Mali, became famous all over the world.

▲ ROCK PAINTINGS
Sub-Saharan Africa is rich in rock paintings. This one was painted in the West African kingdom of Mali, which flourished between AD1200–1500.

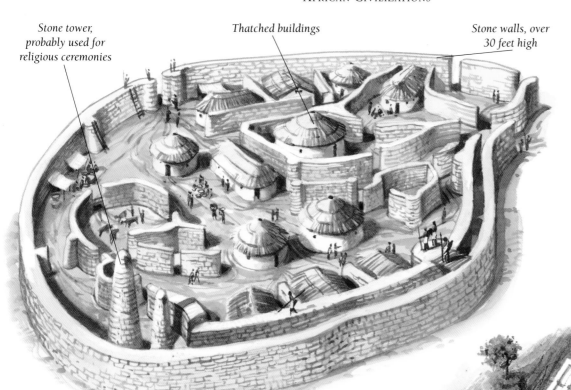

Stone tower, probably used for religious ceremonies

Thatched buildings

Stone walls, over 30 feet high

◀ GREAT ZIMBABWE
The great oval stone enclosure at Great Zimbabwe was the center of the Shona empire. Its stone walls still stand today and contain the remains of several buildings, possibly the ruler's home.

▼ LALIBELA
Some areas of Africa converted to Islam but Axum became Christian in the 4th century. By the 1200s, local masons had carved entire churches, such as this one, from rocky outcrops at Lalibela, southeast of Axum.

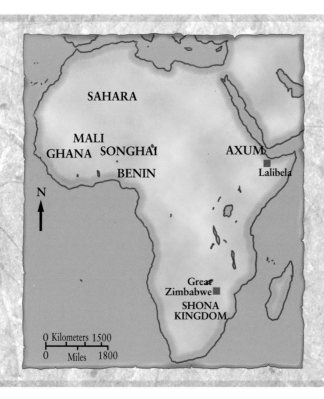

India, the Islamic empire and even China. Further north were still more trading and metalworking kingdoms in what are now Zambia and Ethiopia.

The people of the African kingdoms led lives that were well adapted to their environment. They sought out good land for crops and cattle, and found good sources of metal ore. Their kingdoms lasted a long time and many remained prosperous until the Europeans colonized Africa in the 19th century.

▶ AFRICAN CIVILIZATIONS
The peoples of Africa settled along fertile river valleys and in areas where there were sources of metals such as iron and gold. Soon even the inhospitable Sahara Desert had its settlements, oases and stopping-places for merchants. The Sahara also provided salt, one of the most valuable substances in the ancient world.

SAHARA

MALI
GHANA SONGHAI
BENIN

AXUM
Lalibela

N

Great
Zimbabwe

SHONA
KINGDOM

0 Kilometers 1500
0 Miles 1800

Key Dates

- AD320–650 Kingdom of Axum, East Africa.

- AD700–1200 Kingdom of Ghana, West Africa.

- AD1100–1897 Kingdom of Benin, West Africa.

- AD1200–1500 Kingdom of Mali, West Africa.

- AD1270–1450 Great Zimbabwe is capital of Shona kingdom.

- AD1350–600 Kingdom of Songhai, West Africa.

Minoan Crete

▲ FISHERMAN
A young Minoan fisherman holds fish caught from the Mediterranean Sea. The Minoans were seafarers. Fishing was the basis of their economy.

JUST OVER 100 YEARS AGO, British archeologist Arthur Evans made an extraordinary discovery. He unearthed the ruins of an ancient and beautifully decorated palace at Knossos, on the Mediterranean island of Crete. The palace was enormous. It had hundreds of rooms, courtyards and winding staircases. It reminded Evans of the ancient Greek story of the labyrinth, a maze-like structure built by the legendary Cretan king Minos. He did not know who had built the palace, so he called its builders Minoans, after the mythical king.

Remains in the palace gave many clues so today we know much more about the Minoans. They may originally have come from mainland Greece. They traveled to Crete where, for nearly 1000 years, they created a rich and wonderful culture that reached its height between 2000 and 1700BC. Seas teeming with fish and a rich fertile soil meant that the Minoans had a prosperous and comfortable lifestyle.

The Minoans built many palaces on Crete but Knossos was the largest. The building contained shrines, religious symbols and statues of goddesses. There were several large and lavishly decorated rooms, probably royal throne rooms. Some smaller rooms were full of tall jars, called pithoi, which would have held oil, wine and other produce. Possibly a priest-ruler lived at Knossos, which may also have been a center for food and trade.

Walls in the Cretan palaces were covered in beautiful paintings, many of which have survived. Some show natural scenes and others show the Minoans themselves, working, enjoying themselves and taking part in religious ceremonies.

◀ WALL PAINTING
The palace at Knossos contained about 1300 rooms. Many were decorated with wall paintings like this one showing a beautiful Minoan woman with long braided hair.

◀ SNAKE GODDESS
A pottery goddess from Knossos wears typical Minoan clothing — an open bodice and pleated skirt. Her snakes may symbolize fertility.

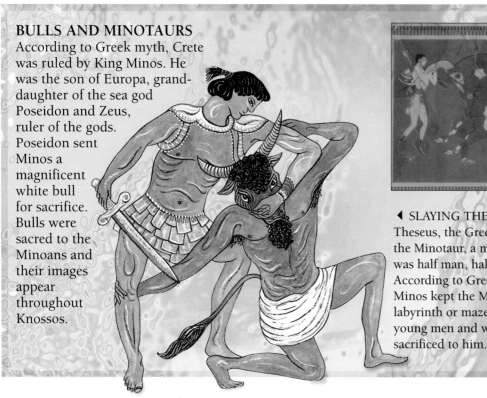

BULLS AND MINOTAURS
According to Greek myth, Crete was ruled by King Minos. He was the son of Europa, granddaughter of the sea god Poseidon and Zeus, ruler of the gods. Poseidon sent Minos a magnificent white bull for sacrifice. Bulls were sacred to the Minoans and their images appear throughout Knossos.

◀ SLAYING THE MINOTAUR
Theseus, the Greek hero, slays the Minotaur, a monster who was half man, half bull. According to Greek myth, Minos kept the Minotaur in a labyrinth or maze. Every year, young men and women were sacrificed to him.

▲ BULL LEAPING
A wall painting shows young Minoan men and women leaping over the backs of bulls. This daring feat was probably part of a religious ceremony that took place in the courtyard at Knossos.

▼ STORAGE JAR
Hundreds of these earthenware storage jars, or pithoi, have been found at Knossos, many as tall as a grown man.

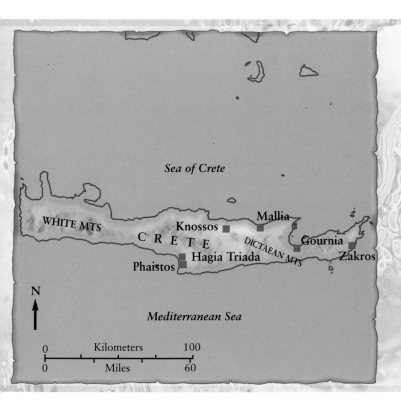

◄ DAILY LIFE
Minoan towns were full of bustle and life. Most were near the coast. Houses were brightly painted and usually two or three stories high. Olive trees grew on the island and olives were used for oil and cooking.

The Minoans were seafarers. They traded with many countries, importing copper from Turkey, ivory and gold from Egypt and lapis lazuli from Afghanistan.

Suddenly, this flourishing culture suffered a disaster. Palace walls collapsed and there were great fires.

Possibly this was due to a massive earthquake or a volcanic eruption on the nearby island of Thera. The Minoans rebuilt their palaces but in 1450BC disaster struck again. Myceneans invaded from mainland Greece and the Minoan civilization was overrun.

Key Dates

- c.6000BC Mainland Greeks arrive in Crete.

- 2000BC Minoans build palace at Knossos.

- 2000–1700BC Minoans build palaces at Phaistos, Mallia and Zakros. Minoan culture flourishes.

- 1900BC Cretans use potter's wheel.

- 1450BC Minoan civilization collapses with eruption on Thera and the arrival of invaders from Greece.

◄ MINOAN CIVILIZATION
Crete is the largest Greek island and the birthplace of the Minoan culture, one of the first European civilizations. The map shows the extent of this glorious civilization. Apart from the Palace of Minos in Knossos, the Minoans also built fabulous palaces in Mallia, Phaistos and Zakros and established trading posts throughout the Mediterranean.

Mycenae

IN ABOUT 1600BC a warlike group came to power in mainland Greece. They were the Mycenaeans, called after one of their largest strongholds at Mycenae in the northeastern Peloponnese. The Mycenaeans created the first Greek civilization. They lived in massive hilltop citadels or fortified settlements, made stunning gold objects and produced soldiers who were famed for their bravery.

The Mycenaeans probably consisted of several different groups of people, each with their own ruler. Each group was based in its own citadel. Mycenae was the largest but there were others at Tiryns and Gla. The people all spoke an early form of Greek and their massive fortifications were built with such huge stones that people later thought that giants must have hauled the stones into place. From their native Greek mainland, the Mycenaeans voyaged far into the Aegean and

▲ MASK OF "AGAMEMNON"
This beautiful gold mask would have belonged to a Mycenaean king. When the king was buried, the mask was placed over his face. Archeologists once thought the mask was a portrait of Agamemnon, a hero of the Trojan War.

Mediterranean Seas. Their merchants traveled west to Sicily and east to the Turkish coast, where they set up a trading post called Miletus. They also visited many of the Greek islands, trading with local people or setting up colonies. Their greatest conquest was the large island of Crete, where they defeated the Minoans. This conquest gave them access to many new trade routes that Minoan merchants had used.

The ruins left by the Mycenaeans look very bleak today, with their bare stone walls on windswept hillsides. But the kings and nobles did themselves proud, building small but luxurious palaces inside their citadels. Each citadel also contained houses for the king's soldiers, officials, priests, scribes and craftworkers. Farmers settled in the hill country and surrounding plains. They supplied the king and his people with food and sheltered in the citadel during times of war.

The Mycenaean civilization continued until about 1200BC when a great fire destroyed the citadel of Mycenae. Although the Mycenaeans hung on for another 100 years, their power began to decline.

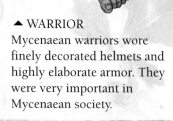

▲ WARRIOR
Mycenaean warriors wore finely decorated helmets and highly elaborate armor. They were very important in Mycenaean society.

THE TROJAN WAR

Ancient Greek myths tell of a great war between Greece and Troy. Paris, Prince of Troy, fell in love and ran away with Helen, Queen of Sparta and wife of King Menelaus. King Menelaus, his brother Agamemnon and a huge army beseiged Troy for 10 years, finally capturing the city. Historians believe the legend is based on a real battle involving the Mycenaeans.

▶ THE TROJAN HORSE
The Greeks tricked the Trojans with a huge wooden horse. They pretended to leave Troy, leaving the horse behind. The Trojans pulled the horse into the city. Hidden inside were Greeks. Late at night, they came out of the horse and captured Troy.

◀ MYCENAE
The Mycenaeans built their huge citadels on the tops of hills, near the coast. Farmlands stretched back on to the inland plains. Huge walls surrounded the citadels. Some said the walls had been built by Cyclops, the legendary one-eyed giant. Within Mycenae was a palace and many other buildings. A town lay outside the fortification.

▲ SEA CREATURES
The Mycenaeans often decorated objects with sea creatures such as dolphins, or the octopus on this stemmed drinking cup. They valued the sea, which they traveled for trade and conquest.

◀ MYCENAEANS
The map shows the main areas of Mycenaean influence and their extensive trading routes. They lived on sites near the coast. Many of their major citadels were on the Peloponnese, the large peninsula that makes up the southern part of the mainland. There were also major settlements at Athens and around Lake Kopais. From these strongholds, the Mycenaeans traveled to most of the islands in the Aegean Sea.

Key Dates

- 1600BC Mycenaean civilization begins to develop in groups on Greek mainland.

- 1450BC The Mycenaeans invade and conquer the Minoans of Crete.

- 1200BC Decline of Mycenaean civilization.

- 800BC Homer's epic poems, the *Iliad* and the *Odyssey*, record some of the traditions of the Mycenaeans.

The Etruscans

▲ ETRUSCAN POT
Etruscan pottery was often beautifully decorated with abstract designs or pictures of animals. Many skilled craftworkers lived and worked in the cities.

ONE OF THE LEAST-known early peoples, the Etruscans lived between the Arno and Tiber rivers in western Italy. From the 8th to the 1st centuries BC, they built a series of cities and grew wealthy by mining copper, tin and iron. We do not know where the Etruscans came from originally, and they remain a mysterious people. They could write, but none of their literature has survived, and many of their cities lie beneath modern Italian towns.

The Etruscans' strength came from living near the coast. They established iron mines by the sea, at Populonia and the nearby island of Elba, and used these as the basis for trade. Skilled seafarers, the Etruscans crossed the Mediterranean to trade with the Phoenician settlers at Carthage, North Africa. They constructed harbors for their ships but built their cities slightly inland to safeguard against pirate attacks.

They also traded with Greece but the Greeks began to set up rival trading colonies in southern Italy. By the

▲ CHARIOT-RACE MURALS
Etruscans may have been the first people to introduce chariot racing, as shown in this tomb painting from Chiusi. Later, it became a popular Roman pastime.

6th century BC, the Etruscans and Greeks were at war. The Gauls, ancient people of western Europe, were also making raids. Etruscan leaders realized that their best protection was to join forces, and 12 of their cities came together in a league to encourage trade and defend each other from attack.

The Etruscans were also skilled artists. Their art was stongly influenced by the Greeks. The most spectacular Etruscan remains are tombs. Rich families built large

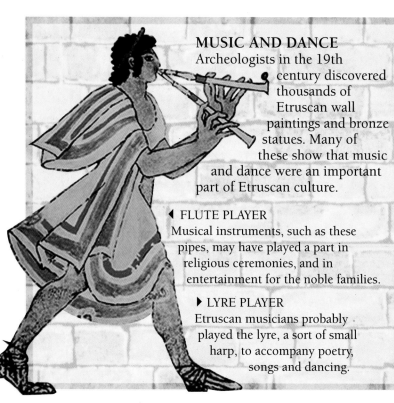

MUSIC AND DANCE
Archeologists in the 19th century discovered thousands of Etruscan wall paintings and bronze statues. Many of these show that music and dance were an important part of Etruscan culture.

◀ FLUTE PLAYER
Musical instruments, such as these pipes, may have played a part in religious ceremonies, and in entertainment for the noble families.

▶ LYRE PLAYER
Etruscan musicians probably played the lyre, a sort of small harp, to accompany poetry, songs and dancing.

▲ ROOF DECORATION
This brightly painted head dates from the 6th century BC. Made of clay and fired in a kiln, it decorated the roof of a building in the Etruscan town of Veii.

Terracotta tiles

Colonnades provided shade in the summer

Buildings were organized around an open area

▶ ETRUSCAN PALACE
Some leading Etruscan families became rich and powerful through the iron trade. As cities grew and prospered, these noblemen ruled over their people from luxurious palaces like this one near Siena.

Rammed earth walls

tombs with several rooms, decorated with portraits of the owners' families. These are some of the best preserved paintings to survive from the ancient world. There were also many fine sculptors in the northern Etruscan cities. They worked in bronze, producing figurines, statues, and items such as engraved mirrors and decorative panels for furniture and chariots.

The Romans — the Etruscans' final enemies — prized this artwork highly. When Rome and her allies conquered Etruscan cities in the 3rd century BC, they took away thousands of bronze statues.

◀ TRADE
The Etruscans traded with Phoenicia and Greece, becoming the first wealthy civilization in western Europe. With profits from the iron trade, they could enjoy luxuries such as this gold vase.

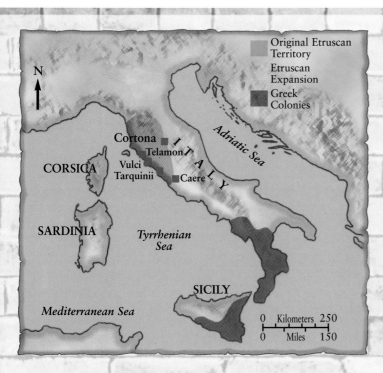

Original Etruscan Territory
Etruscan Expansion
Greek Colonies

N

Cortona
Telamon
Vulci
Tarquinii
Caere
CORSICA
SARDINIA
Tyrrhenian Sea
Adriatic Sea
ITALY
SICILY
Mediterranean Sea

0 Kilometers 250
0 Miles 150

◀ ETRUSCANS
The map shows the extent of Etruscan influence and how this grew. Etruria, the land of the Etruscans, stretched from the River Arno to the Tiber. The major Etruscan cities, such as Caere, Chiusi, and Tarquinia, were independent states with their own rulers. Rome, originally a small town on the edge of Etruria, became a city in the time of the Etruscans.

Key Dates

- 800BC Etruscans set up cities.

- 540BC The Etruscans trade with the Phoenician city of Carthage, and forge an alliance with the Carthaginians.

- 524 and 474BC The Etruscans and Greeks battle over trade in Italy. The Greeks, with colonies in southern Italy, are victorious.

- 413BC The Etruscan league of cities makes an alliance with the Greeks.

- 273BC Romans conquer Caere.

- 265BC Romans destroy Volsinii.

Classical Greece

▲ ZEUS
The Greeks worshipped many gods and goddesses. Zeus, above, was supreme. Greeks thought the gods lived on Mount Olympus, Greece's highest mountain.

THE WAY OUR countries are governed, the books we read, the plays we watch, even many of our sports, all have their origins in the classical Greek civilization, which flourished some 2500 years ago. The Greeks did not have a huge empire. For much of their history their civilization consisted of several separate city-states. But their art, science, philosophy and ways of life have had an enormous influence on our lives.

The Greek countryside is rocky and mountainous. Early Greeks lived near the coast or in fertile plains between the mountains. Gradually, these early settlements became city-states. The Greeks were good sailors and boat-builders and their civilization began to flourish when they sailed to Italy and the eastern Mediterranean to trade with their neighbors. They also set up colonies in these areas and around the coast of the Aegean Sea.

As their wealth increased the Greeks built fine cities. The largest and richest was Athens. The citizens of Athens enjoyed much leisure time and Athens

◀ PARTHENON
The largest temple on the Acropolis, the Parthenon was built in 432BC. The pillars were marble and its beautiful frieze showed a procession in honor of the goddess Athene.

became the center of Greek culture. Greek dramatists such as Sophocles wrote some of the finest plays in western theater. Their musicians created fine music and architects designed elegant buildings and temples. The Greeks also started the Olympic Games.

Greek education was famous throughout the ancient world. Philosophers, or thinkers, came to Athens to discuss everything from the nature of love to how a country should be governed. The Athenians developed a new form of government, in which people had a say in who ruled them. They called it democracy, or government by the people. Not everyone was actually allowed to vote but their system was the ancestor of modern democratic government.

Athens remained strong for several centuries until the Romans began to take over the Mediterranean world. War with another Greek city state, Sparta, also weakened Athens. In 404BC Sparta defeated Athens.

ENTERTAINMENT

The ancient Greeks believed in enjoying themselves. They enjoyed music and art and went to theater regularly. Sport too was very important and had religious significance. The first ever Olympic Games were held in 776BC, in honor of the god Zeus. Like today, they were held every four years.

◀ ATHLETE
A Greek discus thrower. The Olympic Games were only for men. Women were not even allowed to watch. They held their own games, in honor of Hera, goddess of women.

Actors wore these masks – the one on the left for comedy, that on the right for tragedy.

▲ AMPHITHEATER
Greek theaters were large, open-air arenas with rows of stone seats. There were regular drama festivals where playwrights such as Aristophanes, Euripides and Sophocles competed for the award of best play.

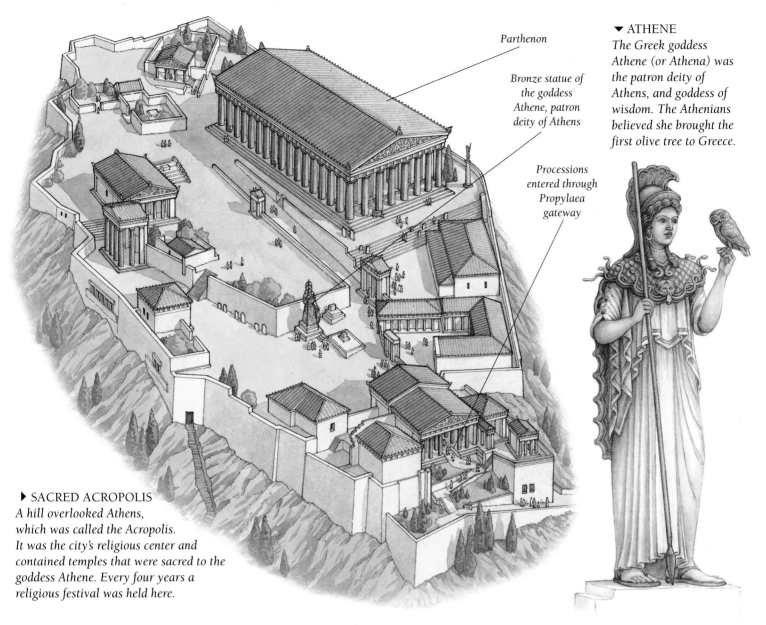

Parthenon

Bronze statue of
the goddess
Athene, patron
deity of Athens

Processions
entered through
Propylaea
gateway

▼ ATHENE
*The Greek goddess
Athene (or Athena) was
the patron deity of
Athens, and goddess of
wisdom. The Athenians
believed she brought the
first olive tree to Greece.*

▶ SACRED ACROPOLIS
*A hill overlooked Athens,
which was called the Acropolis.
It was the city's religious center and
contained temples that were sacred to the
goddess Athene. Every four years a
religious festival was held here.*

◀ ANCIENT GREECE
The Greeks spread out
from their homeland in
the Peloponnese, setting
up colonies in southern
Italy, Sicily, the Aegean,
and the coasts of the
Black Sea.

▼ ELGIN MARBLES
These marble sculptures,
known as the Elgin
Marbles, were taken from
the Parthenon to England
in 1815 by Lord Elgin.
They remain in the
British Museum.

ITALY

MACEDONIA

THESSALY

Aegean
Sea

ATTICA

Ionian
Sea

Smyrna

Eretria

Athens

SICILY

Corinth

Sparta

Miletus

N

Lindos

Mediterranean Sea

CRETE

| 0 | Kilometers | 400 |
| 0 | Miles | 250 |

Classical Greece

THE HEART OF A GREEK CITY was the agora, or market place. This was a central square surrounded by the city's main public buildings – temples, law courts, market halls and shops. Everyone came to the agora to do their shopping, meet friends, listen to scholars, or just gossip. The city council also met in the agora.

Beyond the agora lay streets of private houses. They were usually arranged around a courtyard with overhanging roofs and small windows to keep out the summer sun and winter cold. In the summer, much of the life of the house took place here.

Men and women were not equal in ancient Greece. Women did not have the vote and were allowed little in the way of money or private property. Most women aimed to marry and give birth to a son. Men enjoyed much more freedom. There was even a room in most Greek houses, called the andron, which was used only by the men of the household.

Boys and girls were also treated differently. In the cities, boys went to school from age 7 to 12. They learned reading, writing, music and poetry, as well as sports such as wrestling. Most girls stayed at home with their mothers, where they learned skills such as spinning, weaving and cooking, so that they would be able to run homes of their own.

Life was rather different in Sparta. From early childhood, boys were taught skills to prepare them for fighting and life in the army. All men had to do military service. Girls too were trained for a hard, outdoor life.

When a Greek person died, people believed that he or she would go to Hades, the underworld. The Greeks imagined this as a dark, underground world, surrounded by a river, the Styx. People were buried with a coin, to pay Charon, the ferryman who would row them across the River Styx into the next world.

◀ WOMEN
Greek women wore folded material called chitons, fastened at the shoulder. Few houses had water so, balancing jars on their head, women collected water from the local well or fountain.

◀ VENUS DE MILO
This beautiful statue of Aphrodite is known as the Venus de Milo. Although carved after the time of classical Greece, it still demonstrates the ancient Greek ideal of the perfect body.

LEARNING AND PHILOSOPHY

The Greeks were educated people and valued learning. Western philosophy, which means "love of wisdom" began in ancient Greece. Greek philosophers studied astronomy, science and asked deep questions about the meaning of life.

◀ SOCRATES
The most famous of all the ancient Greek philosophers was Socrates (469–399BC). During discussions, he asked continuous questions, sometimes pretending not to know the answers in an attempt to trip up his opponents.

▲ GOING TO SCHOOL
Boys from rich families were taken to school by a slave called a paidogogos. The tutor used papyrus rolls to teach the child, but the boy would practise writing on a wax tablet, using a pointed tool called a stylus.

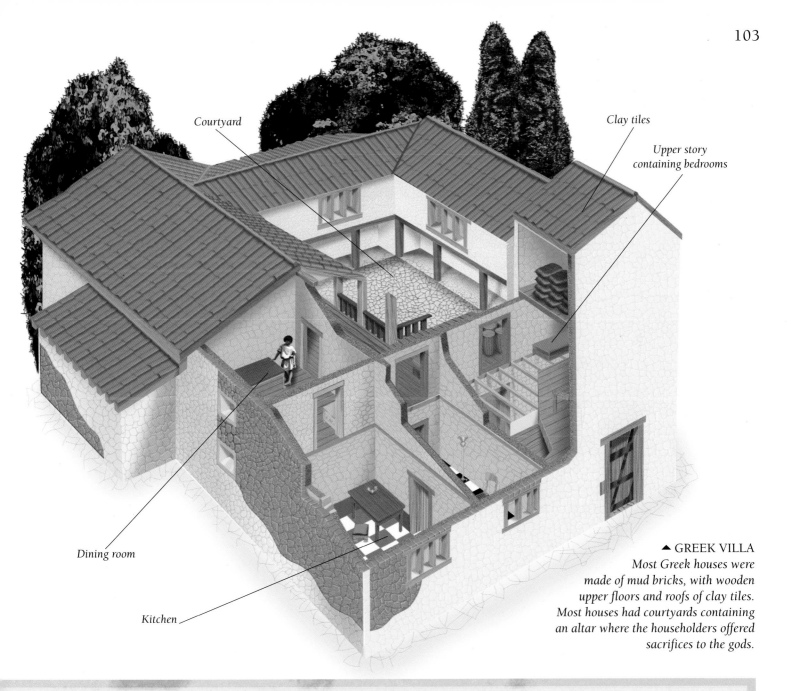

Courtyard

Clay tiles

Upper story
containing bedrooms

Dining room

Kitchen

▲ GREEK VILLA
*Most Greek houses were
made of mud bricks, with wooden
upper floors and roofs of clay tiles.
Most houses had courtyards containing
an altar where the householders offered
sacrifices to the gods.*

▶ SPARTA
Spartan footsoldiers
were heavily armed.
When attacked, they
formed a solid line
or phalanx, spears
pointing outwards.
Sparta was far
inland. Its people
had to be tough to
live in their remote
mountain region.

◀ COINS
The Greeks used silver coins. Slaves
toiled in mines near Athens, digging
out silver by hand. Some coins were
decorated with an owl, symbol of the
goddess Athene.

Key Dates

- 900BC The Greeks begin to trade in
  the Mediterranean.

- 776BC First recorded Olympic Games.

- 700BC Greek city states develop.

- 490BC Persia attacks Athens but is
  defeated at the Battle of Marathon.

- 480BC The second Persian war also
  leads to defeat for Persia.

- 443–429BC Athens flourishes under
  its greatest leader, Pericles.

- 431BC The Peloponnesian Wars
  begin between Athens and Sparta.

- 404BC The Spartans defeat the
  Athenians.

Hellenistic Age

▲ COIN
The head of Alexander the Great (356–323BC), wearing the horns of an Egyptian god appears on this coin. His exploits gained him almost legendary status.

IN 336BC, A YOUNG MAN called Alexander became ruler of the small kingdom of Macedonia, north of Greece. Within just a few years, he and his well trained army had conquered one of the greatest empires of the ancient world. They swept across Asia Minor and marched down the eastern Mediterranean coast to take over Phoenicia (modern Syria) and Judea (modern Palestine). Then they moved on to Egypt, where Alexander was accepted as a child of the Sun God. From there, Alexander and his men went north once more, to take Persia, then the world's greatest empire. Soon Persia too was in Alexander's hands, together with the area of the Indus Valley, on the borders of India. Alexander was preparing to conquer Arabia when he died of a fever, aged only 33.

Alexander was one of the most brilliant generals and powerful leaders the world has known. He was highly educated — his teacher was the Greek philosopher Aristotle — but also a skilled horseman and had boundless energy. After conquering Persia, he would

▲ ALEXANDRIAN LIBRARY
The city of Alexandria contained a fabulous library where many of the works of the great Greek writers were preserved on papyrus rolls. The library burned down in AD391.

have continued into India but his men were exhausted.

By the time he died, Alexander had traveled 20,000 miles on his epic journey of conquest. Everywhere he went, he took with him the Greek culture and way of life, so spreading it over a huge area. He founded cities, often called Alexandria after him, and left behind

◀ BUCEPHALUS
Alexander had a favorite horse, Bucephalus. Legend says the horse was wild and only responded to Alexander.

ALEXANDER
When Philip II of Macedonia was killed, Alexander took over a kingdom that was the strongest in Greece. Philip was about to attack Persia when he died. Alexander inherited his ambition.

▲ DELPHIC ORACLE
The Greeks often consulted an oracle for advice before undertaking a momentous event. The most famous was the oracle at Delphi. Philip II and Alexander consulted her.

▶ ALEXANDRIA
The Castle of Qaitbay stands in the present-day city of Alexandria in Egypt. Alexander founded this city in 332BC. He founded others, many of which were named after him.

◀ BATTLE OF ISSUS
At the Battle of Issus, in 333BC, Alexander with a much smaller force defeated the much larger Persian army under Darius III. It was a tremendous victory, opening Syria and Egypt to Alexander's advance.

▼ TIARA
As the Macedonian army swept across Persia, they took what booty they could carry with them. They especially prized Persian metalwork, such as this gold tiara and other items made from gold and silver worn by Persian nobles.

workers who filled them with classical buildings — temples, theaters, houses, all in the Greek style. For 300 years, this Greek style remained fashionable all over western Asia. Historians now call this period the Hellenistic Age, after Hellas, the Greeks' own name for their country.

Alexander's vast empire did not survive his death. His generals carved it up between them. Ptolemy, ancestor of Queen Cleopatra, ruled Egypt; Antigonous took over Greece and much of Turkey; Seleucus,

founder of the Seleucid dynasty of Persian kings, controlled the area from Turkey to the Indus. Only cities named Alexandria remained to remind people of the great general from Macedonia.

◀ ALEXANDER'S WORLD
The map shows the extent of Alexander's empire and the major routes he took. From its heartland in Greece and the Aegean coast of Turkey, Alexander's empire spread east to the River Indus. The Macedonians founded several Alexandrias in Persia, as well as the more famous one in Egypt.

Key Dates

- 356BC Alexander born in Macedonia.

- 336BC Alexander becomes ruler of Macedonia and puts down uprisings in Greece.

- 333BC Alexander defeats the Persians at the Battle of Issus.

- 332BC Macedonians conquer Egypt. Alexander is accepted as pharaoh.

- 331BC Alexander wins the Battle of Gaugamela, the final defeat of the Persians.

- 326BC Alexander and his army reach the Indus River.

- 323BC Alexander dies of a fever. His empire breaks up.

Ancient Rome

▲ ROMULUS AND REMUS
According to legend, two brothers – Romulus and Remus – founded Rome. Abandoned as babies, they were left to die but a she-wolf suckled them and they survived.

Two THOUSAND YEARS ago a small Italian town grew to become the most important city in the whole of the western world. The name of the town was Rome. Built on seven hills near the River Tiber, Rome was already powerful by the 3rd century BC. It had a well-organized government, a fearsome army and had taken over the whole of Italy. Over the next 200 years, Rome expanded its influence to become the center of a great empire. By AD117, the Roman Empire stretched from Britain to North Africa, and from Spain to Palestine.

At the heart of this great empire was the city of Rome itself. At the center of the city was the forum, a market square surrounded by large public buildings, such as temples, baths and stadiums. The Romans took much from the ancient Greek culture. Many of their public buildings looked similar to Greek ones, with classical pillars and marble sculptures.

Beyond the forum were streets of dwelling places. City land was expensive. Poorer Romans could not afford houses so they rented apartments arranged in multi-story blocks, like modern apartment buildings. On the ground floor of each block were stores full of goods and craftworkers. Between the stores was an entrance way, leading to the apartments above. Some had larger, more expensive, rooms. Others, further up the building, were smaller and cheaper. Few had their own water supply or proper kitchen.

In the countryside too, many ordinary Romans lived in poverty, working the land to supply food for the cities. Here, land was cheaper and more plentiful so the wealthiest Romans built themselves large, graceful villas, or country houses. These often had their own baths and an underfloor heating system.

◀ HUNTING
In the countryside, Romans hunted wild boar with dogs. Hunting provided enjoyment and also gave the Romans a more varied diet.

SOCIETY
Roman society was divided into classes, or social groups. At the top were generals, governors, magistrates and other important officials. Further down were bankers and merchants. Below were craftworkers and shopkeepers. Bottom of the social pile were slaves. Romans were either citizens, free people with rights, or non-citizens.

▼ SHIPS
The Romans used ships for war and trade. Slaves labored to drive them forward by means of banks of oars on either side.

▲ AT THE BATHS
Roman cities had large public bath complexes. There were different rooms with baths of different temperatures, and bathers went from one to the other, finishing up with a cold plunge and an invigorating massage. People went to the baths not only to get clean but also to meet friends and socialize.

◀ STREET SCENE
Some of the best preserved ancient Roman houses are in Ostia, the port of the city of Rome. Sand blowing in from the coast covered the houses, protecting mosaic floors and walls. The town was full of apartment buildings with stores and bars beneath.

Poorer people lived in smaller, upper apartments

Craftworkers made and sold wares in workshops on the ground floor

An entranceway led past stores to a stairway going up to the apartments

Lower apartments had larger rooms and were more expensive

▲ CLOTHING
Most Romans dressed simply and according to class. Outside, Roman citizens only wore a toga, a large piece of white woolen cloth, wound round the body. Roman women wore long linen or woolen tunics.

◀ SHOE
Romans wore leather shoes or sandals, which laced part way up the leg.

▼ NEPTUNE
The Romans worshipped the same gods as the ancient Greeks but gave them different names. The Greek Poseidon, king of the sea, became the Roman Neptune, shown here.

Key Dates

- 753BC According to legend, Rome is founded by Romulus and Remus.
- 509BC Rome becomes a republic.
- 146BC Rome defeats Carthage.
- 58–50BC Julius Caesar conquers Gaul.
- 44BC Julius Caesar is assassinated.
- 27BC Augustus becomes first of the Roman emperors.
- AD117 Emperor Trajan conquers Dacia (Romania). Empire is at its largest extent.
- AD324 Christianity becomes the official religion of the empire.
- AD410 Invading Goths conquer and destroy the city of Rome.

Ancient Rome

As Rome's influence grew, so its government changed. The city had once been ruled by kings but in 509BC, it became a republic, governed by elected consuls. A senate advised the consuls. Under the consuls, Rome's power grew until, by the 2nd century BC, only Carthage,

◀ AQUEDUCT
The Romans built many aqueducts to bring in water from the rivers in the countryside to the city. Rome had many aqueducts and was the only ancient city with a reliable water supply. Roman aqueducts still stand today in cities as far apart as Nîmes, France and Istanbul, Turkey.

the powerful North African trading empire, could stand up to its might. In 146BC the Romans destroyed Carthage. Rome continued to be a republic until 27BC when, after a civil war, Augustus became the first Roman emperor. For the next 500 years, a series of emperors ruled an empire that was the largest in the western world.

There were many reasons for Rome's success. The empire had a strong, well-organized army. The Romans also gained rich spoils whenever the army conquered a new territory. In this way, Rome had access to a wide range of raw materials, including iron from central Europe and gold and silver from Spain. As the Romans conquered new territories, they introduced their own system of government, language and laws into the conquered regions.

The empire also included many talented engineers, who built bridges and aqueducts as well as the first large domes. The Romans developed concrete. They also built a huge network of long, straight roads across the empire, linking all parts of the empire to Rome. Many of these routes are still used today.

By AD220, the power of Rome appeared complete. The Romans seemed to be able to build anything and their army seemed to be able to conquer any country. But in the end, the empire became too large. Peoples from the lands on the fringes of the empire in central Europe began to rebel, and it was difficult for the army to move quickly and crush their revolts. Rome's vast empire began to fall apart. In AD395, the empire divided into two and within a few years the last Roman emperor was overthrown.

ROMAN ARMY
Without their powerful army, the Romans would have had no empire. The Roman army conquered new territories and defended frontiers. It also worked on huge engineering projects such as bridges and roads.

◀ LEGIONARY
The best-trained soldiers in the Roman army were the 150,000 legionaries. They were highly disciplined,and wore metal armor.

▶ JULIUS CAESAR
Caesar was a consul who ruled Rome as dictator. He conquered Gaul (France) and invaded Britain. His enemies assassinated him in 44BC.

▲ TRAJAN'S COLUMN
Roman legions attack Dacians in this detail from Trajan's Column in Rome. Made of marble, the column was built to the orders of Emperor Trajan, who led a campaign against the Dacians in AD117.

▶ COLOSSEUM
The Roman emperors staged great "games" to win the favor of the Roman people. The Colosseum in Rome, shown here, was the most famous arena. Opened in AD80, it could hold up to 50,000 spectators who crowded in to see gladiators fight.

▼ GLADIATOR
Specially trained, gladiators fought each other to the death or were forced into combat with wild beasts from all over the empire. Slaves and prisoners of war were used as gladiators.

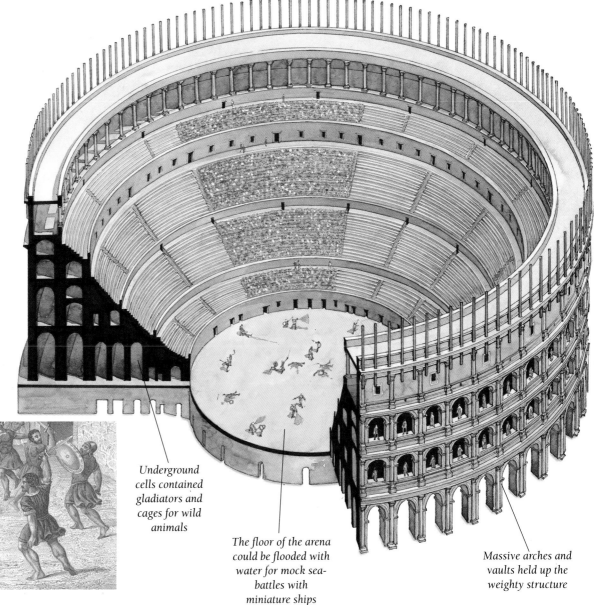

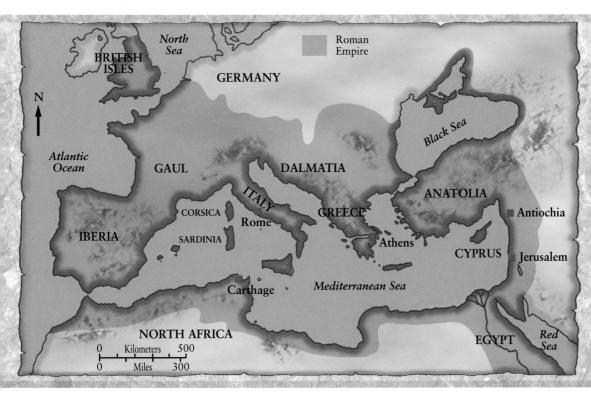

Underground cells contained gladiators and cages for wild animals

The floor of the arena could be flooded with water for mock sea-battles with miniature ships

Massive arches and vaults held up the weighty structure

Roman Empire

North Sea

BRITISH ISLES

GERMANY

N

Atlantic Ocean

GAUL

Black Sea

DALMATIA

ITALY

CORSICA
Rome
SARDINIA

GREECE

ANATOLIA

Antiochia

IBERIA

Athens

CYPRUS

Jerusalem

Carthage

Mediterranean Sea

NORTH AFRICA

EGYPT

Red Sea

0 — Kilometers — 500
0 — Miles — 300

◀ ROMAN EMPIRE
At its largest extent, in around AD117, Rome's empire stretched right across Europe into western Asia. Hadrian's wall, northern England, was the northern frontier. Egypt was the empire's southernmost point. In AD395, the empire, which was too large, divided. The eastern empire became known as the Byzantine Empire.

Early Dynastic China

CIVILIZATION IN CHINA grew up quite separately from the rest of the world. In many ways, Chinese civilization was far in advance of Europe and western Asia, whose people did not know what was happening in China. The Chinese invented many things, including metal working and writing, without any contact with other peoples. This made the Chinese way of life quite distinctive.

Periods of Chinese history are named after dynasties or ruling families. One of the earliest was the Shang dynasty, which began in about 1650BC. Many of the key features of Chinese daily life evolved at this time, such as farming and ancestor worship. The Shang Chinese also became skilled at working in bronze and jade.

They developed a form of writing, which later became the written characters still used in China today.

China is a vast country and the Shang dynasty controlled only northern China. The ruling priest-kings were supremely powerful. To the Chinese, they were god-like figures, who could communicate with their ancestors in heaven.

The Shang built many capital cities, possibly

▲ RITUAL VESSEL
This bronze container was used for religious offerings. An ancestor spirit, in the form of a tiger, stands protectively over a man. Other beasts, probably also spirits, cover the tiger's skin.

▶ BRONZE CASTING
Shang Chinese pour molten bronze into a mold. The Chinese had developed bronze casting by about 1650BC and used bronze for making dishes and other items. The king appointed special officials to run the industry.

BELIEFS
The ancient Chinese believed spirits controlled everything. They also worshipped their dead ancestors. One teacher who influenced Chinese beliefs was Confucius. Another was Lao-tze (b. 604BC), founder of Taoism (The Way). This teaches the need to be in harmony with earth, nature and the cosmos.

▶ ORACLE BONE
When a priest wanted to ask ancestor spirits a question, he wrote the question on a piece of bone. He put the bone into the fire until it cracked, then "read" the marks. They were the first form of Chinese writing.

◀ CONFUCIUS
One of the greatest of the Chinese philosophers was Confucius (551-479BC). He taught his followers to help and respect others, to value the family and to respect elders.

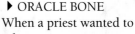

◀ YIN AND YANG
Yin and yang symbol. Traditional Chinese beliefs are based on the idea that everything and everyone contains yin — darkness — and yang — lightness. Health and well-being occur when they are balanced.

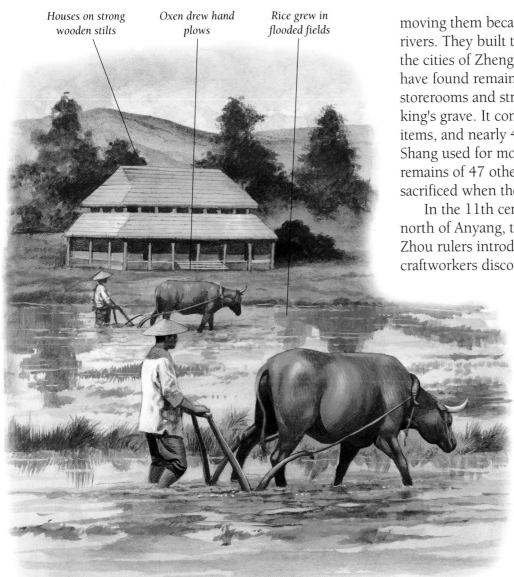

Houses on strong wooden stilts

Oxen drew hand plows

Rice grew in flooded fields

moving them because of floods from China's great rivers. They built the first at Erlitou, then founded the cities of Zhengzhou and Anyang. Archeologists have found remains of wooden houses, a palace, storerooms and streets at Anyang. They also found a king's grave. It contained pottery, bronze and jade items, and nearly 4000 cowrie shells, which the Shang used for money. Also in the tomb were the remains of 47 other people, probably servants sacrificed when their ruler died.

In the 11th century BC, the Zhou dynasty, from north of Anyang, took over from the Shang. The Zhou rulers introduced coins into China and Zhou craftworkers discovered how to work iron. They also invented the crossbow. The Zhou ruled for around 800 years, letting local lords look after their own areas. But the lords began to fight each other. The Zhou dynasty ended and China entered what is known as the Warring States period.

◀ FARMING
For thousands of years the Chinese have farmed the fertile land around the Yellow River, which often floods. The Shang Chinese grew millet, wheat and rice. They also domesticated cattle, pigs, dogs and sheep.

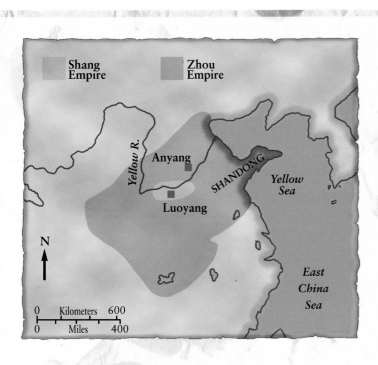

◀ EARLY DYNASTIC CHINA
The map shows the territories of the Shang and Zhou dynasties. The Shang homeland was by the Yellow River, where its waters left the mountains to flow down on to a broad fertile plain. Here they built their main cities — Anyang was a Shang capital. The Zhou came from farther north but also occupied the plain. They made Luoyang their capital city.

Key Dates

- 1650–1027 BC Shang dynasty. China's first great Bronze Age civilization develops.

- 1027–256 BC Zhou dynasty. The kingdom is divided into many states and the king rules through local lords.

- 481–221 BC Warring States period. Local noblemen clash in large-scale battles. China becomes weaker.

- 221 BC The first Qin emperor unifies China.

Qin China

▲ LUCKY DRAGON

The dragon was a Qin symbol of good luck. When he came to the throne, Qin Shih Huangdi made the creature his own symbol. Ever since, the emperor, the dragon, and the idea of good fortune have been linked closely in China.

B Y THE THIRD century BC, war had torn China apart. Seven different states fought each other. For years, no state was strong enough to win a decisive victory and take control of China. Then, in 221 BC, the armies of Qin defeated their enemies and brought the seven states together under their leader, Zheng. He took the title Qin Shi Huangdi, the First Sovereign Emperor of Qin.

The First Emperor ruled for only 11 years. But the changes he made lasted much longer and helped later dynasties, such as the Han and Yüan, to rule effectively. His empire was so large, and contained people of so many different backgrounds, that Zheng had to be ruthless to keep China united. Troops executed anyone who disagreed with his policies. They also burned books by writers who disagreed with the emperor.

Another way of making this huge country easier to govern was to create national systems that all

▲ TERRACOTTA ARMY

The First Emperor's tomb contained 7500 life-size terracotta models of the emperor's army, from foot soldiers and crossbowmen to charioteers and officers. Each was based on a real-life soldier. Automatic crossbows were placed by the entrance to fire if anyone tried to rob the tomb.

people could use. The First Emperor ordered that everyone in China should use the same systems of weights, measurements and writing. He also began a program of building roads and canals, so his officials and merchants could travel easily around the country.

The Xiongnu, a nomadic people from the north of China, were always threatening to invade. So the emperor built the Great Wall to keep out the invaders. He ordered his builders to join up many existing walls along China's northern frontier. Working on the wall

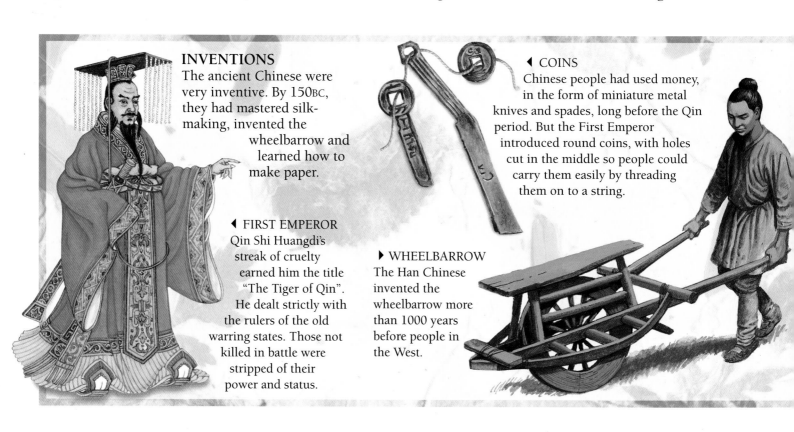

INVENTIONS
The ancient Chinese were very inventive. By 150 BC, they had mastered silk-making, invented the wheelbarrow and learned how to make paper.

◀ FIRST EMPEROR
Qin Shi Huangdi's streak of cruelty earned him the title "The Tiger of Qin". He dealt strictly with the rulers of the old warring states. Those not killed in battle were stripped of their power and status.

◀ COINS
Chinese people had used money, in the form of miniature metal knives and spades, long before the Qin period. But the First Emperor introduced round coins, with holes cut in the middle so people could carry them easily by threading them on to a string.

▶ WHEELBARROW
The Han Chinese invented the wheelbarrow more than 1000 years before people in the West.

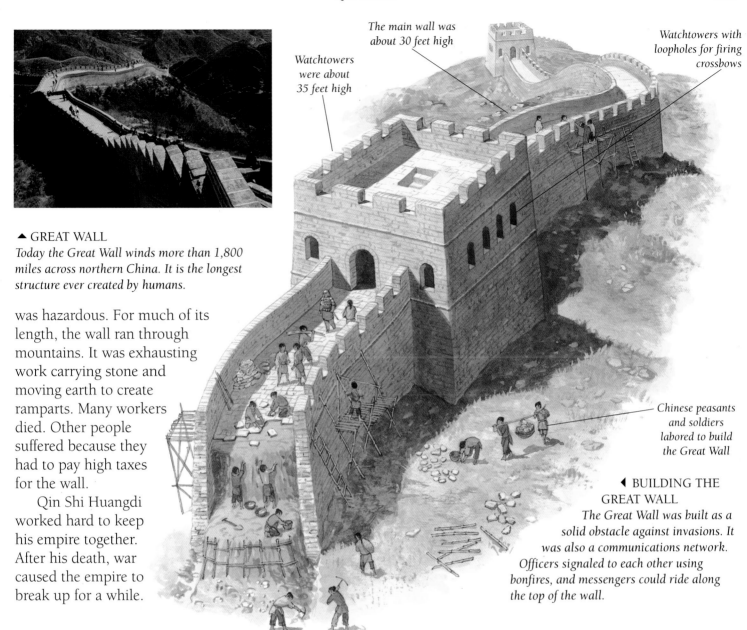

The main wall was about 30 feet high

Watchtowers were about 35 feet high

Watchtowers with loopholes for firing crossbows

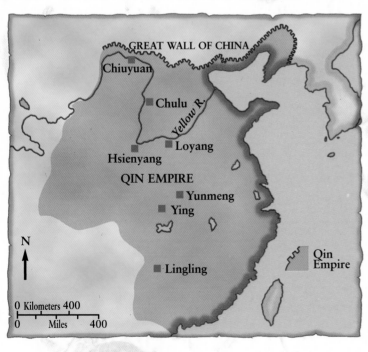

▲ GREAT WALL
Today the Great Wall winds more than 1,800 miles across northern China. It is the longest structure ever created by humans.

was hazardous. For much of its length, the wall ran through mountains. It was exhausting work carrying stone and moving earth to create ramparts. Many workers died. Other people suffered because they had to pay high taxes for the wall.

Qin Shi Huangdi worked hard to keep his empire together. After his death, war caused the empire to break up for a while.

Chinese peasants and soldiers labored to build the Great Wall

◀ BUILDING THE GREAT WALL
The Great Wall was built as a solid obstacle against invasions. It was also a communications network. Officers signaled to each other using bonfires, and messengers could ride along the top of the wall.

◀ QIN EMPIRE
The map shows the extent of the Qin Empire. From the heartlands along the banks of the Yellow River, the empire of the Qin stretched north to the fort at Juyan, south to Panyu (near modern Canton), and west into the province of Sichuan. Qin is pronounced chin, the origin of the name China.

GREAT WALL OF CHINA
Chiuyuan
Chulu
Yellow R.
Loyang
Hsienyang
QIN EMPIRE
Yunmeng
Ying
N
Lingling
Qin Empire

0 Kilometers 400
0 Miles 400

Key Dates

- 246BC Zheng becomes ruler of the kingdom of Qin.

- 230-222BC A series of victories brings the armies of Qin control of most of the warring states.

- 221BC Qin defeats the last of the warring states. Zheng becomes the First Emperor.

- 213BC The First Emperor orders books by authors opposing his rule to be burned.

- 210BC Qin Shi Huangdi dies.

- 209–208BC A peasant rebellion reduces the power of the Qin government.

- 207BC Qin empire breaks up.

Han China

▲ BRONZE HORSE
This beautiful bronze horse was made nearly 2000 years ago by skilled Chinese craftworkers.

THE PERIOD OF THE Chinese Han dynasty was a time of exciting change. Technology and industry improved, farming became more efficient, and Chinese merchants traded along routes that stretched right across the huge continent of Asia. These developments were so wide-reaching that even today, many Chinese people think of the Han period as the true beginning of China.

The Han emperors took over the government of the Qin dynasty. They organized China into a series of local provinces, each with its own commander. The Qin dynasty had ruled by force but the Han emperors found more peaceful ways of wielding their power. When Han ironworkers discovered how to increase the temperature of their furnaces, they were able to make a much wider range of better quality products. The emperors saw the value of this and put all the iron foundries under state ownership. This gave them control of all the tools and weapons that were produced.

The emperors also tried to control trade, especially the rich trade in silk, which Chinese merchants carried along the overland routes across central Asia. Neighboring areas were only allowed to trade with China if they paid regular tribute to the emperor.

▲ MEASURING EARTHQUAKES
This wonderful object was used to detect earthquakes. The slightest tremor loosened a trigger in a dragon's jaw. The jaw opened, releasing a ball into a frog's mouth below.

CIVIL SERVICE
The first Han emperor, Gaozu (r. 206–195BC) was not highly educated, but he knew he needed well qualified officials to run his empire. He started the civil service with a small group of scholars, who recruited more and more officials.

◀ EXAMINATIONS
Emperor Wu Di (r.140–87BC) thought of the first civil service exams. He founded a special university where candidates could study the writings of Confucius, which they had to learn by heart in order to pass their exams.

▶ GOOD MARKS
The circles on this 19th-century Chinese exam paper indicate where the tutor thought the student's calligraphy was particularly good.

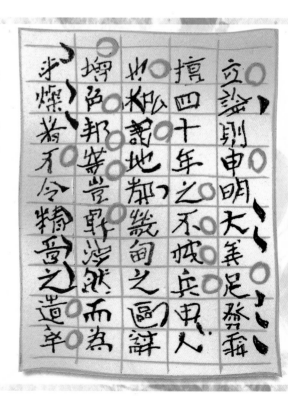

The Han emperors also set up a civil service to administer the empire. They created a huge number of officials, who got their jobs by taking an examination. Candidates had to answer questions on the teachings of the philosopher Confucius. This civil service, with its system of examinations, lasted some 2000 years — much longer than the Han dynasty itself.

▶ PRECIOUS SILK

The Chinese used silk for kimonos, wall hangings and, before the Han invented paper and ink, even as a writing material. Silk making began in China some 4000 years ago. The Chinese kept the details of its production secret and earned a huge income from trading in the luxurious fabric.

The most important of all the changes that took place under the Han emperors were in technology. Paper and fine porcelain, or china, were both Han inventions. Scientists of the Han period even made the world's first seismograph for predicting earthquakes. They also invented a water clock, the wheelbarrow and the stern-post rudder, for better steering of boats at sea. At the same time, merchants brought many new materials into China, from wool and furs to glass and pearls. Peaceful and wealthy, Han China was probably the most advanced civilization of its time.

▼ THE JADE PRINCESS

This body of a Han princess, wrapped in jade, dates back from the 1st century BC. The Chinese believed jade was magical. They thought it would preserve anything wrapped in it for ever.

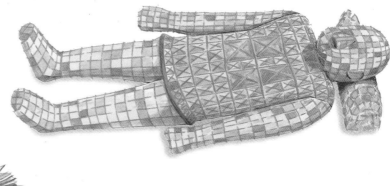

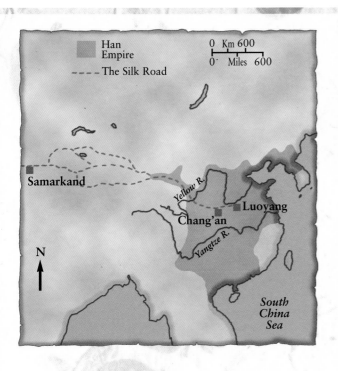

◀ HAN EMPIRE
The Han empire stretched far into the northwest, along the routes of the silk merchants into central Asia. The Han emperors also pushed into the south, where population increased towards the end of the Han period. The earliest Han capital city, and site of the imperial palace, was at Chang'an. Later the capital moved to Luoyang.

Han Empire

---- The Silk Road

0 Km 600
0 Miles 600

Samarkand

Yellow R.

Luoyang

Chang'an

Yangtze R.

N

South China Sea

Key Dates

- 207BC Gaozu overthrows the Qin dynasty. The Han dynasty rules from the city of Chang'an.

- 140–87BC The reign of Han Wu Di. He defeats the northern nomads. The Han empire reaches its largest extent.

- 124BC Competitive examinations for the civil service begin.

- 119BC Iron industry nationalized.

- AD25 Later Han period begins. The emperor moves the capital to Luoyang.

- AD105 An official called Cai Lun develops the paper-making process.

- AD220 Power struggles weaken the court and the Han empire collapses.

Early Japan

◀ FARMING RICE
Early Japanese cultivated rice in wet paddy fields. Rice farming probably came to Japan from Korea between 500 and 300BC.

▲ POTTERY FIGURINE
Jomon potters showed their skill making figurines like this.

FOR THOUSANDS OF YEARS after the last Ice Age, the people of Japan survived by hunting and gathering. Archeologists call these early people the Jomon. They used tools made of stone and bone and by about 10,500BC, had produced some of the world's first pottery, even though they did not use the potter's wheel. During the 3rd century BC, a new people arrived in Japan, probably from the mainland of Asia. Known as the Yayoi, they were the first people in Japan to grow rice in irrigated fields. They also brought metal working to Japan as well as domesticated animals, woven cloth and the potter's wheel, and established a new, settled agricultural society.

The Yayoi people began farming rice on the southern Japanese island of Kyushu. Soon their farming way of life had spread to much of Japan's main island, Honshu. Yayoi farmers used stone tools, such as reaping knives, and made hoes and spades out of wood. Bronze was used mainly for weapons and finely decorated

IMPORTED SKILLS
Settlers who came from mainland Asia brought important skills to early Japan. These were bronze and iron casting, useful for making effective tools. They also brought the potter's wheel, so the Japanese could make earthenware objects like jugs and pots, and they introduced land irrigation for growing rice.

◀ BRONZE BELL
Bells like this, covered with decorative patterns and simple pictures of humans and animals, were made in both the Yayoi and Yamato periods. Unlike western bells, they did not have clappers, so must have been rung by beating.

▲ FISHING
Japanese fishermen pursue a whale through high seas in this typically stylized image. Early people in northeastern Japan relied on fish for much of their diet. Whale was an important food source.

▼ TOMB HORSE
When a Yamato emperor died, the people surrounded his burial site with thousands of pottery objects, such as this horse. They were meant to protect the tomb and its contents.

◄ SHINTO
A Shinto temple in Nikko, Japan. Shinto is the traditional religion of Japan. It dates back to very early Japan and was based on a love of nature and belief in spirits, called kami.

items such as bells and mirrors. From this evidence, archeologists believe that only rich or high-status Japanese, such as chiefs, priests and warriors, used metal items. Their owners may have used many of these bronze items, including bells, in ceremonies to celebrate the passing of the seasons or rituals performed during rice planting and harvesting.

By the 3rd century AD, some of the warrior-chiefs had gained power over large areas of Japan. These powerful families became the leaders of the next

Japanese culture, the Yamato. They claimed to be descended from the sun goddess and their power soon stretched across the whole of Japan. They led their soldiers on horseback, and copied the government of the Chinese emperors, with large courts and ranks of officials. The Yamato built hill-top settlements to defend themselves and huge burial tombs, surrounded by moats, were also used for self-defence. These tombs, filled with armor, jewelry and weapons, indicate the great power and wealth of the Yamato emperors.

◄ EARLY JAPAN
The Yayoi rice farmers spread northwards from southern Japan. They are named after the section of modern Tokyo where remains of their culture were found. The later Yamato culture began on the Yamato plain in southeastern Honshu. The greatest number of Yamato remains, especially palaces and tombs, is still to be found in this area.

Key Dates

- 8000BC Jomon culture of hunter-gatherers dominates Japan.

- 200BC The Yayoi people begin to introduce rice farming.

- AD250 Rise of the Yamato culture.

- AD350 The Yamato emperor rules the whole of Japan.

- AD538 The first Buddhists to settle in Japan arrive from Korea.

- AD604 After a period of weakness, Prince Shotoku Taishi strengthens imperial power and introduces new forms of government based on Chinese models.

- AD710 The Yamato period ends and the state capital moves to the city of Nara.

The Khmers

▲ GLAZED JAR
This Vietnamese jar was made around the 11th century AD. It has a finely-cracked cream glaze, decorated with brown leaf sprays.

DEEP IN THE JUNGLES of Cambodia stand the remains of some of the largest temples and palaces ever constructed. They are reminders of the great civilization of the Khmers, who flourished between the 9th and 15th centuries AD, and were ruled by kings so powerful that their people believed them to be gods.

The Khmers lived in a difficult, inhospitable part of the world. Dense tropical forests covered much of their country and every year the monsoons flooded their rivers, making it difficult to grow crops. But they began to clear the forests and adapted to the rains, growing rice in the flooded plains on either side of the great Mekong River.

As time went on, the Khmers learned how to dig canals and reservoirs, to drain away and store the flood water. Then they could water their fields during the rest of the year, when there was little rain.

While their farmers were busy in the fields, the

▲ ANGKOR WAT
The greatest of all the Khmer temples was Angkor Wat. Started by King Suryavarman II in 1113, it covers a vast area. It contains several courtyards lined with shrines and topped with huge towers. The picture shows a detail from the Elephant's Terrace.

Khmers were opening up trade routes through Siam (Thailand) into India. As a result of these links, Khmer artists and architects copied Indian styles, and the Khmers began to adopt the Hindu religion.

RELIGIOUS TEMPLE

The Khmer kingdom lasted for 500 years. Angkor Wat was its most fabulous achievement. The Khmers were Hindus, who believed in gods such as Vishnu, Shiva and Brahma. Their images appear in reliefs all over the temple. Also at Angkor Wat were statues of Nagas, mythical seven-headed snakes. The Khmers believed they were kindly water spirits.

▶ ANGKOR STATUE
The sculptors who worked at Angkor Wat created fabulous work. This intricate stone carving forms part of a massive gateway to the temple. It has survived for hundreds of years in the Cambodian jungles.

▲ ASPARAS
Carved in relief on the walls and in the courtyard of Angkor Wat, these dancing women were known as *asparas*. Covered in jewels and wearing towering headdresses, they entertained kings.

◀ CUTTING TREES
The Khmers had to clear large areas of tropical forest for farming and to build their temples. They used elephants to move and carry heavy trees. They also used elephants in warfare.

The godly status of the Khmer kings gave them enormous power and made most people eager to work for them. From the 12th century onwards, the kings began enormous building projects — temples covering many acres, surrounded by huge lakes and long canals. Thousands of laborers, toiling in groups of 25 or more, hauled massive blocks of stone through the forest to the building sites to create towering temples. They also built hospitals, reservoirs and roads.

The Khmer kingdom lasted until the 15th century, although the people had to fight off several invasion attempts by neighbors jealous of their wealth. Finally, in 1431, an invading army from Siam proved too strong for the Khmers, who fled to a small area in the south of the country.

◀ KHMERS
The kingdom of the Khmers occupied much of modern Cambodia, plus the southern part of Vietnam. Around one million people lived in and around the capital, Angkor. The rest of the population occupied the floodplains of rivers such as the Mekong.

Key Dates

- AD802 The Khmer empire is founded under King Jayavarman II (r.802–850).

- AD881 King Yasovarman I builds the earliest surviving Khmer temple.

- AD1113 Work starts on building Angkor Wat.

- AD1177 The Cham sail up the Mekong River and attack Angkor Wat.

- AD1200 King Jayavarman VII builds a new temple, Angkor Thom.

- AD1431 Siamese invaders destroy Angkor; the Khmer empire collapses.

North American Civilizations

THE EARLY CIVILIZATIONS of North America are famous for their burial mounds, remains of which still exist today. These huge structures contain thousands of tons of earth. Large numbers of people must have labored for months or even years to build them. The most famous of the North American civilizations were the Hopewell people, who were based in the Ohio River valley, and the mound builders of the Mississippi area.

Hopewell mounds were gathered together in groups. At Hopewell itself, 38 mounds form a complex of 45 hectares. Most are round or rectangular mounds. They contain several bodies. The Hopewell people left offerings and belongings in the graves with their dead. These included tools, beads, jewelry and ornaments.

Some of the graves were made from raw materials that came from far away because the Hopewells traded over long distances. They imported sea shells from Florida, obsidian (a naturally occurring form of glass) from the Rockies, and flint from Illinois. In return they made goods such as pipes, pottery figurines and copper ornaments as far as southeastern Canada.

After about AD400, the Hopewell trading network began to break down, and the civilization went into decline. No one knows why this happened. Perhaps the population was too large for the local food supply. The climate became colder which may also have cut down the food supply.

But by this time another mound-building group were living in the Mississippi area. They mainly lived in small settlements but created a large city, of perhaps 30,000 people, at Cahokia. This city consisted mainly

CROPS

The most important crop for the early North American civilizations was maize. Together with beans and squash, it may have come into North America from Mexico. Most early North Americans relied on agriculture, which enabled them to create more permanent settlements.

◀ STONE PIPE
Native Americans may have used this carved stone pipe, dated about 100BC, to smoke various plants, including tobacco. Archeologists found the pipe in Ohio.

▼ HOMES
Houses made from a framework of wooden poles, covered with thatch, provided homes for early Native Americans in the river valleys of southeastern North America.

▲ MASK
The Kwakiutl, Native Americans from the northwest Pacific coast, carved this elaborate mask. Unlike the Ohio peoples, they relied mainly on fishing for their food.

of wood and thatch houses on the fertile river flood plain. In the central area were more than 100 earth mounds. The largest was the vast Monk's Mound, which was more than 90 feet high and topped by a wood and thatch temple. Cahokia was probably the home of local chiefs, whose period of greatest power lasted some 200 years, from 1050 to 1250AD.

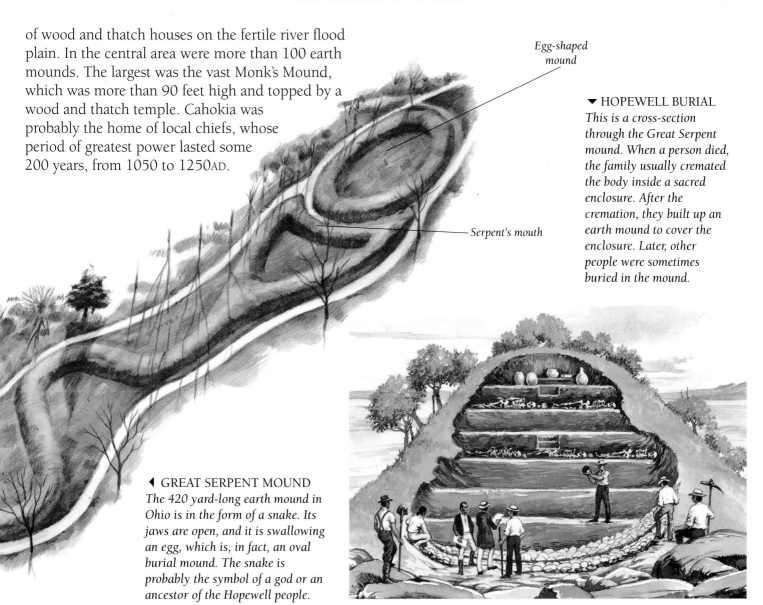

Egg-shaped mound

Serpent's mouth

◀ GREAT SERPENT MOUND
The 420 yard-long earth mound in Ohio is in the form of a snake. Its jaws are open, and it is swallowing an egg, which is, in fact, an oval burial mound. The snake is probably the symbol of a god or an ancestor of the Hopewell people.

▼ HOPEWELL BURIAL
This is a cross-section through the Great Serpent mound. When a person died, the family usually cremated the body inside a sacred enclosure. After the cremation, they built up an earth mound to cover the enclosure. Later, other people were sometimes buried in the mound.

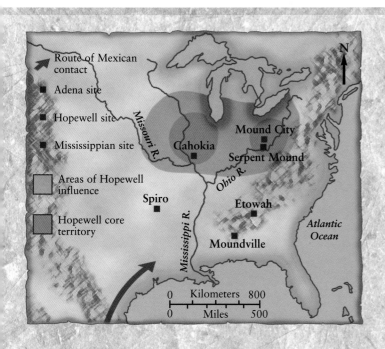

Route of Mexican contact
■ Adena site
■ Hopewell site
■ Mississippian site
☐ Areas of Hopewell influence
☐ Hopewell core territory

Missouri R.
Cahokia
Mound City
Serpent Mound
Ohio R.
Spiro
Mississippi R.
Etowah
Atlantic Ocean
Moundville

N

0 — Kilometers — 800
0 — Miles — 500

◀ NORTH AMERICA
The Hopewell people had their main centers in Ohio and Illinois. The Mississippi people came from the area where the Mississippi and Missouri rivers joined. But the influence of both peoples spread much farther. Archeologists have found their goods all over eastern North America, from Florida in the South to Canada in the North.

Key Dates

- 200BC Beginnings of Hopewell civilization.

- AD400 Hopewell civilization declines.

- AD400–800 Maize growing spreads across southeastern North America.

- AD900 Rise of the Mississippi civilization.

- AD1050–1250 Cahokia is a major center of Mississippi civilization.

- AD1250 Power shifts to Moundville, west-central Alabama.

People of the Andes

I T SEEMS AN UNLIKELY PLACE to settle. The high Andes mountains make travel, building and farming difficult. But in the 12th century BC, a group of people started to build cities and ritual centers in these harsh conditions. We know these people as the Chavín, after their city at Chavín de Huantar. During their most prosperous period, their settlements spread for many miles along the coastal plain.

At Chavín, near the Mosna River, they built a large temple complex with a maze of corridors and rooms. Here they hid the images of their gods, who were often beings that combined human and animal features — jaguars, eagles, and snakes. Archeologists think that people came to the temple to ask the gods about the future, and that priests inside the hidden rooms replied by blowing conch-shell trumpets.

The Chavín were powerful for around 500 years, after which several local cultures sprang up in the region. The Huari people took over much of the Chavín's territory and a civilization of sun-worshippers emerged at Tiahuanaco, Bolivia.

▲ GATEWAY OF THE SUN
The Gateway of the Sun stood at the entrance to the temple at Tiahuanaco, near Lake Titicaca, Bolivia. It was carved out of one enormous piece of stone.

TIAHUANACO

The Tiahuanaco civilization emerged near Lake Titicaca, where they built an extraordinary city and temple complex. On the shores of the lake, the Tiahuanaco people drained large areas of marsh to make farmland to feed the city's population. With the Huari, they controlled the Andes region.

◀ ANIMAL POT
Tiahuanaco's potters were some of the most skilled in South America. They made many of their pots in animal shapes.

▲ TEMPLE WALL
The main buildings at Tiahuanaco included a huge temple whose walls were decorated with stone heads. Tiahuanaco was probably also a bustling city as well as an important ceremonial site.

◀ JAGUAR CULT
Fearsome deities appear in all early Central American civilizations. The jaguar was especially sacred.

The Olmec

THEY WERE KNOWN AS THE PEOPLE of the jaguar. The Olmec came from a small area by the Bay of Campeche in central Mexico. Like the Chavín of South America they worshipped gods that were half-human and half-animal. A jaguar figure seems to have been their most favored, and most feared, deity.

The Olmec were the ancestors of the later Mexican civilizations, such as the Maya and Toltec. Like them, the Olmec cleared the tropical forest to farm maize, squash, beans and tomatoes. Like them too, they built their temples on tall pyramids, expressed

◀ JAGUAR SPIRIT
The image of the jaguar spirit appeared on all sorts of Olmec objects, such as this pot.

◀ COLOSSAL HEAD
Archeologists have found huge heads, such as this, at many Olmec sites. About 4.5 feet tall and carved from a single piece of rock, they were probably portraits of Olmec rulers. Olmec sculptors also used precious materials such as jade to carve human heads.

their beliefs in stone carvings, and were a strong warlike people.

But the Olmec did not use warfare to build a large empire. They probably used their army to protect the extensive trade links they set up in central America. This trade brought them a plentiful supply of raw materials, especially rocks such as basalt, jade and obsidian. Olmec sculptors used these materials to produce massive carved heads and decorative reliefs showing their gods.

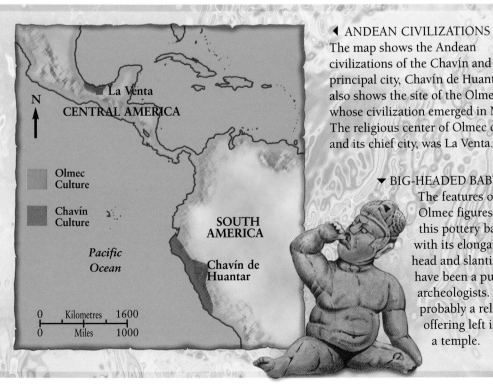

N ↑
CENTRAL AMERICA
La Venta

Olmec Culture

Chavín Culture

SOUTH AMERICA

Pacific Ocean

Chavín de Huantar

| 0 | Kilometres | 1600 |
| 0 | Miles | 1000 |

◀ ANDEAN CIVILIZATIONS
The map shows the Andean civilizations of the Chavín and their principal city, Chavín de Huantar. It also shows the site of the Olmecs, whose civilization emerged in Mexico. The religious center of Olmec culture, and its chief city, was La Venta.

▼ BIG-HEADED BABY
The features of Olmec figures like this pottery baby, with its elongated head and slanting eyes, have been a puzzle to archeologists. It was probably a religious offering left in a temple.

Key Dates

- 1200–900BC The Olmecs rule north-central Mexico.

- 850–200BC The civilization of Chavín de Huantar is at its peak.

- 200BC Many small, independent cultures develop in the valleys of the Andes.

- AD500–1000 Civilizations of Huari and Tiahuanaco.

The Maya

▲ CHAC
One of the most important of the many Maya gods was Chac, the god of rain.

DURING THE 19TH century, archeologists in Mexico were amazed when they stumbled across tall, stone-built, pyramid-shaped temples and broad plazas. They belonged to the Maya, an ancient Mexican people. The Maya created wonderful cities and were scholars. They invented their own system of writing and were skilled in mathematics and astronomy. But they were also a violent people. Their cities were continuously at war with each other. They took prisoners, who were later sacrificed to their gods.

The Maya lived in Mexico before 2000BC. But their cities became large and powerful much later, after AD300, in what historians call the "Classic" phase of their civilization. They developed efficient farming, producing maize, squash, beans and root vegetables to feed their rising population of city-dwellers.

By the Classic period, some Maya cities were huge, holding up to 50,000 people. The people lived in mud-brick houses around the outer edges of the cities. Most of the houses had only one or two rooms, and little in the way of furniture — just thin reed mats to sit on and slightly thicker mats for mattresses.

The chief Maya cities included Palenque, Copan, Tikal and Chichen Itza. In the heart of each of the cities was a complex of pyramid-shaped temples. The Maya continually rebuilt these temple-pyramids, adding more earth and stone to make them larger and taller.

The Maya survived for hundreds of years, but eventually constant civil war ate away at their wealth and power. Chichen Itza declined around 1200 and by the 16th century AD, when the Spanish conquered Mexico, only a few small Maya towns were left.

▲ TIKAL
Tikal was one of the largest cities of the Mayan civilization. Its ruins lie in the tropical rain forest of what is now northern Guatemala.

CRAFTS AND SKILLS
The Maya were skilled craftworkers. They produced fine pottery, carved stone reliefs and jade ornaments. They used razor-sharp flints for stone carving. Some flints were highly decorative and therefore buried as offerings to their gods.

◀ COSTUME
A Maya warrior wears a distinctive headpiece and carries a wooden spear. The Maya wove cloth from plant fibers such as cotton, and used plants to produce colorful dyes.

▼ CODEX
The Maya developed a series of picture symbols for writing, called glyphs. They carved these on stone tablets and also wrote them in books, called codices, made of paper, cloth or animal skins. They were the first Americans to develop picture writing.

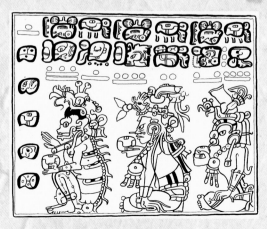

▲ CALENDAR
Astronomers and mathematicians, the Maya also invented calendars. One was a solar calendar, like ours, based on 365 days in the year. The other had a year of 200 days and was used for religious ceremonies.

▲ WALL OF SKULLS
These carvings come from a 200 foot-long wall at Chichen Itza. The wall once supported a fence on which heads of sacrificial victims were displayed, skewered on poles.

▲ WARRIOR
The people of Chichen Itza had an army of warriors who were feared all over the Yucatan peninsula. Their prisoners of war were often sacrificed to the gods.

Stepped pyramid

Shrine

Temples containing bodies of past rulers

Sacred temple

Ball court

▼ MAYA CITY
The center of a Maya city contained tall pyramid-shaped temples. Staircases led up each face of the pyramid to a shrine. Special courts were included in the temple complex, including a ball court for playing games.

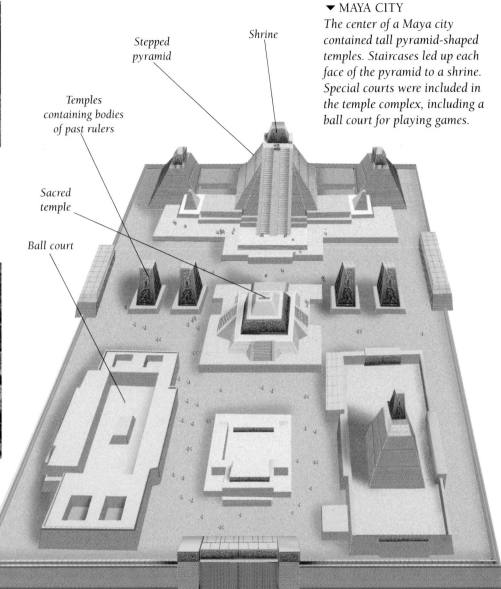

◀ THE MAYA
The Maya came from the Yucatan, the large peninsula that sticks out from the eastern coast of Mexico. They built most of their cities here and in the area to the southeast, now part of Guatemala and Honduras.

Key Dates

- 300BC–AD300 Many of the Maya cities are founded.

- AD300–800 "Classic" phase of Maya civilization flourishes.

- AD900 Most Maya cities are in decline.

- AD900–1200 Cities in the northern Yucatan flourish under the warlike Toltecs, from Tula

CLASHING SHIELDS

Human beings have continued to seek ever more effective ways of defeating their enemies, from the use of clubs and spears to siege machines and cannons. Clashing Shields examines the development of weapons and warfare in the ancient world.

BY **WILL FOWLER**

Introduction

▲ ARMOR
This Japanese warrior wears armor made from bamboo wood. Today armor is made from plastic or nylon.

▼ KEY DATES
The panel charts the progress of weapons and warfare from the Stone Age to the 1600s.

THE USE OF WEAPONS is almost as ancient as humanity. Many early weapons came from hunting tools such as spears and bows, but probably the oldest and most useful weapon is the knife or dagger. A flint dagger from Scandinavia and dated around 1800 B.C. is one of the earliest examples found in Europe, but daggers have been made from stone, bone, wood, metal and plastic. Today, soldiers are armed with bayonets or combat knives, weapons whose origins can be traced back to the simple dagger.

The development of weaponry and warfare runs alongside the development of early civilizations. As Stone Age people moved out of caves and simple shelters they banded together to form tribes and clans and built villages. Bronze replaced stone and flint for tools, and then iron replaced bronze. People began to acquire valuable possessions such as food stocks and animals, agricultural equipment, clothing and cooking utensils, and finally precious and attractive adornments and decorations. For the first time, weapons were needed, not just for hunting, but for self-defense and attack against other humans. The horses which herdsmen used to move cattle also allowed armed warriors to travel further and faster than people on foot. Raids and ambushes by horsemen, as well as movements by nomadic mounted tribes, became part of daily life.

To reduce the chance of death or injury, men used shields and armor, made from toughened animal hide,

▼ FORTIFICATIONS
Legionaries patrol Hadrian's Wall. Once territory had been won or taken, rulers needed to defend their lands or empires. Castles and walls guarded by troops were built all over Europe.

THE FIRST WEAPONS

10,000–5000 B.C. Cave paintings in Spain show men armed with bows in combat.

3500 B.C. The Royal Standard of Ur, Sumerian pictures made from shells and precious stones, shows men armed with clubs, axes and spears.

2500 B.C. First fortified city, Ur of the Chaldees in Modern Iraq.

1680 B.C. The Hyksos introduce horse-drawn chariots to Egypt.

Assyrian siege towers

1800 B.C. Flint daggers made in Sweden.

Hittite chariot

1600 B.C. Bronze weapons in Sweden and Greece.

1469 B.C. The first record of a battle, at Megiddo, between Egypt and the Canaanites.

1000 B.C. Assyrians make use of iron for weapons.

500 B.C. In China, Sun Tzu writes the first book on military theory.

GREEKS AND ROMANS

Mediterranean galley

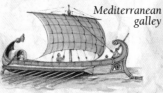

490 B.C. The Battle of Marathon fought between the Greeks and the Persians. Both army and navy are used and the Greeks defeat an enemy once thought to be unbeatable.

401 B.C. Battle of Cunaxa between Greeks and Persians uses chariots with scythes near Babylon. The Persians won.

387 B.C. First siege of Rome by Gauls. The City is burnt but the government buildings remain.

327 B.C. Alexander the Great crosses the river Hydaspes and defeats the Indian king Porus.

216 B.C. Hannibal of Carthage uses elephants at the Battle of Cannae against the Romans. It was his greatest victory.

206 B.C.–AD220 Crossbows widely used in China.

A.D. 408–410 The Goths under Alaric besiege Rome and sack it on August 24, 410.

Roman legionary

wood or wood strengthened with metal. This ancient equipment forms a model for the plastic shields used by modern-day police to protect themselves from the oldest of weapons—the thrown stone. The breastplates worn by ancient cavalries are copied by the "flak jackets" worn by many soldiers and helicopter crews today.

Tribal raids to steal goods or settle territorial disputes led to the building of fortifications. The fences and ditches built to control wild or domesticated animals were just as effective against raiding parties. Wood was easy to get and to work with, but could be set on fire by attackers, and would rot in time. Stone or mud brick was tougher and more enduring. Today, fortifications may no longer be towering castles, but we still use sandbag parapets, trenches and bunkers.

Ancient weapons relied for their effectiveness on human or animal strength although heavy shields and armor made maneuvering awkward. Warfare stayed much the same until the late 1800s when the internal combustion engine was invented.

▲ ANIMALS
Before the invention of the combustion engine, animals— usually horses—were used to transport troops, weapons and supplies. In the Crusades in the Middle Ages, both European knights and Saracen warriors fought on horseback. A medieval knight wore such heavy armor that he had to be lifted onto his horse by crane.

▼ TECHNOLOGY
Gunpowder was probably invented in China in the 10th century. The Arabs made the first known guns in about 1300. From the 1400s, muskets were developed in Europe and were gradually improved to allow them to be carried into battle.

VIKINGS TO THE MIDDLE AGES

500 Saxon raids on Britain from north Germany.

778 Battle of Roncesvalles. The Franks under Charlemagne beaten by Basques and Gascons.

700s to 1000s Norse raids on Britain and Europe.

The Norman conquest

1066 The Battle of Hastings. William of Normandy invades Britain and seizes power.

1095–99 The First Crusade. European Christian armies fight for the Holy Land.

1120 Welsh archers use longbows for the first time at Powys.

1190 Mongols under Genghis Khan begin expansion south and west from the Gobi Desert.

1330 First steel produced by accident in the Middle East while making iron.

1326 First illustration of cannon appears in manuscripts in Europe.

1337 Hundred Years War between England and France begins.

Medieval cannon

GUNPOWDER AND AFTER

1400 Handguns first produced in Europe.   *Hand cannon*

1400–1600 Rise of halberdiers and pikemen in Europe. Simple breech loading guns in use.

1411 Earliest illustration of a simple matchlock.

1415 Battle of Agincourt. The last great victory of the longbow.

1420s Jan Zizka and the Hussites pioneer the use of war wagons and shoulder-fired guns.

1453 Massed artillery used by Turks at the Siege of Constantinople.

1500 Metal shot gains widespread use.

1505 First battleworthy pistol developed in Germany.

1547 Flintlocks developed in Spain.

1595 English begin to use fire arms and cannon.

1635 Flintlocks perfected in France.

1620 Swedes first use light leather-bound cannon. First tactical use of artillery.

Clubs, Maces, Hammers and Flails

▲ CLUBS AND MACES AT HASTINGS
The Bayeux tapestry showing Norman cavalry, armed with maces and clubs, at the Battle of Hastings in 1066.

THE EARLIEST KIND of weapons were clubs, maces and hammers. People could hold them in their hands. They could not break down and nothing could go wrong with them. The club is the oldest weapon. The earliest clubs were lumps of stone picked up from the ground. Prehistoric people used them as both tools and weapons. Clubs could be used to crush seeds for food. They could also be used as weapons to hunt animals or to fight with enemies. In South Africa, there are wall paintings made around 6000 B.C. showing two human figures with long heavy sticks that look like clubs. People made clubs from a variety of materials—long, heavy animal bones, or thick lengths of wood taken from trees, bushes or plants, for example.

When people learned how to make bronze, iron and steel, they used these metals to make stronger weapons. Using metal, the simple club was turned into a mace. A mace had a weighted, spiked or pointed end. This could be used to batter through an enemy's shield or armor. It could be used in hand-to-hand fighting or by soldiers on horseback. Today in the United States, a ceremonial mace, made of ebony and silver, is used in the House of Representatives. In Britain, the scepter carried by the queen on special occasions is also a kind of mace.

The war hammer was like an ordinary carpenter's claw hammer, but had only one claw. This was a kind of spiked pick. The shaft, or handle, of a war hammer was up to a yard in length. A soldier using a hammer could reach out from his saddle to strike his enemy. Using the sharp claw of the hammer, the soldier could then puncture his enemy's metal helmet. This kind of blow to the head could be fatal, killing instantly.

The flail was first used by farmers to thresh corn. It was made into a weapon which is a mixture of mace and club. Between one and three lengths of chain were attached to one end of a thick metal stick. Weighted spikes were attached to the end of each length of chain. When the flail was used, the chains whipped through the air, and struck the enemy in several places at once.

▲ THE MACE
This elaborately crafted mace is a weapon of war but may also serve as a symbol of political or military status.

SIMPLE WEAPONS FOR CLOSE COMBAT
In its most primitive form, a club or contact weapon extends the reach of a person in close combat and replaces their feet or fists as weapons. It can be made from any spare wood or timber. Later the use of metal and the positioning of the weight at one end made these contact weapons much more effective in battle.

◀ THE SHILLELAGH
This Irish chieftain holds a shillelagh, a type of club made from hard wood like blackthorn or oak. Clubs are the simplest of contact weapons. In a more sophisticated version, they are still used today in the form of police night sticks.

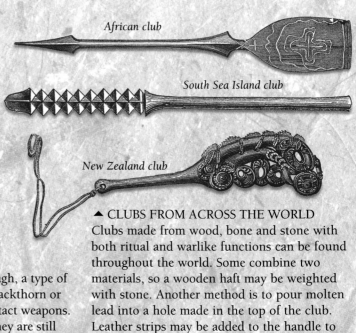

African club

South Sea Island club

New Zealand club

▲ CLUBS FROM ACROSS THE WORLD
Clubs made from wood, bone and stone with both ritual and warlike functions can be found throughout the world. Some combine two materials, so a wooden haft may be weighted with stone. Another method is to pour molten lead into a hole made in the top of the club. Leather strips may be added to the handle to improve grip, or a loop for the user's wrist.

◀ THE ROUT OF SAN ROMANO
This detail from a painting by the Italian Renaissance artist Uccello shows armor-clad horsemen wielding maces, hammers and bows.

▲ HAMMER VERSUS MACE
Even though medieval knights wore complicated armor, they still fought with simple weapons. In this picture you can see how the hammer and mace were used, and how powerful they look.

16th-century war hammer

▲ WAR HAMMER
The spike on the war hammer was designed to penetrate armor. The flat end was used for smashing in helmets.

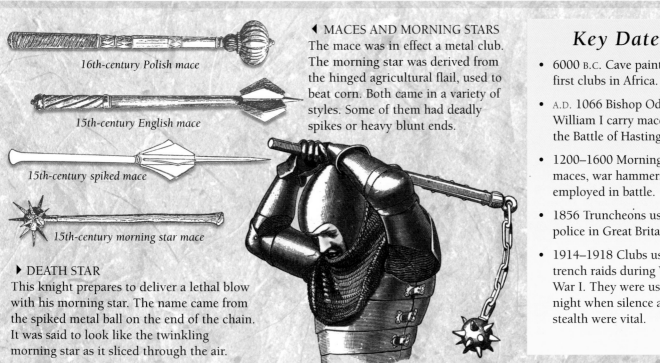

16th-century Polish mace

15th-century English mace

15th-century spiked mace

15th-century morning star mace

◀ MACES AND MORNING STARS
The mace was in effect a metal club. The morning star was derived from the hinged agricultural flail, used to beat corn. Both came in a variety of styles. Some of them had deadly spikes or heavy blunt ends.

▶ DEATH STAR
This knight prepares to deliver a lethal blow with his morning star. The name came from the spiked metal ball on the end of the chain. It was said to look like the twinkling morning star as it sliced through the air.

Key Dates

- 6000 B.C. Cave paintings of first clubs in Africa.

- A.D. 1066 Bishop Odo and William I carry maces at the Battle of Hastings.

- 1200–1600 Morning stars, maces, war hammers employed in battle.

- 1856 Truncheons used by police in Great Britain.

- 1914–1918 Clubs used in trench raids during World War I. They were used at night when silence and stealth were vital.

Axes and Throwing Weapons

THE AX WAS FIRST USED as a woodsman's tool for felling trees. The first axes, like the first clubs, were made from sharp stones or flints. They were simply cutting tools. Later they were fixed to shafts or handles, which made them more powerful. They could be swung first to put more force behind the blow.

Axes were first made by tying sharp flints into forked or split branches. When people learned how to use bronze, iron and steel, they made stronger, sharper axes. By the time of the Iron Age, ax heads could be cast with a socket to fit the handle. Then the blade was hammered and ground to a sharp edge. Axes are still made in the same way today.

Axes have always been symbols used by powerful kings and rulers. The double-headed bronze ax was used as the symbol of the Minoan civilization in Crete. Pictures of the ax were used in wall paintings and as decoration on pottery.

The hand ax had a short handle. It could be used to hack the enemy in hand-to-hand combat. Soldiers could also throw the ax, although

▲ DECORATIVE AX HEADS
The simple wedge shape of an ax head has often been decorated for war or ritual throughout the world.

◄ KNIGHT WITH AX
Medieval knights often rode into battle armed with a heavy battle-ax. This had a sharp blade and a spike. The ax was attached to the knight's arm with a chain. These axes could cause terrible injuries to both men and horses.

this meant they might lose it. A good example of a fighting ax was the tomahawk used by Native North Americans. Tomahawks were first made of stone, then later of steel brought by traders. They were used for hunting and fighting. The tomahawk had a long handle which gave it a powerful swing. British soldiers fighting in North America in the 18th century adopted the tomahawk for their own use.

The last time an ax was used in combat in Europe was at the battle of Waterloo in 1815 between the

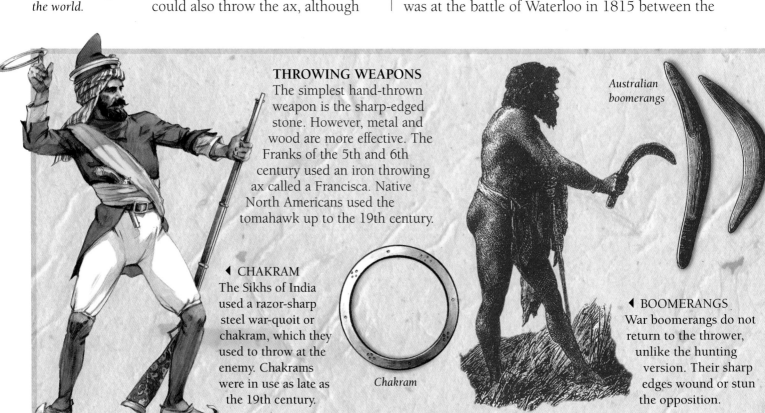

THROWING WEAPONS
The simplest hand-thrown weapon is the sharp-edged stone. However, metal and wood are more effective. The Franks of the 5th and 6th century used an iron throwing ax called a Francisca. Native North Americans used the tomahawk up to the 19th century.

Australian boomerangs

◄ CHAKRAM
The Sikhs of India used a razor-sharp steel war-quoit or chakram, which they used to throw at the enemy. Chakrams were in use as late as the 19th century.

Chakram

◄ BOOMERANGS
War boomerangs do not return to the thrower, unlike the hunting version. Their sharp edges wound or stun the opposition.

▼ NORSE RAIDERS
Norse raiders disembark from their longships and race into action armed with their single-headed war axes. These iron-bladed weapons were often elaborately decorated.

French and the British, together with the Prussians. During the battle, French troops used axes to break down the door of the farm at Hougoument, which was being held by the British infantry.

The ax is still in use today. In some armies, it is the badge of the assault pioneers. These are soldiers who do engineering work. The badge shows crossed axes. Firefighters also use axes which look rather like ancient war axes. They have spikes and blades and are easy to hold and use in one hand.

▼ THROWING KNIFE
The leaf-shaped throwing knife was a war weapon used throughout Africa from Nigeria through the Congo to the Sudan. As it turned through the air in flight the blades of the throwing knife were intended to strike the victim in a sawing action. The disadvantage of a throwing weapon was that if it missed, it could be thrown back.

African throwing knife

◄ WAR BLADE
This African throwing knife had a steel, double-edged blade. The short handle was bound with grass or a leather thong to give the warrior a good grip. The knife was designed purely as a weapon, unlike an everyday knife, and could not be used off the battlefield for day-to-day tasks or hunting.

Key Dates

- 2000–1700 B.C. Double-headed ax used as symbol for the civilization of Minoan Crete.

- 700 B.C. Evidence that slings were used in Assyria.

- A.D. 400–500 Francisca throwing axes found in England.

- 700–1100 Single- and double-bladed axes used by Norse raiders.

- 900–1400 Heavy, long-handled battle-axes used by knights.

- 1700s Iron-bladed tomahawks manufactured for North America.

- 1800s Chakrams in use in India.

Slings, Bows and Crossbows

T HE SLING, LIKE the longbow and crossbow, is a "stand-off" weapon. This lets a soldier attack his enemy while remaining out of reach himself. Slings were used in early sea battles. Piles of sling stones were discovered at Maiden Castle, Dorset, England, where the Celtic defenders fought the Romans in A.D. 44.

▲ DAVID AND THE GIANT GOLIATH
The shepherd David defeated the Philistine warrior Goliath by stunning him with a sling stone.

Bows are among the most ancient weapons in the world. Ancient cave paintings, dating from 10,000 and 5000 B.C., from Castellon in Spain show figures of men using bows for fighting. Bows have been found in Denmark dating from 2000 to 1500 B.C. and in Egypt from around 1400 B.C.

The bow was also used for hunting. Many of the skills of the hunter were also those of the warrior. Experienced archers could fire accurately from horseback or chariot.

In the 16th century, Henry VIII of England ordered that young men should practice shooting their bows every Sunday after church. Most bows were made from yew wood.

The triumph of the English and Welsh longbow was in three battles against France: Crécy in August, 1346;

Poitiers in September, 1356; and Agincourt in October, 1415. English and Welsh archers were able to keep the French mounted nobles under a constant rain of arrows from 800 feet. As horses and riders crashed to the ground, others became entangled with them and they all became easy targets.

When muskets and rifles were first invented, the longbow, fired by a skilled archer, was still more accurate. It was not until the American Civil War that firearms became more effective. Muskets were adopted because it was easier to train soldiers to use them.

◀ TAKING AIM
A crossbowman takes aim. He operated the trigger, which held back the string with a hook called a nut, with his right hand. If the weapon was used to hunt game a stone was used in place of the bolt.

◀ TAKING COVER
A crossbowman takes cover with his weapon and equipment stowed in a shield carrier.

STAND OFF WEAPONS

The crossbow and longbow allowed ordinary foot soldiers to engage enemies at long range. This meant that mounted knights and foot soldiers could be killed before they could use their swords, lances or axes. Both longbows and crossbows could penetrate armor at short range, which meant that they could bring down a knight in full armor.

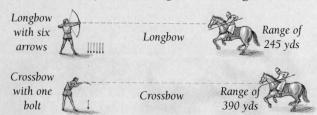

Longbow with six arrows   Longbow   Range of 245 yds

Crossbow with one bolt   Crossbow   Range of 390 yds

▲ SHOOTING RANGE
The expert longbowman could fire up to six aimed arrows in a minute to a range of about 245 yards, or twelve less accurately.

On the other hand, the skilled crossbowman had a longer range at 390 yards, but a far slower rate of fire. He could only shoot one bolt a minute.

Using the Crossbow

Spanning

Fitting the bolt

Taking aim

▲ THREE STAGES
It took much longer to load a crossbow than to aim and fire an arrow. There were three stages to loading and firing a crossbow. Spanning was the first stage. It involved pulling

the bow string back and locking it. Then the bolt was fitted into the slot. Finally the bow was aimed and fired. With mechanical assistance as many as four bolts could be fired in a minute.

▼ LONGBOWS IN ACTION
English and Welsh longbowmen protected by a palisade of stakes fire at advancing French knights.

Some armies used men armed with crossbows. The crossbow is a short bow attached to a piece of wood or metal called a stock. The bowstring was pulled back by hand or mechanically and held in place by a hook and trigger mechanism. The short arrow, or bolt, was fitted into a slot and aligned with the string. The crossbowman had only to aim and operate the trigger.

The first description of a crossbow appears in a book called The Art of War by the Chinese military thinker Sun Tzu, writing in 500 B.C. In 1139 Pope Innocent II tried to ban the use of the crossbow against Christians because of the terrible injuries it caused. Richard I of England died in 1199 from gangrene caused by a crossbow bolt.

Barbed arrowhead *Forked steel tip*

▲ ARROWHEADS
Archers used different shaped arrowheads. Barbs and forks were popular. Barbs ensured that the arrow stayed lodged in the target and made withdrawal difficult. The forked steel tip was used in the Far East.

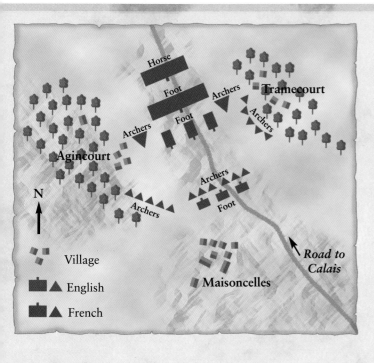

Village

■ ▲ English

■ ▲ French

◄ LONGBOWS SAVE THE DAY
The Battle of Agincourt was the last great victory of the longbow against mounted soldiers. Wet weather slowed down the French knights and the English and Welsh archers stopped two attacks before Henry V's forces attacked from the rear. The French were defeated and lost about 5000 of their men.

Key Dates

- 10,000–5000 B.C. Cave paintings in Spain show archers in battle.

- 500 B.C. Sun Tzu writing about military doctrine mentions crossbows.

- A.D.1100 Crossbows widely used in Europe.

- 1199 King Richard I of England killed by a crossbow at Chaluz.

- 1200s Longbow enters wide use in England and Wales.

- 1914–1918 Crossbows used for firing grenades in the trench warfare during World War I.

Daggers and Knives

SMALL, LIGHT AND EASY TO CARRY, daggers and knives are hand-held weapons. Daggers and knives make very good secret weapons as they can be used in complete silence. They were used on their own for hand-to-hand fighting, or for throwing.

Although the dagger design was based on the knife, there is an important difference between the two. The knife is a simple tool, sharp along one edge of the blade, it may have a relatively blunt point. It can be used for everyday tasks like cutting up meat for example, as well as being used as a weapon. A dagger is double-edged and tapers along its length to a sharp point. It may have a guard between the blade and the handle to protect the user's hand. It is always classified as a weapon.

The earliest daggers were made from flint. Early daggers were also made from sharpened wood or bone. Daggers made from bronze, iron and steel lasted longer.

◀ SWORD AND DAGGER
A fully armored knight equipped with a sword and dagger. The sword was suitable for hacking and the dagger for thrusts to gaps in the armor.

▶ MURDER WEAPON
Lurking in the shadows, an assassin armed with a stiletto awaits his victim. This dagger was easy to conceal and deadly if it penetrated a vital organ.

Stiletto

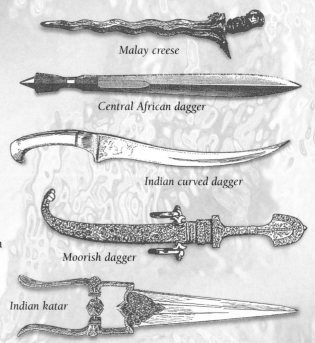

DAGGER DESIGN

As a weapon, a dagger or knife was inexpensive and very effective in even unskilled hands. It could be used for agricultural or domestic work if necessary. A dagger consists of the blade, the cross guard that protects the user's hand and knuckles, the grip or handle and the pommel. In a fight, the pommel at the base of the grip could be used in the same way as a hammer on an opponent's head. Dagger designs vary from country to country. The Indian katar or push dagger was designed to be used in a punching action.

Pommel

Grip or handle

Blade

◀ A BLADE FROM THE BRONZE AGE
This Swedish dagger dates from around 1350–1200 B.C. and shows all the basic design principles of a hand-held edged weapon. It has a separate riveted hilt, distinct pommel and double-edged blade with fullers or blood grooves. Later designs would have a full-length tang, an extension of the blade, built into the handle. This gave the dagger greater strength and better balance.

Malay creese

Central African dagger

Indian curved dagger

Moorish dagger

Indian katar

▶ A DUEL
Duels were considered an honorable way to settle an argument. The stilleto is used here to block the sword thrust.

In the 14th and 15th centuries sword fighters used daggers with their swords. A swordsman would hold the dagger in his left hand to block and deflect his enemy's sword. He would then make a thrust with the sword in his right hand.

Swordsmiths were the people who made swords and daggers. The daggers they made were almost works of art. They had beautiful inlays and precious and semi-precious metals and jewels set in the handles. The best known swordsmiths were the Saracens of Damascus in Syria. They used a method of hammering layers of steel together. This made blades of swords and daggers very hard and sharp and created a pattern rather like watered silk, known as Damascene.

In the 20th century the dagger and the knife are still used by soldiers in combat. In World War I the United States Army was issued with the Fighting Knife Mk 1 which protected the user's knuckles with a guard which could be used as "knuckle dusters" or "brass knuckles." Modern combat knives are more like multi-purpose tools, with a screwdriver, saw edge, and wire cutter as well as a sharp knife blade.

▲ TOLEDO, CITY OF STEEL
This Spanish city was a center for beautifully designed swords, daggers and armor which were manufactured for many centuries and exported through Europe.

▶ SWORDBREAKER
A 17th-century Italian swordbreaker was a dagger made for special use in a sword fight. It was designed to trap an opponent's sword thrust in its notched blade. The dagger would not be used just to parry a sword thrust. A vigorous twist of the wrist could either break the thin blade of the trapped sword, or wrench it from the user's hands.

Cross guard

Notched blade

Key Dates

- 2000 B.C. Bronze daggers were manufactured throughout Europe.

- 500 B.C. First Iron Age weapons produced and used widely.

- A.D. 1600s–1700s Stiletto manufactured in Italy. It was copied and used throughout Europe.

- 1700s–1900s Dress daggers worn as part of military or political uniforms.

- 1820s Bowie knife invented in the United States by Jim Bowie. Its classic design forms the model for most modern sheath knives.

- 1940s–1990s Combat knives issued to soldiers as multi-function tools.

Swords, Sabers and Scimitars

ONE OF THE MOST ANCIENT weapons in the world, the sword is now a symbol of rank for officers on ceremonial parades. Tools shaped like swords were used in farming work and to cut down trees. Like other working tools they were adapted to use in fighting. The kukri from Nepal is an ancient weapon that remains in service today with Gurkha regiments of the British army. Its broad, curved blade is ideal for chopping and even digging, but it is also a very good weapon for close combat.

Early swords were used to slice rather than to thrust. For many centuries European swords had a short, straight blade which tapered to a point. It was sharp on both edges. They were first made in bronze, later iron and finally steel. The short Roman steel sword called a gladius was about 20 inches long. It was like a long, wide-bladed dagger. The gladiators who fought in the Roman circus or arena with these swords, got their name from the gladius.

Swords in the Middle Ages were longer. They were about 30 to 35 inches long with a cross-shaped handle and tapering blade. Long swords could be used to thrust at the enemy but most soldiers fought by hacking at each other. Swords could be used by soldiers on foot or horseback.

Very strong men used the two-handed sword, which was very long, with a broad blade. Swordsmen used both hands to fight with it. Scottish chieftains in the mid-16th century used a long, double-edged, two-handed sword called the claidheamh múr, or claymore.

◀ VIKING WEAPON
A Viking sword from the 10th century. Its hilt is covered with silver leaf.

◀ TWO-HANDED
Medieval knights in close combat. One of them is armed with a hand-and-a-half, or two-handed sword.

▲ SWORD SKILLS
A Japanese samurai warrior from the 15th century. Samurai warriors usually wore two swords and a distinctive headdress.

SWORDS
Swords today are made from steel and have been made from bronze, stone and even wood. Although not used in war, in many cultures, they remain the symbol of power and status within military organisations. Sword fighting techniques vary according to the design of the blade. The Japanese favour a chopping action, while the thin bladed rapier is best suited to a thrust.

▶ SAMURAI WEAPON
The Japanese traditionally used single-edged daggers and swords of different lengths. The traditional long-bladed sword is called a katana.

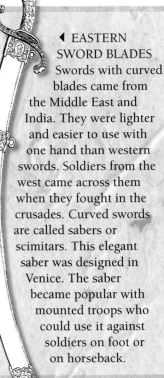

◀ EASTERN SWORD BLADES
Swords with curved blades came from the Middle East and India. They were lighter and easier to use with one hand than western swords. Soldiers from the west came across them when they fought in the crusades. Curved swords are called sabers or scimitars. This elegant saber was designed in Venice. The saber became popular with mounted troops who could use it against soldiers on foot or on horseback.

◀ DEATH AT DAWN
A Victorian print shows the victor of a duel armed with a rapier. His victim's weapon shows the guard or side rings designed to protect the hand.

▶ HEAVY BLADE
An Asian warrior armed with a bow and broad-bladed sword. The sword has the weight closer to the tip, which makes it ideal for a chopping action.

Knights and soldiers discovered the sword-making techniques of the Middle East during the crusades. This led to improved sword design in the west. Soldiers in the Middle East used a curved sword called a scimitar. These had long, narrow blades and very sharp edges.

The guard in front of the sword handle was made to protect the fighter's hand. Around 1600, Venetian sword makers produced a new guard design called the basket hilt. This was a curved, perforated guard that protected the whole hand. The basic design is still used today on many modern ceremonial swords.

The mounted soldiers of the cavalry charged towards their enemy with their swords pointing forward for a straight thrust. However, long swords became difficult to use once the soldiers were fighting close to each other. There was no room to make a good stroke. The sabre was developed as a cavalry weapon. It had a short, curved blade and was used to slash and thrust. The blade cut as it went up and as it came down.

In Renaissance Europe, noblemen and courtiers wore weapons almost as fashion accessories. Rapiers were very popular. These were light, very narrow swords known with elaborate guards. The fashion lasted from about 1530 through to 1780.

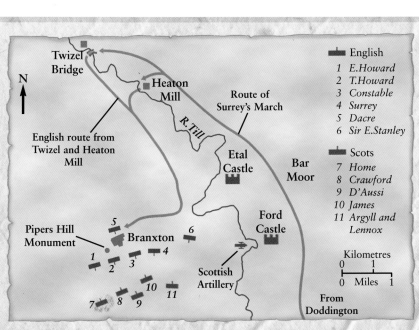

▲ THE BATTLE OF FLODDEN 1513
This battle between the English and the Scots, took place in Northern England. The Scots fought with the two-handed claymore sword.

English
1 E.Howard
2 T.Howard
3 Constable
4 Surrey
5 Dacre
6 Sir E.Stanley

Scots
7 Home
8 Crawford
9 D'Aussi
10 James
11 Argyll and Lennox

Key Dates

- 1300 B.C. Bronze swords used in war.

- 650–500 B.C. Iron swords in use.

- A.D. 900s Viking double-edged swords used in Viking raids all over Europe.

- 1300s Curved Turkish sabres in use as a cavalry weapon.

- 1500s Rapiers in use.

- 1500s Scottish two-edged swords in use.

- 1600s Venetian basket-hilt swords in use throughout Europe.

- 1850 Kukri in use with Nepalese soldiers.

Spears, Poles, Pikes and Halberds

PREHISTORIC HUNTERS used spears to kill animals for food. They were more powerful and accurate than simple stones and could be thrown from safe distances. The earliest spears were simply straight saplings (very young trees) which were sharpened at one end. In the Far East, bamboo wood was used. It was light and strong and could be hardened in a fire to give a very sharp point. Flint, stone or metal points fixed onto a spear made it even more effective.

There were soldiers armed with spears in most ancient armies. Another name for the throwing spear is javelin. Throwing

▲ THE QUARTERSTAFF
This was the simplest weapon ever made. It could be cut from saplings. In Europe in the Middle Ages, the staff was used more in competitions and brawls than in war.

spears have one drawback. Once they have been thrown at the enemy, you cannot get them back. In fact, the enemy may use them to throw at you. The Romans solved this problem by inventing a spear called a pilum. This had a long, thin neck near the point. When the spear hit a target, it snapped at the neck. Then it could not be used by the enemy.

Longer, heavier stick weapons were used to fight with rather than to throw. In medieval times, country people used large sticks called staffs for walking. Various types of blades were attached to these to make weapons for both cavalry and

▶ PIKE WALL
Pikemen in the 17th century lined up to form a barrier for cavalry. This tactic gave musketeers time and space to reload their weapons behind the pike wall.

POLE ARMS

The advantage of pole arms like spears, pikes or halberds is that the user can stab, chop or even entangle his enemy at a safe distance. Peasants often fitted a pruning bill to the shaft of a quarterstaff to make a simple pole arm during revolts and insurrections.

◀ PIKEMAN
A pikeman in the splendid uniform of the 17th century. In addition to his helmet, he might also have a breastplate for extra protection. Some pikes were nearly 4.8m long, the same length as those used by the Macedonians around 350 B.C..

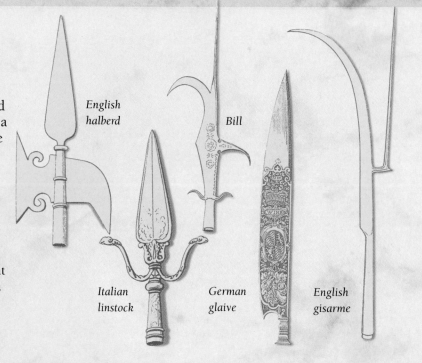

English halberd

Bill

Italian linstock

German glaive

English gisarme

infantry troops. A spear point would make a lance, used by cavalry. Knife blades and axes were also used as well as billhooks, which were tools for cutting hedges. A trident was made by attaching a sharp-pointed fork (like a pitchfork). Halberds were long poles with a spear point and an ax head mounted behind it. Pikes were long, heavy pole weapons with long blades of various designs.

In the 14th and 15th centuries, the Swiss developed specialized pike tactics. Using a pike that consisted of a twenty-foot shaft and a three-foot iron shank, Swiss soldiers marched in columns which had a front line of 30 men but could be 50 to 100 men deep. The massed pikes could stop a cavalry attack. Many rulers and generals hired Swiss pikemen to fight in their battles. Today, the Pope's Swiss Guard, armed with pikes, is all that is left of this force.

The bayonet fitted to the muzzle of modern army rifles is based on the pike. Bayonets were first used by soldiers with muskets. Although muskets were effective firearms, they took time to reload. By attaching long pointed blades, called bayonets, to their muskets and forming themselves into a hollow square with bayonets pointing outward, soldiers could break up a cavalry attack and protect each other while they reloaded.

◀ SWISS GUARD
The Swiss Guard at the Vatican still carry pikes and wear uniforms similar to those worn in the 15th and 16th centuries.

▶ CLOSE COMBAT
Two soldiers fighting with halberds. One tries to use the curved beak to trip his enemy while the other uses the spike as a spear.

▶ ON THE MOVE
An Etruscan warrior armed with a sword and throwing spear. The classic tactic for these lightly-armed men was to throw their spears, then to run forward as the spears were in flight. By the time the spears reached their target, the Etruscan soldier was within sword reach. The enemy was hit twice in one move.

▲ ISLAND WEAPONS
Spears have been used throughout history in many different cultures. This islander from New Caledonia in the Pacific Ocean is ready to throw one spear and holds two more in reserve.

Key Dates

- 600 B.C. GREEK hoplites use short throwing spears.

- 350 B.C. The sarissa (light spear) used in Macedonian phalanx formations.

- 200–100 B.C. Roman foot soldiers use the pilum, or heavy javelin.

- A.D. 900–1400 Lances used by knights for jousting and war in Europe.

- 1400s Pole ax enters service.

- 1400–1599 Halberd widely used.

- 1600s Pikes enter service.

- 1815 Cavalry lances adopted by Britain from France.

Ancient Firearms

FIREARMS ARE WEAPONS that use gunpowder and shot. The earliest firearms in the west were made around the beginning of the 15th century. They worked like mini cannons and were small enough to be carried by a soldier on foot or on horseback. They looked a lot like the modern hand-held flare used to signal an emergency at sea. They had a short barrel attached to a handle.

▲ MATCHLOCK
The matchlock was used in Europe until the 18th century and in parts of India until as late as the 20th century.

▶ MOUNTED FIREPOWER
The wheellock was ideal for mounted soldiers who would need to keep one hand free.

By the late 15th and early 16th centuries, the standard firearm was about five feet long with a barrel, stock and butt. The stock supported the metal barrel and the butt rested in the crook of the firer's shoulder when the gun was being used.

The arquebus was a bigger weapon, often used mounted on a simple tripod. It usually needed two people to operate it. One aimed it and the second put a lit taper into the touch hole or vent. The soldiers who had to carry these heavy weapons were very eager for craftsmen to make them lighter and easier firearms. The matchlock was the first improvement. This weapon was fired using a fuse or length of cord which had been soaked in a chemical called saltpeter. This made it burn slowly. The cord was coiled into a curved lever called a serpent. A shallow pan filled with gunpowder had a thin tube leading into the barrel of the weapon. To operate the matchlock, the soldier lit the cord, opened the spring-loaded cover to the

HAND GUNS
Improved metal technology and designs made hand guns more reliable and easier to carry. Tactics for infantry and cavalry changed to suit these firearms. Weapons were still made by craftsmen. After the Napoleonic wars, muskets and guns began to be mass produced.

▲ POWDER HORN
Gunpowder was stored in a powder horn to keep it dry. Many of them were made from hollow animal horns. They had a spout through which an exact measure of powder was dispensed.

▶ HAND MADE
The lead ball fired by muskets was easily made using a simple mold. Once the molten lead had hardened, the handles of the mold were opened and the new ammunition was ready. Soldiers made their own ammunition as needed.

Mould

Shot

Inside a rifled gun barrel

Bullet spinning from the barrel

▲ RIFLING
Rifling was a system of grooves inside the barrel of a firearm which gave the bullet a spin as it left the barrel. This made the gun more accurate. Rifled weapons were still rare in the early 19th century. Now rifling is used in every modern gun.

◄ MUSKETEERS
Musketeers armed with the heavy Spanish style matchlock weapon that required a fork rest for easy handling. This weapon was used by armies throughout Europe from about 1567 for over 100 years and the musketeers were an elite within the army.

▶ WHEELLOCK
This firearm used a spring-loaded wheel and pieces of iron pyrites to produce sparks which ignited the gunpowder at the moment of firing. But they were expensive and not in common use.

pan and then pulled the trigger. This brought the burning cord, or match, down into gunpowder, which exploded.

The matchlock was not a practical weapon for a soldier on horseback who needed to have one hand on the reins. So the wheellock was developed. It worked like an old-fashioned cigarette lighter. When the trigger was pulled the pan of gunpowder was uncovered. A metal wheel rubbed against a lump of iron

pyrites and produced a stream of sparks. A mounted soldier could carry two or three short-barrelled wheellock pistols in holsters on his saddle or tucked into the tops of his riding boots.

The snaphaunce, miguelet and flintlock were later firearms. They used flint and steel to produce a spark. The flintlock was in use until the mid-19th century. A shot could be fired every 20 seconds from a smoothbore flintlock musket, but the weapon was inaccurate beyond 85 yards.

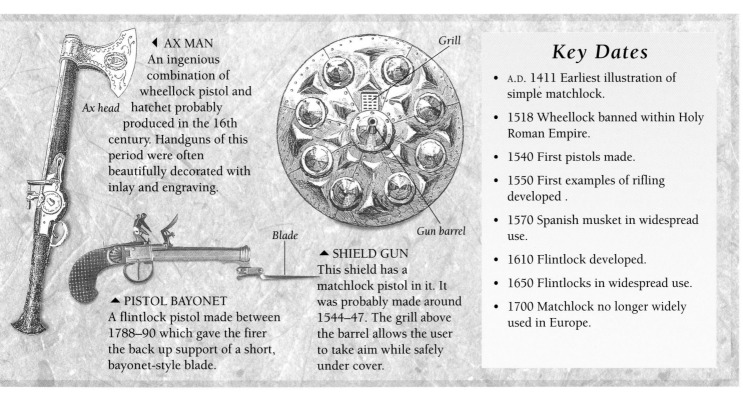

◄ AX MAN
An ingenious combination of wheellock pistol and hatchet probably produced in the 16th century. Handguns of this period were often beautifully decorated with inlay and engraving.

Ax head

▲ PISTOL BAYONET
A flintlock pistol made between 1788–90 which gave the firer the back up support of a short, bayonet-style blade.

Blade

Grill

Gun barrel

▲ SHIELD GUN
This shield has a matchlock pistol in it. It was probably made around 1544–47. The grill above the barrel allows the user to take aim while safely under cover.

Key Dates

- A.D. 1411 Earliest illustration of simple matchlock.

- 1518 Wheellock banned within Holy Roman Empire.

- 1540 First pistols made.

- 1550 First examples of rifling developed .

- 1570 Spanish musket in widespread use.

- 1610 Flintlock developed.

- 1650 Flintlocks in widespread use.

- 1700 Matchlock no longer widely used in Europe.

Armor

▲ ANCIENT ARMOR
A figure dressed in classical armor of Greece and Rome with a breastplate covering his torso and shinpads called greaves protecting his lower legs.

S OLDIERS WORE ARMOR to protect the head, neck, eyes and chest. Early armor was made from bronze. Later iron and steel were used. Japanese warriors wore armor made from bamboo wood. There is a problem with armor. It must be thick or heavy enough to protect the soldier wearing it, but light enough for him to move around easily.

The ancient Greeks were the first to use bronze armor. They used it to protect their forearms, legs and chest. A Roman legionary wore armor which covered his chest, stomach, back and shoulders. This protected his lungs, heart and the important blood vessels in the neck. Although his arms and legs were not protected, he could still move and run quickly and easily.

A cheap way to make armor was to sew metal plates onto a heavily padded tunic. By the time of the Battle of Hastings in 1066, nobles and soldiers wore chain or link mail. It protected them from sword, arrow or spear thrusts. It could also

move with their bodies. Mail was made by linking iron rings together to make a kind of metal fabric. Norman and Saxon soldiers both wore a tunic that covered the arms and body as far as the knees. A hood made from mail covered the head. Underneath ring mail, soldiers wore padded jackets. This stopped the mail being pushed into their skin by the force of a sword thrust.

Plate armor became very popular in medieval Europe. The whole body was covered with plates that were either strapped on to the wearer or hinged off one another. This was called a suit of armor. Each suit was made to fit exactly. Although the metal was heavy, its weight was so well balanced that a knight could walk about in reasonable comfort when wearing it. The parts of the armor that were most likely to be struck by a sword were specially angled so that

▲ JAPANESE WARRIOR
Japanese armor consisted of bamboo plates sewn to a padded jacket. Mythical motifs decorated the helmet.

PROTECTION
Chain mail was both light and sword-proof, but was never as strong as plate armor. The answer to this problem, for many centuries, was to use chain mail in areas such as the neck and limb joints and plate armor in slabs on the chest, back, legs and arms. The top of the head was protected by plate armor.

◀ NORMAN MAIL COAT
A Norman soldier wearing chain mail coat and helmet, light and flexible armor made from linked steel rings.

◀ INDIAN MAIL HELMET
This helmet uses a combination of plate and chain or ring mail to protect the head and neck. It is similar to the helmets worn by the Saracens.

▶ SHARK ARMOR
Shark's teeth stitched onto a simple tunic made strong armor for warriors of the Sandwich Islands in the Pacific.

▲ BRIGANDINE
The brigandine was a kind of 16th century flak jacket. It was a short, flexible coat with protective rivets on the inside and a rich fabric on the outside.

Simple rivets   Plates

Leather fasteners

Roman foot soldier

◀ ROMAN BREASTPLATE
Roman armor was made of plates held together with bronze hinges. In later versions, these were replaced by simple rivets and strong hooks.

◀ MOUNTED ARMOR
Knights might be well protected, but their horses could easily get hurt in battle. To protect them, they wore their own armor.
The same care and attention that went into making armor for the knight was given to that for his horse. How much armor they both wore and how richly it was decorated, showed the owner's wealth.

the sword blade would slide off without doing harm.

This kind of armor was very expensive. Both the knight who owned it and the armorer who made it wanted it to look beautiful as well as to work well. It was engraved and inlaid with metals such as brass and even gold. Enamel was used to color the metal plates so that knights appeared in black, green or even red armor.

Even though plate armor was worn in medieval times, soldiers still used chain mail to protect parts of the body that armor could not cover. Later, cavalry troopers, armed with sabers and ready to engage in hand-to-hand fighting, wore chain mail around their necks to prevent their throats being slashed open.

▶ A SUIT OF ARMOR
Knights had their armor specially made to fit. Armor was made up from lots of separate pieces. It was laced or strapped together and hung off a gorget. This was a metal collar that protected the neck and shoulders. A suit of armor from the 16th century was made up of at least 16 pieces and took a long time to put on. Knights needed a squire to help them get ready for battle. Armor was very heavy but, it was so cleverly made that the knights could still move around fairly easily. Most of the names of the pieces of armor are from the French language.

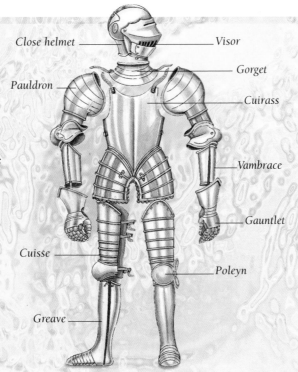

Close helmet — Visor
— Gorget
Pauldron —
— Cuirass
— Vambrace
— Gauntlet
Cuisse —
— Poleyn
Greave —

Key Dates

- 1500–1200 B.C. Bronze Mycenaean armor.
- 460 B.C. Corinthian armor.
- 102 B.C. Mail armor used by Romans.
- A.D. 75–100 Roman legionary interlocked plate armor widely used.
- 1100s Norman mail armor.
- 1300s Jointed plate armor.
- 1500s Horse armor widely used.
- 1600s Pikemen's armor.
- 1990s Body armor made from plastic or nylon is used today by police forces and armies.

Shields

▲ GREEK PROTECTION
A Greek hoplite of 600 B.C. equipped with a round bronze hoplon shield. Bronze was easy to work, but was softer than iron.

BODY ARMOR was part of the wearer's "clothing". A shield was a piece of moveable armor. It was normally carried by or strapped to the left arm, while a weapon was held in the right hand. It could be used to push aside an opponent's sword or spear. Like all armor, a shield has to be strong enough to defend its user yet light enough for him to carry easily. It also has to be made in a shape that will give the user most protection.

The earliest shields were made from animal skin stretched over a wooden frame. They were something like the shields carried by African warriors in the 18th and 19th centuries.

The first metal shields were made of bronze. The ancient Greeks used large round shields. In ancient Britain, Celtic warriors used round bronze shields and figure-of-eight shaped shields. Circular shields were used by cavalry in both ancient Greece and Rome. Round

▲ RIOT PROTECTION
Modern German police with polycarbonate riot shields and helmets as protection against rocks in riots.

▼ GALLIC SHIELD
The Norman inverted tear-drop shaped shield covered the torso, but left the legs free.

shields were used later by the cavalry in the armies of the Middle and Far East. The Vikings also had round shields.

Roman legionaries used an oblong shield that was slightly curved. It was large enough to protect a man from his shoulders to his knees. The shields could fit together. A group of legionaries lined up in rows of four could fit their shields together and form a very strong barrier. Used in this way, the shields made a kind of temporary tank.

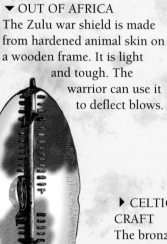

SHIELDS
Shields could be used to block a sword blow or protect the head and shoulders from arrows. The Greeks and Romans had finely crafted shields. In medieval times, shields were plainer but made from tougher materials.

◀ INSIGNIA
Knights wore insignia on their shields and armor to identify themselves on the battlefield. Here a simple bar and two dots are repeated, like a brand name, on the knight's shield, lance and the trappings of his horse.

▼ OUT OF AFRICA
The Zulu war shield is made from hardened animal skin on a wooden frame. It is light and tough. The warrior can use it to deflect blows.

▶ CELTIC CRAFT
The bronze Celtic shield is like a Roman design. The metal decoration on the front shows the wealth and position of the shield's owner.

▲ THE TOUGH TORTOISE
The Roman interlocked shield pattern called a tortoise allowed troops to approach the enemy fortifications under cover. Soldiers would then climb on their shields to attack the enemy walls.

Well protected, the whole unit moved forward to attack with their short swords.

The Romans developed a shield technique for attacking walls and castles. The soldiers fitted their shields together above their heads making what was called a testudo, or tortoise. Once the "tortoise" had reached the walls of the castle, the shields provided a platform for men to climb up to the fortifications.

By the time of the Norman invasion of Britain in 1066, shields had changed to a distinctive kite shape. The shield tapered downward, so the user could move his legs, but protected his upper body. Both cavalry and infantry used this type of shield.

The medieval shields were smaller. English and Welsh archers used a small round shield while knights had shields which were flat along the top edge and tapered to a point. This shape is now the accepted pattern for modern heraldry. It was in this period that shields were painted with the coats-of-arms of their users so they could be recognized by their followers on the battlefield.

▲ MOON POWER
The raised symbols of the sun and moon on this Persian shield were meant to give extra power to the user.

▶ ANCIENT PERSIAN SHIELD
This shield from Persia has cut-outs at arm level. These allowed the soldier to attack with his spear while he was still protected by his shield.

◀ BUCKLER SHIELD
This round German shield called a buckler has decorative studs called bosses set in an unusual random pattern.

Key Dates

- 1750-1600 B.C. Wood and hide shields used by Mycenaean soldiers.

- 480 B.C. Bronze and wood shields used by Athenian hoplites.

- 400 B.C. Celtic shield fittings found in England.

- 400 B.C. Hide shields replace bronze types for Athenian troops.

- 300 B.C. Roman soldiers equipped with hide and wicker shields.

- A.D. 1000–1200 Norman and Norse troops use tear-drop shields.

- 1400s Shields with coats-of-arms used by knights.

Helmets and War Hats

SOLDIERS HAVE ALWAYS worn helmets of some kind to protect their heads and eyes in combat. They came in all shapes and sizes, to suit the kind of weapons soldiers were likely to come up against. Ancient helmets were designed to protect soldiers from attack by cutting weapons such as swords or thrusting weapons such as spears or arrows. Some helmets were simple round metal hats. Others were more like iron masks. The ancient Greeks invented the nosepiece. This was a strip of armor running from the brim of the helmet along the bridge of the nose. It was still in use in the 17th century. The Romans favored helmets with deep cheek pieces. These were hinged flaps that hung down the sides of the helmet, covering the ears and cheeks, but leaving the front unrestricted. This made it easier for the wearer to see clearly as he was fighting.

In the 11th century, the Normans wore conical helmets with nosepieces. They also wore a chain mail hood which completely covered the ears and back of the neck. This gave them added protection.

▲ SAXON HELMET
This helmet from the 7th century comes from the Saxon burial ground at Sutton Hoo. It is inlaid with silvered bronze.

PROTECTING THE HEAD

Because the head incorporates the brain and face with important organs such as the eyes, ears, nose and mouth, it has always been protected in war. Helmets were made from bronze, iron or steel. Today they are made from modern plastics and polymers, which are light but very strong.

◀ THE GREAT HELM
By the mid-14th century the helm was the helmet most widely used by mounted knights. A visor pulled down to protect the face. Helms often sported elaborate crests at the top showing the owner's coat-of-arms. Today's motorcycle helmets resemble the helm.

Assyrian war hat

Hoplite helmet

Assyrian helmet

▲ ANCIENT HELMETS
Helmets began as simple metal hats. Later, hinged flaps were added to give protection to the cheeks, nose and neck without making it too difficult for the soldier to see or move. The flaps were often decorated.

◄ SPEED OR STRENGTH
During the crusades of the 11th and 12th centuries, European knights, who wore heavy armor and helmets, met Saracen warriors who wore lighter mail coats and small helmets that fitted close to their heads.

The most magnificent helmets were made during the medieval period in Europe. Ordinary foot soldiers had simple armor including a plain helmet but royalty and noblemen had splendid armor and helmets. The helmets were engraved and inlaid and were made with angles to deflect sword blows and a hinged visor that protected the wearer's eyes. A three-dimensional model of the family crest was often set on top. These elaborate helmets were like badges to show the nobility of the wearer.

By the time of the English Civil War (1642–1651), helmet design had changed. There was neck and earflap protection, a hinged peak and a face guard. The helmet was known as a "lobster-tail pot" because it looked like a lobster shell.

When the helmet was revived in World War I, the British army adopted the style of the brimmed war hat worn by archers at the Battle of Agincourt (1415). It was called the "kettle."

▶ LOBSTER POT
The pot or lobster-tail pot helmet worn by Parliamentarian cavalry in the English Civil War gave them their nickname of "Roundheads."

▶ MEDIEVAL HELMETS
Armorers in the Middle Ages produced helmets and armor for wealthy and discriminating customers. Some designs were very fanciful. Others had carefully constructed angles and shapes which could deflect sword or mace blows.

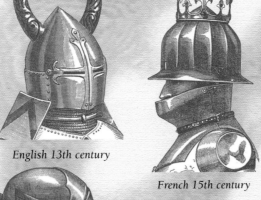

English 13th century

French 15th century

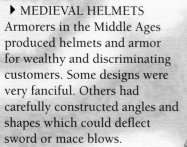

French 12th century

French 13th century

German 15th century

Key Dates

- 1700–1100 B.C. Bronze helmets in use in Mycenae.

- 55 B.C.–A.D. 100 Roman cavalry and infantry helmets introduced.

- 1000–1100 Norman helmets with nosepiece.

- 1300s Basinet hinged helmet.

- 1350s Helms in use by European knights in battle and in tournaments.

- 1400s Kettle-hat or war hat.

- 1500s Nuremberg close helmets.

- 1600s Pot or lobster-tail pot helmet worn by Cromwell's Roundhead army in the English Civil War.

Animals at War

ELEPHANTS, HORSES, DONKEYS, bullocks and camels have all been used to fight wars. Most of them were used to carry soldiers or pull wagons. Elephants were used rather like modern tanks. An elephant could trample enemy soldiers, while archers riding in a large basket on its back could pick off targets with their arrows.

▼ HANNIBAL'S TANKS
The most famous elephants in war belonged to Hannibal the Carthaginian general. In 216 B.C. he brought them from Spain to fight against Rome at the battle of Cannae in southern Italy.

WAR BEASTS
Elephants are not aggressive by nature but could be used to frighten troops who had never seen them before. A panicking elephant could trample its own soldiers. In India, handlers called mahouts carried a spike. If their elephant went out of control, they killed it.

◀ ELEPHANT POWER
The elephant has three natural weapons: its great weight, its huge tusks and its powerful trunk.

▲ THE HEAVY BRIGADE
Elephants were used on the front line of battle to frighten the enemy infantry and to block cavalry charges. Like modern tanks, they were protected from close range attack by special groups of foot soldiers.

▼ ARMOR
The Indians put armor on their elephants as well as fighting towers on their backs.

One of the earliest battles to use war elephants was fought at Arbela, now modern Irbil, in 331 B.C. The Persian leader Darius led an army, including 15 war elephants, against Alexander the Great of Macedonia. Alexander's troops were frightened of the elephants at first, but so well-disciplined that they did not run away but fought and won the battle.

War elephants had been used in India by the Hindus from around 400 B.C. They were as important as chariots on the battlefield. At the battle of Hydaspes in India in 327 B.C., Porus, the Rajah of Lahore, led elephants against Alexander the Great. This time, Alexander's horses were frightened by the elephants. However, his foot soldiers attacked the elephants with battleaxes. The animals panicked and the Macedonians won.

The most famous war elephants belonged to Hannibal, the Carthaginian general. He fought against Rome in the Second Punic War (218–203 B.C.). The elephants were used in several battles but Hannibal was eventually beaten.

Elephants were first seen in England in A.D. 43 when the Romans used them to invade.

War elephants were still in use in India during the 18th century. The elephants had iron plates fixed to their heads and were driven forward like four-legged battering rams to break down the gates of the town of Arcot in 1751. They panicked when they were fired at.

▲ CAMEL ARMY

The camel has been used for transport in battle in the Middle East. It has lots of stamina and can move fast. Camels can also travel a long way without much food or water. Here, camel-mounted soldiers use lances and swords in a lively battle.

◀ OVER THE ALPS
Hannibal marched with his elephants across the Pyrenees and the Alps to attack Imperial Rome. When he set out from Saguntum in 218 B.C., he had 50,000 infantry, 9000 cavalry and about 80 elephants. By the time he reached the Po valley in northern Italy six months later, only a few elephants were still alive. Hannibal had lost 30,000 infantry and 3000 cavalry.

Key Dates

- 327 B.C. Battle of Hydaspes. Alexander the Great meets Indian elephants.

- 275 B.C. Battle of Benevenetum, Italy. Carthage uses elephants for the first time against Rome.

- 218 B.C. Hannibal crosses the Alps.

- 202 B.C. Battle of Zama. Hannibal defeated and his elephants taken.

- 190 B.C. Battle of Magnesia. Syrian war elephants panic and confuse their own troops.

- A.D. 43 Roman Emperor Claudius uses elephants to invade Britain.

Horses in Battle

HORSES MADE IT POSSIBLE for armies to move around quickly. They could pull wagons and siege weapons or carry loot and possessions. On the battlefield, they could be ridden by scouts or messengers taking news to and from the generals planning the battle. Large horses, working together as heavy cavalry, were unstoppable on the battlefield.

The first people to use the horse in war were the Assyrians around 800 B.C. They used them as cavalry, to pull chariots and for hunting. The Romans bred from European, Middle Eastern and African stock to produce racehorses, hunters, chargers and harness-horses.

The saddle with stirrups, which were probably invented in China, reached Europe in the 2nd century AD and transformed mounted operations forever. They made it easier to ride a horse. A Roman soldier on foot could cover about 5 miles a day. When he was on a horse, he could travel twice as far as that.

The horse also made it possible for groups of people to move far away from their home lands. In the 13th century, the Mongols roamed from Central Asia as far as Vietnam, the Middle East and Europe.

There were two kinds of cavalry, the light and the heavy. The difference between them was based on the size of the horse. Most ancient armies had both light and heavy cavalry. About two-thirds of the Mongol riders

▲ PARTING SHOT
Horse archers from Parthia, an ancient country now part of Iran, used to pretend to retreat then turned and fired their arrows backward to take the enemy by surprise.

◀ A LIGHT SKIRMISH
Persian light cavalry troops, carrying round shields and armed with lances and maces, fight a running battle.

HORSES AT WAR
Horses have been used in war for centuries. They can pull wagons and guns as well as being ridden. They are strong and fast, but can be stopped by long-range weapons.

▶ BAREBACK WARRIOR
The fast, lightly-armed Numidian cavalry played an important part in the victories of Hannibal during the Punic Wars with Rome. They fought and rode bareback.

◀ HEAVY DUTY
German knights in the heavy armor worn in medieval battles. This protected both horse and rider.

▼ JOUSTING TOURNAMENT
Today, tournaments and battles are re-enacted by "knights" on horseback.

▶ AT THE CHARGE
The horse wears a piece of head armor called a chauffron. Its spike is almost as much of a weapon as the rider's lance. Both are pointed toward the enemy when the horse charges.

were light cavalry. They had small, fast horses, wore protective helmets and carried bows and arrows. The heavy cavalry had big, strong horses, wore mail armor or heavy leather clothing and were armed with lances.

Armies in medieval Europe had only foot soldiers and knights on horseback. To carry a knight in full armor the horse had to be big and strong. The knights were a kind of heavy cavalry. By the 16th century the armies of Europe had concentrated on heavy cavalry. The French called them gendarmerie and the Germans called them Schwarzreiter or "Black Riders." It was when they fought with Turkish armies in the 17th century that Europeans began to see how useful a light cavalry could be and to set up light brigades of their own. The Hungarian light cavalry, called hussars, wore Turkish-style uniforms.

The heavy cavalry wore helmets and breastplates, rode large horses and carried a pistol and heavy saber. The light cavalry had no armor and rode horses chosen for their speed. The riders carried two or even three pistols and a light sword.

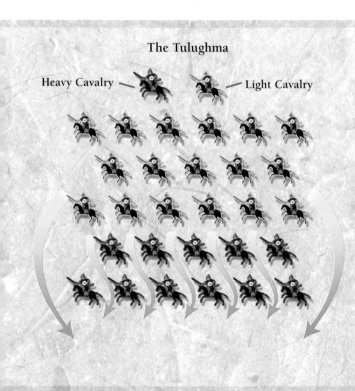

The Tulughma

Heavy Cavalry — Light Cavalry

◀ MONGOLIAN WAR TACTICS
The Mongolian army used light and heavy cavalry and many different tactics. This one is the tulughma. The heavy brigade led the charge and broke up enemy lines. At the same time they protected the ranks of light cavalry behind them. When the enemy ranks were broken, the lighter horses ran through or around their own heavy ranks.

Key Dates

- 500 B.C. Persians employ lancers and horse archers.

- 53 B.C. Parthian horse archers defeat Romans at Carrhae (modern Iraq).

- A.D. 100s Stirrups are introduced.

- 200–400 Horse archers and lancers used by Romans.

- 977–1030 Mahmud of Ghazni uses cavalry horse archers in north India.

- 1000–1200 Crusaders use Moslem mercenaries called Turcopoles.

- 1396–1457 French cavalry, gendarmes, in action.

- 1500–1600 German "Black Riders" in action in Europe.

Chariots and War Wagons

horses, the archer riding beside him was free to concentrate on fast and accurate firing at the enemy. Not all chariots were two-man vehicles. If there was only one rider, he would tie the reins around his waist to keep his hands free so he could use his weapons. Some chariots, pulled by three or four horses, could carry several men, armed with a variety of weapons. Used all together, chariots could break up ranks of enemy infantry. Some later chariots had the protection of armor. They may also have had blades or scythes fitted to the hubs of their wheels to prevent enemy infantry or cavalry approaching too close. The drawback with chariots, like many wheeled vehicles, was that they could bog down in mud and it was hard for them to cross rough ground.

Between 1420 and 1434 the Hussites, a group of people from Bohemia

CHARIOTS WERE A CLEVER WAY to combine speed and action. Most of them were pulled by horses. The driver was called a charioteer. For the armies of ancient Egypt, Assyria, Persia, India and China, chariots were the weapon of surprise, racing in and out of battle. Most chariots held two people, the driver and the bowman. With the driver to handle the horse or

▲ ROMAN CHARIOT
The chariot was not used a great deal in war. It was a popular sight at the public Games held in Rome and other major cities of the Empire.

▶ EGYPTIAN TACTICS
An Egyptian courtier on a hunting trip fires his bow and arrows from a moving chariot. The same skills would be used in war.

▲ WARRIOR QUEEN
Boudicca, chieftain of the British tribe called the Iceni, used war chariots in her battles against invading Romans.

WHEELS OF WAR
Chariots were first used in the Bronze Age in the 15th century B.C. in the Middle East. They could be pulled by two to four horses, but the larger number were harder to control. They could move easily on the flat deserts of Egypt and around the Euphrates, but they were not ideal transport in muddy, broken or rocky terrain. The war wagons used by the Hussites in Europe in the 15th century A.D. were almost like the first tanks. They were formed into circles like mobile forts. Soldiers fired cannons and muskets from the shelter of the wagons.

▲ LEONARDO'S TANKS
Leonardo da Vinci, the genius of the Renaissance, had many ideas that were ahead of his time. This sketch shows armored vehicles of various kinds. They look like early versions of modern tanks.

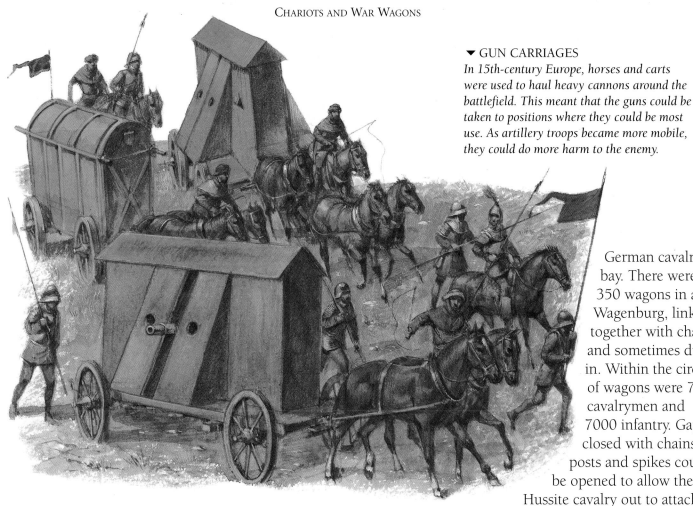

(now the Czech Republic), fought with the Germans. The Hussites were followers of the religious reformer John Huss. Their army, commanded by Jan Zizka, used armored carts. The wagons were formed into a circle of wagons called a Wagenburg, or wagon castle. Behind the wagons, crossbow archers and musketeers kept the German cavalry at bay. There were 350 wagons in a Wagenburg, linked together with chains and sometimes dug in. Within the circle of wagons were 700 cavalrymen and 7000 infantry. Gaps closed with chains, posts and spikes could be opened to allow the Hussite cavalry out to attack.

When the Hussites brought in cannon mounted on special wagons, the German cavalry refused to attack them any more because they were too dangerous.

Some historians have suggested that the Hussite Wagenburg was the first tank in history as it combined fire power, protection and movement.

▲ CHARIOTS OF MARBLE
Many artists have made paintings and sculptures of chariots. This Roman sculpture of a chariot and a pair of frisky horses is in the Vatican Museum.

Key Dates

- 1400 B.C. Chariots used by Egyptians.

- 331 B.C. Persian chariots armed with scythes at Battle of Arbela.

- 327 B.C. Indian chariots used at Battle of Hydaspes.

- 225 B.C. Last use of chariots by Celts in Battle of Telamon, Italy.

- A.D. 60 Boudicca uses chariots against the Romans in Britain.

- 378 Romans use wagons to defeat Goths at Adrianople (modern Turkey).

- 378 Fighting wagons used by Jan Zizka and the Hussites.

Cavalry Weapons

THE WEAPON USED BY A MOUNTED soldier reflected his skills as a rider. The Mongol cavalry riders of Genghis Khan could ride without reins, which meant they were able to use a bow while in the saddle. The lance or spear could be used in one hand. It was long enough for a rider to reach enemy foot soldiers. Cavalry normally rode straight at their enemy using the speed and impetus of the horse to add weight to the lance thrust. The cavalry lance became popular in medieval Europe and continued to be used in battle by horsemen in Poland and Hungary. Polish Lancers used it against the French during the Napoleonic Wars in 1800–1815. Medieval knights used the lance in battle, and practiced their skill in tournaments. The knight's horse also became a target, so craftsmen began to make armor for horses.

Horse armor was called bard. At its simplest it was made up of the chauffron, a plate covering the front of the horse's skull, and the peytral which covered the breast above the front legs. Full horse armor included the crupper and the flanchard. The crupper covered the horse's rump. The flanchard was an oblong plate fixed to the base of the saddle. It protected the horse's flanks and closed the gap between the crupper and peytral.

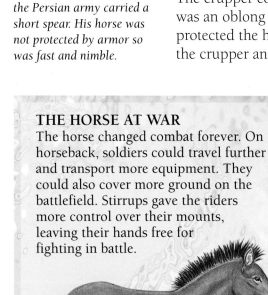

▲ PERSIAN HORSEMAN
The light cavalry trooper of the Persian army carried a short spear. His horse was not protected by armor so was fast and nimble.

▲ SAMURAI BOWMAN
Japanese samurai warriors did not only use swords. Many were also masters of the longbow. A mounted archer on a trained horse had two advantages. He could move fast and he could fire his weapon from a distance, out of the range of his enemy's swords and lances.

THE HORSE AT WAR
The horse changed combat forever. On horseback, soldiers could travel further and transport more equipment. They could also cover more ground on the battlefield. Stirrups gave the riders more control over their mounts, leaving their hands free for fighting in battle.

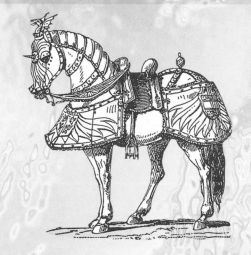

◀ MONGOLIAN PONY
Tough, fast little Asian ponies provided transportation and mare's milk for the Mongol warriors as they crossed Europe.

▲ HORSE ARMOR
Medieval horse armor protected the animal without slowing it down. The rider's legs covered its bare flanks in battle.

▲ A GREAT TEAM
Chain mail protects this horse's neck. The weight of horse, man and armor at the gallop swept them through the ranks of the enemy's foot soldiers.

▼ TOURNAMENT
When jousting for sport, knights used blunted lances so that they would not harm each other.

Chauffron

Blunted lance

Knight's insignia

European cavalry troopers had been using straight swords from Roman times. When fighting in the Middle East, European soldiers came across the curved sword, which was used as a pattern for the curved cavalry saber. This was ideal for the slashing backstroke.

The wheellock pistol was developed in the 16th century. It was designed to be used with one hand so that the rider could shoot while keeping full control of his horse. Because of the noise, flashing and smoke, horses had to be trained to carry men through gunfire.

▶ GOING WEST
In 1190 the Mongol emperor Genghis Khan led his great army westward. It was divided into groups of 10,000 men called hordes. The hordes were named after different colors. By the 13th century they had swept deep into eastern Europe and reached almost as far as Austria. They could not have gotten so far or gone so fast if they had not had such swift horses.

Key Dates

- 400s B.C. Persian mounted archers.

- 400 B.C. Spartan cavalry armed with short javelins.

- 330s B.C. Alexander the Great uses mounted lancers.

- 200s B.C. Hannibal uses Numidian mounted lancers.

- A.D. 1200s Mongol hordes, mounted on horseback, invade Europe.

- 1300s–1500s Jousting lances in use.

- 1400s Heavy horse armor introduced.

- 1600s Sabers introduced as cavalry weapons.

Castles and Fortifications

THERE ARE NUMEROUS EXAMPLES of prehistoric and ancient fortifications throughout the world. The people who built them often used natural features such as hills, cliffs and crags or rivers, lakes and swamps to enhance their strength. Where these features were not present, people created them, making ditches, mounds and later walls and towers. Sometimes castle builders used earlier sites. For example, at Porchester in Hampshire, England, in the 1120s, Henry I built a motte-and-bailey castle using the square fortifications of an earlier Roman Saxon fort.

The outlines of square Roman forts can be seen throughout Europe. These forts were called castra, which is where we get the word castle. Castra were built

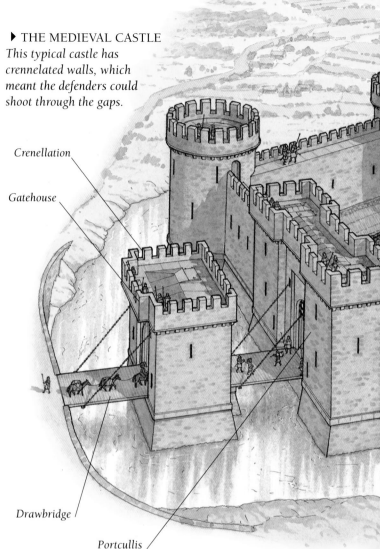

▶ THE MEDIEVAL CASTLE
This typical castle has crennelated walls, which meant the defenders could shoot through the gaps.

Crenellation

Gatehouse

Drawbridge

Portcullis

◀ SCOTTISH CASTLE
Caerlavarock Castle, Scotland, is a classic moated castle. The pattern of stone bricks on the top of the round towers is known as machicolation. It is to protect soldiers inside the towers as they fight off an attack. The moat which surrounds the walls gives even more protection. The castle was hard to storm.

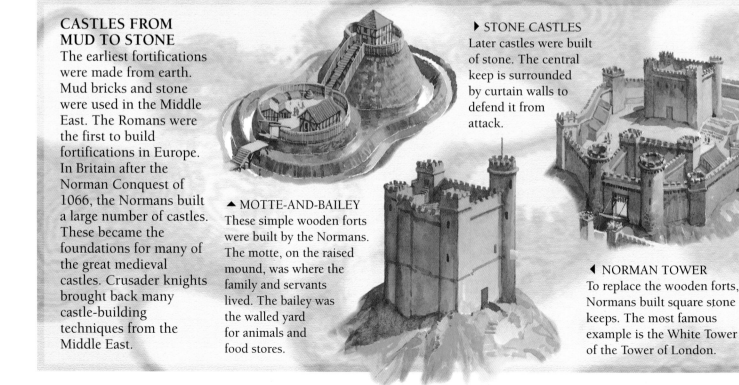

CASTLES FROM MUD TO STONE
The earliest fortifications were made from earth. Mud bricks and stone were used in the Middle East. The Romans were the first to build fortifications in Europe. In Britain after the Norman Conquest of 1066, the Normans built a large number of castles. These became the foundations for many of the great medieval castles. Crusader knights brought back many castle-building techniques from the Middle East.

▲ MOTTE-AND-BAILEY
These simple wooden forts were built by the Normans. The motte, on the raised mound, was where the family and servants lived. The bailey was the walled yard for animals and food stores.

▶ STONE CASTLES
Later castles were built of stone. The central keep is surrounded by curtain walls to defend it from attack.

◀ NORMAN TOWER
To replace the wooden forts, Normans built square stone keeps. The most famous example is the White Tower of the Tower of London.

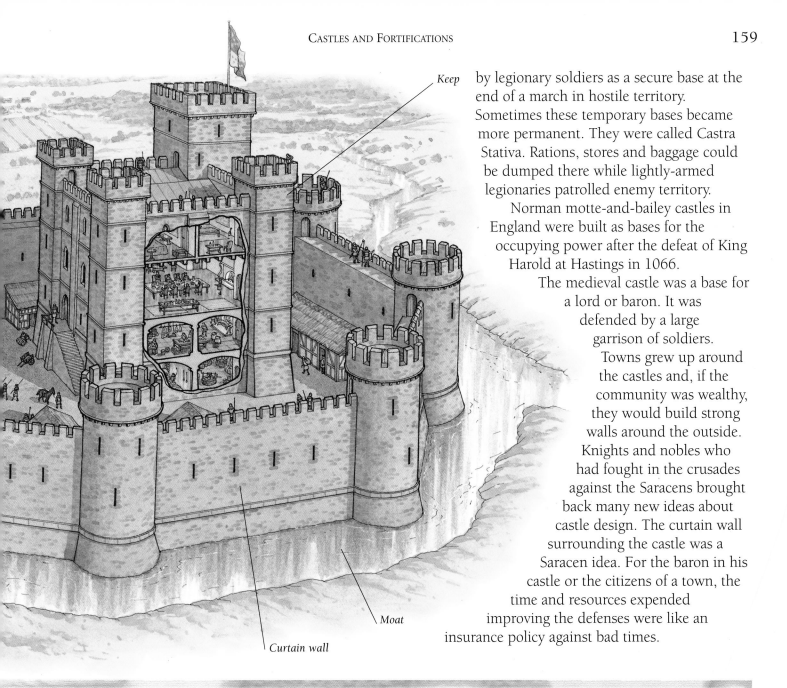

Keep

Moat

Curtain wall

by legionary soldiers as a secure base at the end of a march in hostile territory. Sometimes these temporary bases became more permanent. They were called Castra Stativa. Rations, stores and baggage could be dumped there while lightly-armed legionaries patrolled enemy territory.

Norman motte-and-bailey castles in England were built as bases for the occupying power after the defeat of King Harold at Hastings in 1066.

The medieval castle was a base for a lord or baron. It was defended by a large garrison of soldiers.

Towns grew up around the castles and, if the community was wealthy, they would build strong walls around the outside. Knights and nobles who had fought in the crusades against the Saracens brought back many new ideas about castle design. The curtain wall surrounding the castle was a Saracen idea. For the baron in his castle or the citizens of a town, the time and resources expended improving the defenses were like an insurance policy against bad times.

◀ WELSH CASTLES
In the 13th century, King Edward I of England built a large number of castles in Wales. This was to strengthen his grip on the country. The Welsh people did not care for English rule. Craftsmen were brought from all over England to help in the building work. Edward's wife and queen, Eleanor, gave birth to their first son, the future Edward II, at Caernarfon Castle. He became the Prince of Wales, the first English man to hold the title.

Key Dates

- 2500 B.C. Ur of the Chaldees, first fortified city, built (in modern Iraq).

- 701 B.C. Jerusalem fortified.

- 560 B.C. Athens fortified.

- A.D. 1058–1689 Edinburgh Castle.

- 1066–1399 Tower of London.

- 1181–89 Dover Castle.

- 1196–98 Chateau-Gaillard built by Richard I in France.

- 1200s Krak des Chevaliers, a Crusader castle, built in Syria.

- 1538–1540s Henry VIII builds forts along England's south coast.

Towers, Keeps and Gates

TO DEFEND THEIR CASTLES people built tall towers and keeps. Standing at the top, they could see enemy ships or army columns a long way off. This gave the people in the castle time to prepare for attack. When the enemy arrived at the castle walls, the lookouts on the tower could see down into their camps or siege weapons and fire missiles at them. Towers can be square or round, but always have very thick walls.

Towers are safe places to hide when an enemy attacks. In the 9th and 10th centuries, Vikings raided England and Ireland. To defend themselves, Irish people built high towers in villages or near monasteries. These stone-built towers had no outer defenses. They had arrow slits or embrasures and a simple door built high up the wall that could only be reached using a ladder.

After the Norman Conquest of England, Norman barons built many castles. They were mostly of the motte-and-bailey kind. A curtain wall stood around the bailey. Towers were built at the corners of the wall and at intervals along the sides. Soldiers could use the towers as safe bases. The towers had a thicker belt of stone at the base. This was called a batter. It was there

◀ IRISH DEFENSES
The high towers of Ireland were built as refuges from invading Vikings. They were not intended to hold out against a long siege but were good look-outs and safe places to hide.

▶ BAMBURGH CASTLE
Bamburgh Castle Keep, in Northumberland, England, dates from 1200. The keep was the strongest part of a castle.

THE KEY TO THE CASTLE
The gate was the most vulnerable part of a castle because it was the point of entrance. When it was open, attackers could force their way in, and the castle could be captured very quickly. It was very important that the opening could be closed quickly. An iron gate called a portcullis could be dropped into place in seconds. The drawbridge only needed to be lifted a short way to prevent the enemy crossing the moat.

▶ DRAWBRIDGE
The drawbridge was made from very thick wood. It could be raised very quickly. It was operated by a system of weights which worked in the same way as a see-saw.

◀ PORTCULLIS
The portcullis was operated by a winch. The guards could release it quickly, and let it crash down under its own weight. Spikes on the bottom of the portcullis could trap attackers caught underneath it.

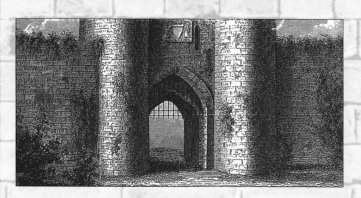

to strengthen the towers against battering rams and make it difficult to mine through the walls.

The gate was the weakest part of the castle. It was protected by a gatehouse and a portcullis. Some gatehouses had two portcullises. Attackers could be lured through the open gate only to find their way barred by an inner portcullis or gate hidden around a corner. Once the attackers were inside, the defenders would lower the outer portcullis and trap them. The passage between the gates became a stone tunnel. In the roof of the tunnel were slots known as "murder holes."

Defenders could shoot arrows, drop rocks or pour boiling oil or water through the holes on to their trapped enemies.

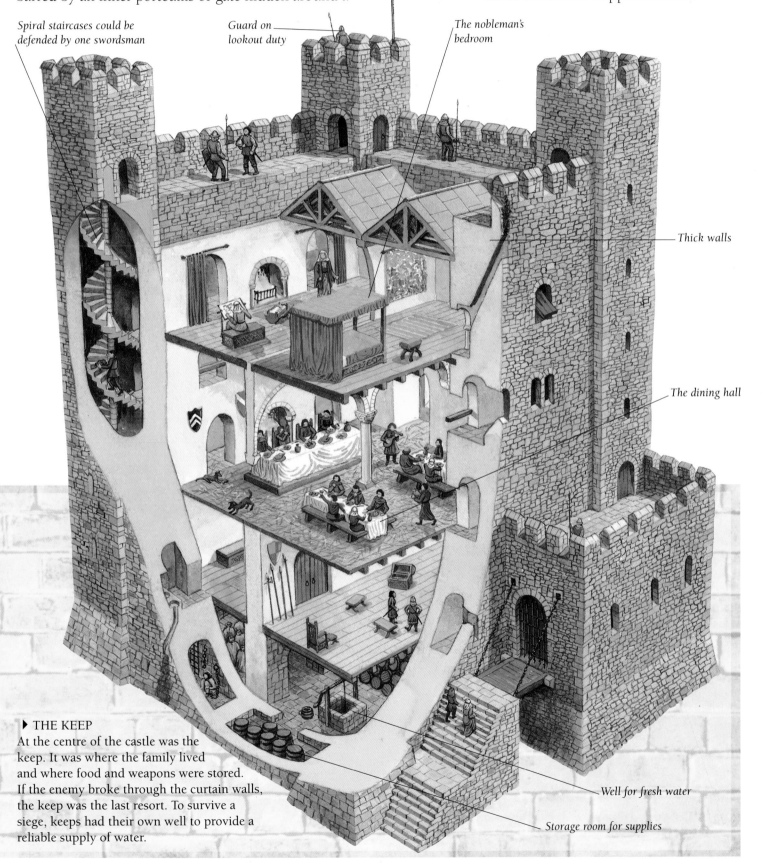

Spiral staircases could be defended by one swordsman

Guard on lookout duty

The nobleman's bedroom

Thick walls

The dining hall

Well for fresh water

Storage room for supplies

▶ THE KEEP
At the centre of the castle was the keep. It was where the family lived and where food and weapons were stored. If the enemy broke through the curtain walls, the keep was the last resort. To survive a siege, keeps had their own well to provide a reliable supply of water.

Walls

CASTLE WALLS were built to a set pattern. Surrounding the castle was a curtain wall. This could be fifteen to twenty-five feet thick and wide enough for people to walk along. On top of the wall was the parapet. The parapet was a wall about one-and-a-half feet thick. In some castles they were built only at the top of the outer face of the wall. Others had them on both sides. They were about six feet high, so that they completely concealed and protected any soldier standing guard on the curtain wall.

Along the parapets were regular gaps which were low and wide enough for an archer to shoot at enemies. The gaps were called crenellations. The sections of raised wall between the gaps, which protected the archer, were called merlons.

At intervals in the wall and in towers of the castle, the builders cut narrow windows from which archers

▲ KEEPING THE NIGHT WATCH
Castles were defended day and night. Norman soldiers on the parapet check on the sentries manning the gatehouse and curtain wall defenses below.

could fire. These were called embrasures. When soldiers began to use cannon, the embrasures were made larger to fit the muzzles of the guns. Circular holes were cut at the base of arrow slits so that both the artillery men and the archers could fire from the same embrasure. This embrasure was known as a "cross-and-orb." Larger embrasures were covered by hinged shutters when they were not being used. From the outside, an embrasure looked like a narrow slit. On the inside, it opened up so that an archer could lean to one side and shoot at targets to the left or right. A variation on this design was the balistraria, a cross-shaped slit for crossbows.

If an enemy force reached the base of a wall the defenders had to lean out to attack them. This would leave them open to attack by enemy archers. The castle builders invented machicolation, which was made to

SLITS AND EMBRASURES
The walls and crenellations of castles were pierced with holes called embrasures. These were made so that the soldiers could fire arrows or crossbow bolts at their enemy below. Later, castle walls were pierced with loopholes for cannon and muskets. The hole was shaped to fit the kind of weapon being fired through it. On the inside face of the wall the sides of the embrasure were angled so that an archer or musketeer could shoot at targets to one side.

▼ ARCHER'S SLIT
The earliest kind of slit was made to fit arrows. Arrow slits also let light and air in to the inside of the castle and through the curtain walls.

▲ CROSSBOW EMBRASURE
This design was used by crossbow archers. It allowed them to aim at targets to the left or right of them, or even to track a moving target before firing their bolts.

▼ LOOPHOLE
When cannons began to be used, arrow holes were changed to fit them. A round hole was cut at the base of a narrow slit.

◀ CARCASSONNE
This walled city in southern France looks much the same today as it did in medieval times. With such strong defenses, the only way an enemy could capture the city would be to starve the citizens.

▲ WINDSOR CASTLE
The towers on each side of the gatehouse at Windsor have machicolations at the top.

protect the defenders. This was a battlement wall built out on stone supports. It had embrasures that faced downward so that defenders could drop rocks and stones on their attackers.

Henry VIII made many changes in the design of fortresses. To fight off the threat of French invasion in the mid-16th century he built a number of forts along the south coast of England. Their walls were not high, but low and massive. This was to provide a wide platform for cannons and large guns to stand on. As the power and range of cannons got better, the walls of fortifications became wider and lower.

◀ WALLS WITHIN WALLS
The Roman general Scipio, also known as Africanus, built a wall with seven forts around the Spanish city of Numantia. He then besieged the city for eight months in 133 B.C. Its 4000 citizens finally gave in after Scipio had blocked off the river access.

▶ CITY WALLS
In ancient times cities were often under threat of attack and invasion. It was common to build fortified walls around the city for protection. This imposing wall surrounds the Morrocan city of Essaouira.

Key Dates

- 1451 B.C. Walls of Jericho stormed.

- 598 B.C. Nebuchadnezzar destroys the walls of Jerusalem.

- 493 B.C. Piraeus, the port of Athens, made secure with fortifications.

- 478 B.C. Athenian city walls restored.

- 457 B.C. Athenian long wall built.

- 393 B.C. Conon rebuilds long walls at Athens following their destruction by the Persians.

- A.D. 93–211 Walls of Perge (southern Turkey) built by Septimus Severus.

- 447 Ramparts of Constantinople rebuilt after earthquake.

Defending Borders

▲ THE GREAT WALL
Large enough to be seen from space, this famous earthwork in China took centuries to build.

MOST FORTIFICATIONS in ancient history have normally protected families and their retainers in castles, or citizens behind curtain walls with fortified gates. When the movement of large numbers of people threatens a civilization, bigger walls have to be built. The Great Wall of China and Hadrian's Wall in England are two very famous examples of land barriers made to defend whole territories.

The Great Wall of China was built over four distinct periods. The building of earthworks in 476–221 B.C. was followed by the Great Wall of Qin Shi Huangdi (221–206 B.C.). The Great Wall of Wu Di (140–86 B.C.) and other emperors was finally finished as the Great Wall of the Mings (A.D. 1368–1644). The Great Wall of China was originally built to delay Mongol attacks along the north frontier long enough for the main force of the Chinese army to get to the threatened area and defeat the enemy.

The Roman Emperor Hadrian toured northern Britain in A.D. 122 and ordered the construction of a physical barrier against the lawless tribes in Caledonia (modern Scotland). At first, the barrier was made from

▶ HADRIAN'S WALL
Named after the Roman Emperor Hadrian, the wall was originally a wooden palisade with a bank and ditch. It was later rebuilt as a stone-faced wall 16 feet high and 8 feet thick. Small emplacements, called mile castles , were placed at every mile along the wall.

Roman legionary

THE WORLD'S EDGE
The Romans and the Chinese had huge empires to guard. Just beyond their borders were people ready to invade. To mark and defend their borders, they built long walls or earthworks. A system of signaling allowed sentries to alert the garrisons if raiders tried to cross the wall. Then soldiers could quickly get to the site to drive them off.

◀ LEGIONARY FROM AFRICA
Roman soldiers were recruited from all parts of the enormous empire. They were often sent on duty far away from their home country. This was to make sure they did not desert.

▲ WALLS AROUND WALLS
The Romans used walls and ramparts as weapons in their siege tactics, closing off a city or fort from any outside assistance or supplies and starving it into surrender. This is the siege of Massilia laid by Julius Caesar in 49 B.C. Massilia is modern-day Marseilles.

◀ MILE CASTLES
Protected from the Picts (the painted people) from the north by Hadrian's Wall, small towns grew up around the mile castles along the wall. There were shops and markets, taverns and baths. Many of the Roman legionaries who manned the wall married and settled down in the towns.

timber and turf. In its final form, Hadrian's Wall was just a stone wall. It ran from Wallsend on the east coast to Bowness in the west, a distance of approximately 73 miles. The wall used natural features such as crags to give it extra height. It varied from 7 to 10 feet in width and was 15 feet high with a crenellated parapet 5 feet above that. There were mile castles along the wall at regular intervals of one Roman mile (4,856 feet) and two guard turrets between them. The mile castle was in a kind of gateway with a garrison of about 16 soldiers. The turrets may have been shelters for soldiers on guard or signal stations. Ten forts were built to house the garrison for the wall.

Hadrian's Wall was an effective military obstacle, and, like similar Roman barriers, it marked the limits of the Roman Empire. Beyond it were barbarians.

▶ JERUSALEM
The walls of the Holy City have been stormed and fought over ever since biblical times. Jerusalem is a city divided into the Jewish western area and the Arab territory in the east. The last battle took place in 1967 during the Six Day War between the Arabs and the Israelis.

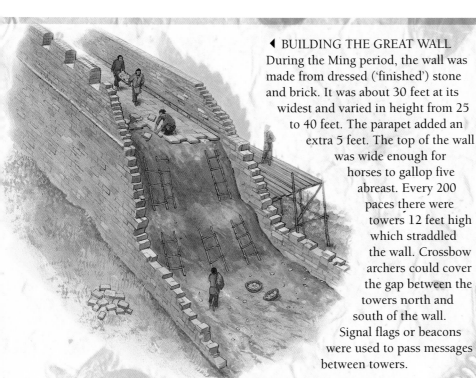

◀ BUILDING THE GREAT WALL
During the Ming period, the wall was made from dressed ('finished') stone and brick. It was about 30 feet at its widest and varied in height from 25 to 40 feet. The parapet added an extra 5 feet. The top of the wall was wide enough for horses to gallop five abreast. Every 200 paces there were towers 12 feet high which straddled the wall. Crossbow archers could cover the gap between the towers north and south of the wall. Signal flags or beacons were used to pass messages between towers.

Key Dates

- 476–221 B.C. Various earth walls built in northern Chinese provinces.

- 221–206 B.C. Emperor Qin Shi Huangdi orders earth walls to be joined together to make the first Great Wall of China.

- A.D. 100 Romans build walls (called limes germanica) across Germany and Romania.

- 122 Emperor Hadrian orders wall to be built at northern edge of Roman Empire.

- 700s King Offa of Mercia, England, builds a dike to separate England from Wales.

Under Siege

▲ OUT OF RANGE
Building a castle on a hill site with a moat and a narrow, easily guarded entry road makes it very hard for an enemy to capture it.

A SIEGE IS WHAT happens when an enemy army surrounds a castle or a city planning to capture it. They can attack, or they can wait until the people inside get too hungry and surrender. A strong, well-stocked castle or fortified town could easily withstand a siege if their besiegers ran out of food. The defenders of a castle or even the wall around a town were higher up than the besiegers so they could see what the enemy was doing. They were also protected by a wooden palisade or a stone wall. From behind these walls, sniper archers could pick off the attackers as they came to the foot of the wall.

If the attackers reached the wall, they tried to make a hole in it so that they could get into the castle or city. Another way to get in was to climb the wall using ladders and grapnel hooks. This was dangerous, because the defenders waited until an attacker was half way up the ladder then pushed it away from the wall.

To attack the enemy camp the soldiers of the castle could use many of the weapons that the besiegers had been using. Each side lobbed rocks or cannon balls at one another. If a battering ram was used, the defenders might try to set fire to it. Another way to disarm it was to use huge tongs hanging from a crane to grab the ram and pull it up inside the castle or curtain walls.

Castles often had secret passages leading to a hidden exit called a "sally port". This could be further down a river or along the coast and from here the defenders might make their escape if the siege became too severe. Sally ports were also very strong doors from which the defenders could launch quick raids on their attackers. The plan was to destroy the enemy's siege weapons, generally by setting them alight. The defenders would also capture prisoners and steal food stocks.

▶ HOT RECEPTION
As storming ladders are raised against a castle, defenders fight back by pouring boiling water or oil on the shed protecting a battering ram crew.

HOLDING OUT
Siege was not always easy for the besiegers. If the castle was well defended and the people inside had lots of water and food supplies, they could sit out any number of attacks. If the siege went on for a long time, the besiegers could run out of food themselves, or die from disease and be forced to stop the siege.

◀ SIEGE SEE-SAW
The tenelon was a crane or see-saw with a basket on one arm. Troops inside the basket could be hoisted over the walls.

▲ WHO'S WINNING?
Every kind of siege weapon is used against the defenders in this castle keep. They are fighting back but seem to be outnumbered and may be running out of food. One of the soldiers is lowering a basket and water pot for supplies.

◀ A CASTLE FALLS
Battering rams, scaling ladders and towers can all be seen in action in this medieval siege. It is the end of the siege. The walls have been finally breached after heavy bombardment and the besiegers are within the walls.

◀ ROMAN SIEGE

The Roman army were very successful at sieges. They invented many techniques and siege engines. In this scene, the besiegers are attacking on three points. A ram batters at the tower. Soldiers advance under cover of their shields locked into the testudo, or tortoise, formation. Some have reached the wall and are scaling it. A tenelon hoists men on to the far tower. The defenders crowd the battlements, but they only have rocks to throw at the enemy.

Key Dates

- 415–413 B.C. Siege of Syracuse. Athenians fail to take city.

- A.D. 70 Siege of Jerusalem, part of the Jewish Wars of the Roman Empire.

- 1189–91 Siege of Acre (Israel), part of the Third Crusade.

- 1487 Siege of Malaga.

- 1544 Siege of Boulogne.

- 1565 Siege of Malta, part of the wars of Islam. Turkish army try to capture Malta from Christian forces. They fail.

- 1688-89 Siege of Londonderry.

Siege Attack

THE ROMANS HAD A VERY SUCCESSFUL method of siege attack. First, they would take a good look at the target fort or city to see if a siege would be practical. They would then surround their objective with an outer belt of defenses so that it could not be relieved by friendly forces and set about systematically destroying it. Several specialty weapons were needed to do this. The most important was the siege tower.

Historic pictures of siege towers often show something that looks like a mobile multi-story building. The height varied. The three iron-clad towers used by the Romans in the Siege of Jerusalem in A.D. 70 were 30 feet high with catapults on top. The towers were fitted with drawbridges that were lowered to span the gap to the castle wall. The military engineers Gaston de Bearn and William de Ricou, employed by the Crusaders

in 1099 in another siege of Jerusalem, designed two towers of about the same height as the Roman towers.

The earliest descriptions we have of siege weapons come from around 400 to 200 B.C. Among them were those developed by the engineer Diades, who worked with Alexander the Great. Diades developed two unusual siege weapons, which do not seem to have been copied by future generations. The first one was a mural hook, also known as a crow. It was slung from a wooden gantry like a ram but it had a huge double

▶ ANCIENT ATTACKERS
Babylonian siege machines batter down the walls of an enemy fortress while archers fire on the walls.

Siege tower

Animal skin covering

Battering ram

▲ SIEGE GRIFFIN
A fantasy siege engine designed to be winched toward the enemy as it fires the cannon from its mouth. The ramp in the chest would be lowered for the assault.

SIEGE TOWERS
In order to reach the top of the walls and take on the defenders, soldiers had to be at the same height and within range. Mobile siege towers could be pushed forward until the soldiers inside them could fire at the enemy and eventually cross simple drawbridges onto the walls.

Mantlet

◀ ALEXANDER
Alexander the Great was a fine general. He laid many sieges. The best known was the Siege of Tyre, a fortified town. It lasted for seven months.

▲ MOBILE SHIELD
The mantlet was either a row of set hurdles, or in this example a mobile shield which could be wheeled close to the enemy wall to give cover to archers.

clawed hook. This was used to pull down the battlements along the top of a city or fortress wall. The second was the tenelon, a kind of crane. A large box or basket hung from it. Soldiers got into the basket and were swung onto the enemy's walls to attack.

Smaller items were also used. Scaling ladders were lightweight ladders, sometimes with hooks at the top. The besiegers used these to assault the walls. The soldiers would run forward, place the ladders in position and scramble up them.

Grapnels or grappling hooks were hooks attached to a length of rope. Soldiers would throw the grapnel so that it hooked over the parapet of the wall and then climb up the rope.

While the soldiers were climbing the walls, archers would keep shooting from behind their mantlets to keep the enemy occupied. Otherwise the defenders would just cut the ropes or push away the ladders.

Another way to get inside was by using a trick. In the Trojan War between the Greeks and the Trojans, the Greeks pretended to give up. They gave the city of Troy a large wooden horse as a parting gift. The Trojans took it inside the city, not realizing that there were Greek soldiers hiding inside the horse. Once inside the city walls, the Greeks jumped out and, after some fighting, they took the city and won the war.

◆ GOING IN
The drawbridge on an Assyrian siege tower crashes onto the enemy wall as the assault party storms in.

◀ ENGINEERS AT WAR
The Romans were masters of the planning and building work as well as the tactics of a siege. The siege of a large city was like a major engineering operation. Large numbers of timber structures had to be made very quickly and put into position. Sieges could go on for many years so any building had to be quite sturdy.

Key Dates

- 612 B.C. Nineveh (modern Iraq), capital of the Assyrian Empire, besieged and destroyed.

- A.D. 1346-47 Siege of Calais. Town officials prepare to die following surrender.

- 1429 Siege of Orleans relieved by Joan of Arc.

- 1453 Siege of Constantinople. Turks take the city ending the Holy Roman Empire.

- 1871 Siege of Paris. Citizens driven to eat zoo animals.

Bombardment

▲ GETTING YOUR OWN BACK
In this medieval picture, trebuchets are used to lob the severed heads of prisoners over the walls of a castle.

BEFORE SOLDIERS had cannons, bombardment weapons were built based on natural forces.

Classical and medieval siege weapons worked on one of three principles: spring tension, torsion or counterweight. Spring tension weapons were like giant crossbows. They used springy wood that bent easily, such as ash or yew.

Torsion means twisting. Torsion weapons were powered by twisted rope. The tighter it was wound up, the more power there was when it was released. This method could be used to fire stones or javelins. The Romans of the 3rd century A.D. nicknamed one of their torsion weapons onager, meaning "wild ass." This was because of the violent kick of the machine's arm when the rope was released. They used a rope made from human hair for this weapon because it was very elastic.

The ballista was a little like a crossbow. The tension was produced by bending two lengths of wood held in coiled cord or braided hair.

The counterweight weapon or trebuchet reached Europe from China around A.D. 500. It was like a giant see-saw with a heavy weight at one end and a sling at the other. A stone or other missile was placed in the sling which was tied down so the heavy weight was in the air. When it was released, the weighted end would drop and lob the stone.

Stones were not the only thing that the trebuchet threw. Burning materials were hurled over the walls to try to start fires. Corpses of humans and animals were also thrown. This was to spread infection and to bring down the spirits of the defenders.

Looking at these weapons today, they seem crude and simple. However, in medieval Europe, with its poor roads and simple carpentry tools, building a weapon such as a trebuchet or a catapult and bringing it into action was a very impressive feat.

▶ WILD ASS
The onager or "wild ass" was developed about the 3rd century A.D. It earned its name from the violent kick from the throwing arm when the ratchet was released.

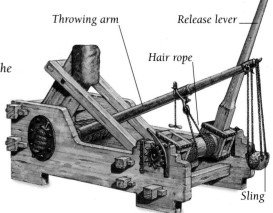

Throwing arm — Release lever — Hair rope — Sling

▲ ARCHIMEDES
A Sicilian scientist, Archimedes designed weapons for the defenders of Syracuse during the siege of 213–212 B.C. His engines were very effective against the Roman fleet.

GUIDED MISSILES
Before gunpowder, muscle power was used to throw missiles at the enemy. Soldiers had to be very strong to stretch or twist the ropes and springs or lift the heavy counterweights that gave catapults and trebuchets their power.

▶ GREEK FIRE
Siege machines could be adapted to throw "Greek fire," a mixture of chemicals, over the walls to burn the enemy.

◀ MASS ATTACK
This machine was designed to fire a barrage of arrows or javelins at one time. It was probably not very accurate.

◀ BALLISTA
The Romans developed the ballista, a weapon to launch missiles at the enemy. It worked rather like a crossbow and could be adapted to suit various kinds of ammunition. A light field ballista such as this could fire stones or javelins.

▼ CATAPULT

Protected by a mantlet, three soldiers tighten the tension on a catapult while a fourth prepares a stone for launching. The largest catapults could fire a 50 pound stone as far as 400 yards.

▶ ROMAN INVASION
In A.D. 43, the Romans invaded Britain in the south. They got as far north as the Plautian frontier, named after the Roman leader Plautus. Maiden Castle in Dorset was the site of a battle between the Britons and the Romans. At this battle, catapults and ballista were used by the Roman army. There had been a fort of some kind on this site since the Stone Age, but by the time the Romans came, it was well fortified by ramps, walls and dikes.

Irish Sea

North Sea

Plautian Frontier Zone

Camulodunum (Colchester)

R.Thames

N

Maiden Castle

Gesoriacum (Boulogne)

Noviomagus (Chichester)

0 Kilometers 150
0 Miles 100

Key Dates

- 400–200 B.C. Catapult introduced into Rome from Syria.

- 211 B.C. Mounted crossbow, possibly designed by Archimedes, in use to defend Syracuse.

- A.D. 100 Greeks build a catapult with an iron frame.

- 101–107 Ballista used by Romans in the Dacian wars (central Europe).

- 300 Onager in use with Romans. It was still used in medieval times.

- 1250s Trebuchet in extensive use.

- 1000–1400 Spring engines used in medieval Europe.

Ramps, Rams and Mining

So that they could bring their weapons in closer to the enemy, besieging troops built ramps outside the walls of the city or castle. Ramps or causeways were needed to cross ditches or moats filled with water. Ideally more than one ramp would be built so that the enemy would not know where the main assault was going to fall. The Romans pioneered the technique of building a ramp, known as an agger, from hurdles, packed earth and stone.

Once the besieging forces had filled in the moat and built a ramp up to the enemy's walls, the battering ram was wheeled into position. The battering ram was one of the oldest siege weapons. It was made from a heavy tree trunk hung on chains from a timber frame. The whole thing was covered by a wooden shelter called a penthouse. The roof and walls of the penthouse were often covered with animal hides that were kept wet as a protection against fire.

The battering ram could have a metal knob, sometimes in the shape of a ram's head, that was mounted at the front end of the tree trunk. By swinging the ram and driving it against the wall, the soldiers operating it would, with time and effort, make a hole.

▲ ROMAN RAMP
The agger or ramp is protected by flanking towers. Soldiers work on the ramp under long protective sheds.

▶ UNDERMINING
Defenders could destroy a ramp by digging a tunnel under its wooden piles and setting fire to them to make the ramp collapse.

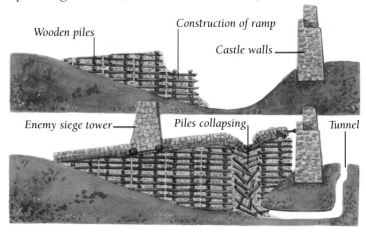
Wooden piles — *Construction of ramp* — *Castle walls*
Enemy siege tower — *Piles collapsing* — *Tunnel*

BATTERING TO VICTORY
The battering ram was the heavyweight siege weapon used to smash holes in the walls of a castle or town. There were many different designs. It was an accepted rule in Roman siege tactics that once the ram had been brought into action, the defenders within the fort or town could expect no mercy when the walls finally came down. So a ram was a frightening weapon in more ways than one.

▲ GREEK BATTERING RAM
This wheeled tower is a two-in-one weapon. The ram batters the wall while the arm above it pulls down the castle battlements.

▶ RAM TOWER
Rams could be carried on the shoulders or mounted on wheels. This ram tower was pushed forward on wheels or rollers until it was within range of the castle wall. The gantry structure allowed the crew to develop a good, powerful swing with the ram.

◀ DEMONSTRATION
This picture shows how an 11th-century ram worked. In a real battle, the ramming crew would be protected from fire and missiles by a penthouse.

◄ HOOKING A RAM
A hook mounted on a crane grabbed the siege weapon, which could be lifted and dropped until it broke up.

Mining was another way to break through a city or castle wall. First, the attackers would build an easy-to-move shelter and put it against the wall. Protected under the shelter, the soldiers could begin to knock down the wall. They supported it with wooden beams so that it did not fall down too soon. When enough of the wall had been weakened in this way, a fire would be lit under the beams. When the beams had been weakened by the fire, the wall collapsed, and the besieging forces could then storm across the gap that had been created. The soldiers inside the castle could dig their own mine beneath the attackers' mine shaft. They could try to make the enemy's mine collapse, or fight underground.

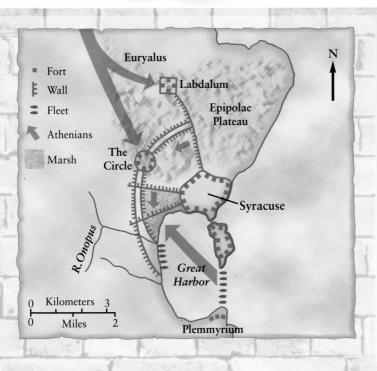

► SYRACUSE
The map shows the Siege of Syracuse in 415 B.C. by the Athenians. They built the square fort at Labdalum and a circular fort with surrounding siege walls. But Syracuse held out and inflicted Athens greatest defeat. The Athenians lost nearly 200 ships and 40-50,000 soldiers.

Key for map:
- ■ Fort
- Wall
- Fleet
- Athenians
- Marsh

Euryalus
Labdalum
Epipolae Plateau
The Circle
R. Onopus
Syracuse
Great Harbor
Plemmyrium

0 Kilometers 3
0 Miles 2

N

Key Dates

- 429–427 B.C. Plataea, in Greece, besieged using ramps and defeated by Spartans.

- 214–211 B.C. Siege of Syracuse (Sicily). Archimedes, born in Syracuse, designs some of the defense machinery.

- 52 B.C. Siege of Alesia in Gaul. Vercingetorix the Gaulish leader finally surrenders to Romans.

- A.D. 72 Siege of Masada, Jerusalem. Romans build ramps to get over the huge walls of the fortress. Many defenders choose to kill themselves rather than be captured.

Gunpowder Arrives

S OLID GUNPOWDER turns quickly into gas when burnt. If it is loose, gunpowder produces a flash, a cloud of white smoke and not much noise. If it is enclosed, the noise and the explosive force increases. This produces energy which can be used to push a solid object along a tube, or to blow up a building. The first use of gunpowder

in battle in Europe was by the British at the Battle of Crécy (1346). King Edward is said to have had three to five guns which were called roundelades or pots de fer because of their bottle or pot shape. Early weapons fired stones or arrows similar to crossbow bolts.

Cannon design did not change much over three hundred years. Gunpowder was poured into the open end or muzzle, and then packed down with a rammer. The packed gunpowder was secured in place with batting, which was rammed home. A cannon ball was then loaded. Loose gunpowder was poured down the touch hole, a small hole at the closed end of the cannon. It was lit using a slow match, a length of rope soaked in saltpeter, which would burn slowly. The explosion that followed pushed the cannon ball out of the gun muzzle. It could reach ranges of between

▲ POWDER RECIPE
The formula for gunpowde—one part sulphur, six parts saltpeter and two parts charcoa—was first written down by the Englishman Roger Bacon around 1242.

▶ WHEELED CANNON
Protected by a penthouse, this cannon sits on a simple frame that allows the crew to move it around the castle to fire stones at the enemy battlements. The cannon is held in place with guy lines and pegs which absorb the recoil when it fires and ensure it is correctly aligned.

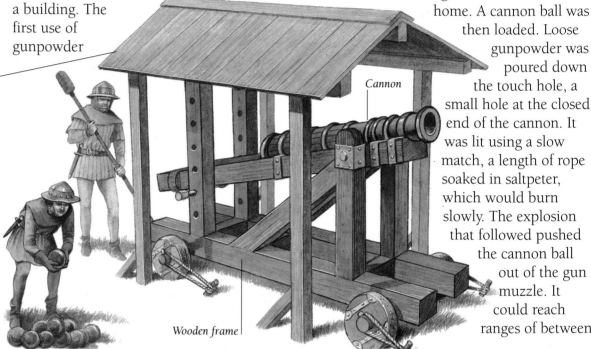

Penthouse

Cannon

Wooden frame

EXPLOSIVES
Gunpowder was first used in Europe for weapons in the 14th century. It had been used in China since the 11th century to fuel battlefield rockets. It was more powerful than ropes, counterweights or springs, but gave off big clouds of smoke.

Double cannon

▶ HAND MORTAR
A 16th-century short-barreled weapon used for lobbing shot into enemy ranks.

◀ DOUBLE SHOT
These cannons are on a static mount and would be fired in quick succession against a wall or gate—almost like a double-barreled weapon.

Hand mortar

Serpentine

▲ HAND CANNON
The hand cannon was first used in 1364 and was the first step towards hand guns as we know them today. The gunner had to support his heavy firearm with a forked pike to keep it steady.

▶ SNAKE GUN
This drawing by the artist Dürer shows a cannon called a serpentine as it was thought to look like a snake or serpent. Many early cast cannon were shaped to look like serpents.

220 yards and 765 yards depending on the size of the cannon and the ball. By the 1860s, ranges for a 12 pound cannon ball fired using a 2.5 pound charge had increased to 1,640 yards.

The ninth Siege of Constantinople by the Turks from April to May 1453 is the first example of the power of cannon. Constantinople was then the capital of the Eastern Roman Empire. It was ruled by Constantine XI. The Turkish leader was Sultan Muhammed II. A Hungarian engineer called Urban made a very long bronze cannon for the Turks.

◀ ENGLISH GUNS
One gunner raises the mantlet as the other prepares to light the touch hole to fire the stone ball.

▲ CANNON WITH COVER
Early cannon were built in a similar way to beer barrels. Lengthwise cast iron strips were bound with iron hoops and mounted in a static wooden carriage.

It measured 26 feet and was capable of throwing a 1,455 pound stone a mile. Loading and firing took some time, so the weapon could only fire seven times a day. After 12 days of heavy bombardment, the Turks had broken through the walls of the city. Constantinople fell on May 29, 1453.

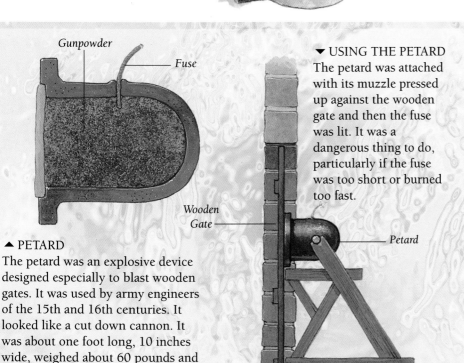

Gunpowder

Fuse

▲ PETARD
The petard was an explosive device designed especially to blast wooden gates. It was used by army engineers of the 15th and 16th centuries. It looked like a cut down cannon. It was about one foot long, 10 inches wide, weighed about 60 pounds and had a touch hole and open muzzle.

▼ USING THE PETARD
The petard was attached with its muzzle pressed up against the wooden gate and then the fuse was lit. It was a dangerous thing to do, particularly if the fuse was too short or burned too fast.

Wooden Gate

Petard

Key Dates

- 1242 Roger Bacon writes down the formula for gunpowder.

- 1324 Cannon believed to have been used at siege of Metz, in France.

- 1342 Reports of cannon at siege of Algeciras, Spain.

- 1346 Confirmed use of cannon at the battle of Crécy, France.

- 1450–1850 Most cannon were cast in bronze, iron or brass.

- 1500 Metal shot had replaced stone.

- 1571 At the battle of Lepanto, Greece heavily gunned galleys were used.

War at Sea

▲ OAR POWER
There were many kinds of warship design. This is a Greek galley with a single bank of oars.

THE MEDITERRANEAN Sea was central to the ancient world. Its name means "in the middle of the earth." Many countries depended on it for food and trade. Whoever controlled the sea therefore, had power over all the countries which surrounded it. The Mediterranean has hardly any tides. Ships were not dependent on the tide coming in to launch and could not become stranded when the tide went out. The sea became part of the battlefield. Fighting methods and weapons were much the same as they were on land. The key to sea fighting was transportation. Fast boats with a reliable power source usually won the battle. The Greeks, Romans, Persians and Carthaginians all developed warships which could deliver troops quickly to the scene of the battle. As each would try to stop the other, they adapted land weapons for use at sea, such as grappling hooks, siege towers and catapults.

A good general used sea power to help his land battles. The tactics developed by the ancient sea

▼ OARS AT WORK
There were three layers of galley slaves in a trireme. To be effective they had to be able to row in time, so they probably used a drum to keep the time. Clearly the best position was on the top row.

SEA POWER
Most warships relied on banks of galley slaves to row them into action. Some ships had sails which could be used when the wind was favorable.

◀ XERXES
This Persian king came to power in 486 B.C. and launched a massive land and sea assault on Athens and her allies in 480 B.C. but he was defeated.

▶ THE BATTLE OF SALAMIS
This classic sea battle was fought in 480 B.C. between the Athenians led by Themistocles and the Persians under Xerxes.

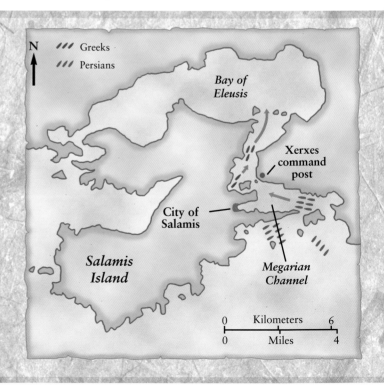

N
/// Greeks
/// Persians

Bay of Eleusis

Xerxes command post

City of Salamis

Salamis Island

Megarian Channel

| 0 | Kilometers | 6 |
| 0 | Miles | 4 |

captains still work today. The Athenian plan for the Battle of Salamis was so successful that it is taught in miltary school. The sea battle at Lepanto in 1571 was fought between Austria and the Turks; it was the last time galleys were used in war. Austria captured 130 Turkish galleys and destroyed 80 more. The battle ended Turkish control of the Mediterranean.

Different kinds of ships and skills were needed to deal with larger seas, more extreme weather and tides. Countries with coastlines on the Atlantic or Pacific built boats that could land in shallow water if the tide was out. The Vikings who sailed the Atlantic owed their success to their long, flat-bottomed boats which could land almost anywhere.

Boats were used to deliver troops to a land battle or invasion. Vikings, Saxons, Danes and Normans invaded Great Britain by sea between 800 and 1066. During the Crusades in the Middle East, knights were brought from Europe by sea. Ships were also used to help in the sieges of coastal cities.

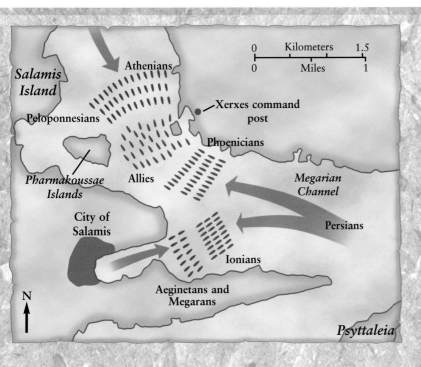

◀ TACTICS

The Persian fleet of 1000 ships had trapped the 370 Greek triremes in the Megarian Channel. The Greeks retreated northward, luring the Persians into the narrow waters near Salamis. Once there, the Persian fleet could not maneuver. The Greeks turned and went on the attack. They sank 300 Persian galleys and lost only 40 ships of their own.

Key Dates

- 486 B.C. Battle of Salamis. Greeks beat Persians.

- 31 B.C. Battle of Actium. Caesar Octavian defeats Mark Antony in Roman Civil War.

- A.D. 1340 Battle of Sluys between French and English as part of 100 Years War. Warships become battlefields.

- 1571 Battle of Lepanto. Austrians beat Turks.

- 1588 England defeats Spanish Armada.

Sail or Oar?

IN THE ANCIENT WORLD, trading ships used sails and windpower to move around the seas. Captains of warships could not rely on winds and tide alone. They used manpower as well. Greek, Roman, Turkish and Spanish ships used massed oarsmen. Others, such as the Anglo-Saxons, Norsemen and Normans, used a combination of sail and oars. The French and British preferred sail-powered vessels and improved their design through the centuries.

The Greeks were first with the oar-driven warship. They used vessels called triremes which had three rows of oars and 150 rowers. Athenian sailors developed a way of fighting using their rowing skills. They would approach an enemy ship at full speed, come alongside and at the last minute pull in their oars. This smashed

◀ ARMED GALLEY
A Roman sculpture shows the banks of oars with armed soldiers at the ready on deck.

▲ THE MARY ROSE
Henry VIII's flag ship was armed with cannons low down which could fire broadsides.

A HARD LIFE
Few people wanted to row a galley. Criminals in countries such as Italy or Spain in the 15th and 16th centuries were often condemned to the galleys as a punishment. Prisoners of war were also made to row in their enemy's galleys.

▶ OARS AT WORK
There were three layers of galley slaves in a trireme. To be effective they had to be able to row in time, so a drum was used to beat out the rhythm.

▲ GALLEY SLAVES
Chained to their benches in the dark, hot smelly hull of their boat, galley slaves could be worked until they died. Their bodies would be thrown over the side.

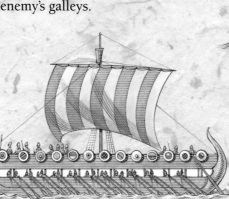

◀ MEDITERRANEAN GALLEY
Fast, light, unarmed boats were used to transport troops. If the boat was sunk in battle, the soldiers and the rowers were picked up by their own side and the boat was abandoned.

▶ FLOATING BATTLES
Spanish and English ships engage in battle in 1372 as part of the 100 Years War. The warships sailed very close together and the soldiers fought across the decks as if on land.

all the oars on the enemy ship, which were still sticking out.

The oarsmen in the galleys were normally slaves. Some were convicted criminals, but many were prisoners of war. By the time of the Battle of Lepanto (1571) the Turks had smaller galleys called galiots with 18 to 24 oars, and the Venetians had developed a large vessel called a galleas. Galleys were equipped with sails so that with favorable winds they could operate without using the oarsmen.

The Scandinavian raiders who roamed as far away as the Mediterranean and Black Sea used both wind and manpower. Under Bjarni Herjolfsson, a Viking longboat reached North America in A.D. 985. The Vikings could row their long, narrow boats when there was no wind or they were close inshore. Because the vessels were light and almost flat on the bottom they could land on gently shelving coasts or even mud flats.

By the 14th and 15th century, all warships in northern Europe relied on wind power. The sailors working in the tidal, stormy waters of the English Channel and North Sea needed to be very skillful.

Under Henry VIII ship design began to change. By the time of the Armada, British warships were sleek and low. They were about 115 feet long and 33 feet wide and were called galleons. Like the galley, they were ships built specially for war. New designs in sails and rigging made the vessels even more seaworthy. The galleon was able to make long distance voyages and so it became the vessel used by navigators and explorers.

▲ FAST AND FURIOUS
Vikings used their fast boats to make lightning raids. They were able to sail as far as America. The chance of plunder and easy targets made the risky journey worthwhile.

Viking warrior

Key Dates

- 241 B.C. Lilybaeum. After a long siege, Rome defeats Carthage, and Carthaginians lose 120 ships.

- A.D. 655 Battle of the Masts. Moaviah governor of Syria attempts to capture Constantinople from the sea.

- 841 Vikings reach Dublin.

- 1027 Normans land near Naples and establish stronghold.

- 1281 Mongol invasion of Japan defeated by "divine wind" or "kamikaze."

- 1588 Spanish Armada in running battles with the English fleet along the south coast of England.

Ramming and Grappling

Before GUNPOWDER ALLOWED SHIPS to stand off at a distance and bombard one another, warships used light siege weapons, archers and slingers. The siege weapons could kill and injure people and damage sails and rigging. The archers and slingers acted as snipers, finding targets on the enemy ships.

Ramming could cause major damage. From the Greeks in 600 B.C. to the Spanish Armada of 1588, galleys powered by oars were fitted with a long ramming beak. The trick was to drive this into the hull of the enemy ship.

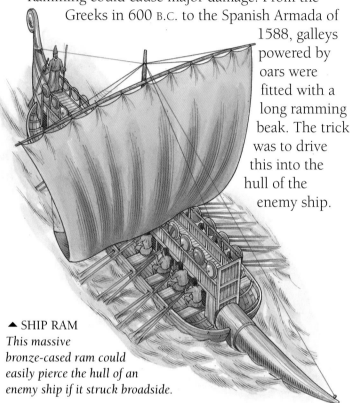

▲ SHIP RAM
This massive bronze-cased ram could easily pierce the hull of an enemy ship if it struck broadside.

▲ GREEK FIRE
Fire can be used as a weapon at sea. "Greek fire," an inflammable chemical, was used by Byzantine ships around the 4th century.

The Romans introduced a new weapon in 260 B.C. at the Battle of Mylae in Sicily. The corvus or "crow" was a hinged gangplank with a weighted hook. It could be swung out over an enemy ship and dropped so that it was stuck in the deck. Then a boarding party raced across the corvus on to the enemy ship. The Romans won at Mylae and took control of the Mediterranean.

Grappling irons, hooks with heavy chains, were later used in sea battles to assist boarding. Once the ships were alongside and the boarding parties in action, the fight became a land battle at sea, with hand-to-hand combat. Medieval ships showed this in their design with crenellated wooden "castles" in the bow and stern.

WAR AT SEA
Before gunpowder changed war, ships could ram the enemy, or slice off their oars. Other weapons were the corvus and twin-hulled siege vessels which could carry fighting towers.

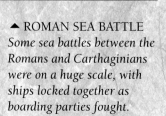

◀ DECORATIVE RAM
This finely worked prow with its ram shaped like a row of swords shows the quality of the work on classical warships.

▲ ROMAN SEA BATTLE
Some sea battles between the Romans and Carthaginians were on a huge scale, with ships locked together as boarding parties fought.

▲ FIRE SHIP
This ingenious little ship is designed to carry a tub of burning tar into the middle of an enemy fleet at anchor. It could damage rigging and sails and had the potential to sink ships much larger than itself. The English sent fire ships like this one against the Spanish Armada when it was at anchor.

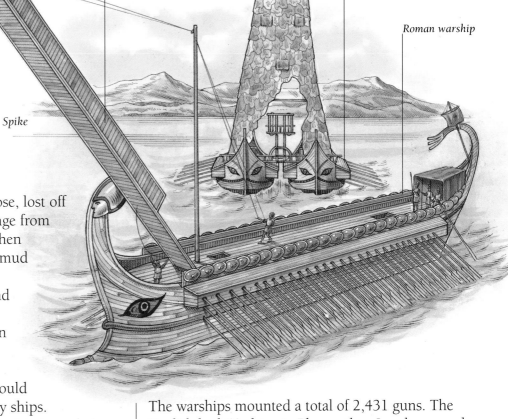

▶ CROWS AND TOWERS
The Romans developed a grappling weapon called a corvus, the Latin word for crow. It looked something like a crow's big beak. It was a hinged gangplank with a hook which sank into the enemy ship's deck. Special twin-hulled siege vessels could carry fighting towers to the enemy.

Corvus — Siege tower — Twin-hulled ship

Spike — Roman warship

This is why the front of a ship is known as the forecastle or fo'c'sle.

The English warship the Mary Rose, lost off Portsmouth in 1545, marks the change from ancient to modern warfare at sea. When she was recovered in 1982 from the mud into which she had settled, her weapons included both longbows and cannon. The ship was designed without castles but with gun ports on the lower decks. Heavy broadside cannons stood on these gun decks. When they opened fire, their shot would damage the hulls and masts of enemy ships.

In the running battle with the Spanish Armada in 1588, the English Royal Navy demonstrated that modern ship design, skilled sailors and good weather could shift the odds in favor of a smaller force. The Spanish had 20 great galleons, 44 armed merchant ships, 23 transports, 35 smaller vessels, four galleases (a double sized heavily armed galley) and four galleys.

The warships mounted a total of 2,431 guns. The English had 68 ships in Plymouth, a London squadron of 30 ships and an additional squadron of 23 in the eastern English Channel. Aside from seafaring skills and ship design, their strength lay in their 1,800 heavy cannons, mostly long-range cannons called culverins.

In running battles up the Channel the English finally prevented the Spanish from landing in England.

◀ ARMADA
Before dawn on July 28, 1588, the English sent fire ships into the Spanish fleet off Flanders as part of their running battle with the Armada. It forced the Spanish to cut their anchor cables. In the great sea battle that followed, only a storm prevented the English fleet from capturing or destroying 16 of the most damaged Spanish ships.

Key Dates

- 480 B.C. Battle of Salamis, Greece. Greeks defeat Persians.

- 262 B.C. Battle of Mylae, Sicily. Romans win and take control of the Mediterranean Sea.

- 241 B.C. Battle of Lilybaeum, Sicily. Romans defeat the Carthaginians.

- 31 B.C. Battle of Actium, Greece. Romans defeat Cleopatra and the Egyptians.

- A.D. 1571 Battle of Lepanto. Christian Allies defeat Turks.

- 1588 Defeat of the Spanish Armada by the English.

Sailing to War

CARRYING SOLDIERS AND THEIR WEAPONS, vehicles, horses and food by sea and landing them on an enemy shore is called an amphibious operation. Amphibious means able to work on land and in water. In ancient times, this was a simple operation. Coasts weren't always defended and boats were flat enough to land directly on sand or shingle shores.

As ships became bigger, they had to remain off shore and troops transferred to smaller boats before they could land. Horses could swim ashore on their own, but artillery and wagons posed an extra problem. In bad weather these operations could be dangerous and so sailors and soldiers looked for sheltered anchorages where they could land and unload in safety.

One of the earliest recorded amphibious operations were the Punic Wars of 264–241 B.C. between the Carthaginians, who lived in what is now Tunisia, and the Romans, in modern Italy. Both sides transported men and horses across the Mediterranean. The Carthaginian general Hannibal even took about 80 war elephants by ship from North Africa into Spain.

There were earlier operations. The most famous is described in Homer's Iliad, an epic poem that includes both myth and fact. To lay siege to Troy (a city located in what is now Turkey) the Greeks, under Agamemnon, had to sail across the Aegean Sea. Archeological evidence of both Troy and the Trojan Wars dates the sea crossing to around 1200 B.C.

BATTLES BY LAND AND SEA

Islands could not be attacked without the use of ships. Sometimes the landings were the beginning of a long campaign. They could be part of the siege of a fortified port, or the means of escape for a battle fought on the coast. Vikings used their boats like a modern "getaway car," raiding a settlement and escaping quickly.

▲ NATURAL LIFT
A Sumerian warrior uses an inflated animal skin as a float to help him to cross a fast-flowing river.

▲ HELEN OF TROY
The wife of the king of Sparta was so beautiful that her face was said to have "launched a thousand ships." She was kidnapped by Paris of Troy, which began the Trojan Wars.

◀ TROOP CARRIERS
Boats like this one were used to ferry troops across the Mediterranean to fight battles on land.

At Marathon in 490 B.C. a Persian invasion fleet landed a force of 20,000 on the Greek coast near Athens. They were defeated by the Athenians, who numbered only 11,000, but despite heavy losses they were able to reach their ships and escape.

In Europe there was usually no need for soldiers to travel by sea. The waves of raids by the sea-going Saxons between A.D. 205 and 577 and the Viking raids between 800–1016 reached eastern England and northern France. They were not so much amphibious operations as military "smash and grab raids," The Anglo-Saxons and the Vikings eventually settled in the territories they had been raiding.

For island countries, such as Britain, that might be threatened by enemy landings, it was a good idea to build watchtowers and fortifications at the harbors and likely landing sites.

▲ THE NEW WORLD
In the 16th century, Spanish and Portuguese explorers sailed west and invaded large areas of South America.

▼ INVASION
In 1066, William of Normandy transported 9000 men with all their horses and equipment for his invasion of England.

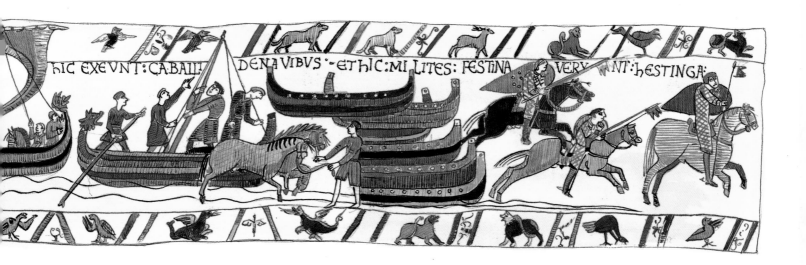

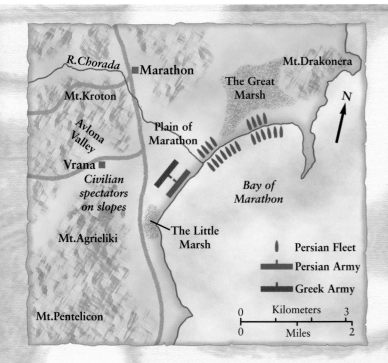

◄ THE BATTLE OF MARATHON
In 490 B.C. Persia invaded Greece. The Persian leader Darius worked his way down from modern day Turkey in the north, with a force of 150,000 men in ships. He landed an army 20,000 strong near Marathon. The Greeks met them on the coastal plain with about 11,000 soldiers and lost only 192 to the Persians' 6400.

Key Dates

- 490 B.C. Battle of Marathon. The Greeks defeat the Persians.

- 415 B.C. Athenians land in Sicily and besiege Syracuse.

- 54 B.C. First Roman invasion of Britain.

- A.D. 43 Second Roman invasion of Britain.

- 400s Raids on England by Jutes, Angles and Saxons.

- 700s–800s Vikings raid Europe.

- 1027 Normans land in southern Italy.

- 1066 Normans invade England.

JOURNEY
WITHOUT END

Journey Without End looks at the great explorers and adventurers who battled against adversity to discover the oceans and continents of the world.

BY SIMON ADAMS

Introduction

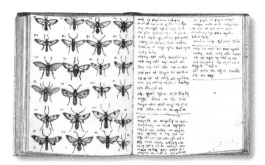

▲ SCIENCE
Explorers in the 18th century set out to record the world they found. Illustrators were taken on expeditions to catalog the wildlife of the islands that they discovered.

▼ KEY DATES
The panel charts voyages of discovery on Earth, from the first sea voyages in the Mediterranean 3,500 years ago to the conquest of the South Pole in 1911.

EVER SINCE THE FIRST PEOPLE walked on the Earth they have explored the world they lived in. In the beginning, hundreds of thousands of years ago, this was to hunt and gather food; later on it was to find new pastures for their animals. But food was the reason for exploring, and people rarely went far from the place they were born.

When the first civilizations began, in the Middle East, people began to live in towns and cities. Farmers grew crops, and traders bought and sold goods that were not available in their own area. It was these intrepid merchants, from ancient civilizations like Phoenicia and Egypt, who were the first explorers. The Phoenicians sailed out from the Mediterranean into the North Atlantic, while the Egyptians ventured south into the Indian Ocean, looking for opportunities to trade and to establish permanent trading posts or colonies.

Throughout history trade has remained the driving force of discovery. It was the search for a new trade route to China and India that sent Vasco da Gama around Africa into the Indian Ocean, and Columbus across the Atlantic. Explorers like Hudson and Bering braved the Arctic Ocean trying to find ways around the top of North America and Siberia. And it was trade that sent Magellan around the world and European sailors into

▼ CONVERSION
Many European explorers set out to convert the local people they encountered to Christianity.

EUROPE

Phoenician galley

c.1400B.C. Phoenician sailors explore Mediterranean.

c.330B.C. Pytheas sails from France to Thule.

A.D.300s First Barbarian invasions of Roman Empire.

1419 Henry "The Navigator" establishes school of navigation in Portugal.   *Pilgrims*

ASIA

Caravanserai on the Silk Road

c.500B.C. Silk Road opened.

138B.C. Chang Ch'ien, from China, travels into Central Asia.

A.D.399 Fa Hsien travels from China to India and Ceylon.

1099 First Christian crusaders visit Palestine.

1271–95 Marco Polo visits China.

1325–54 Ibn Battuta, from Algeria, travels around Islamic world.

1405–33 Zheng He, from China, leads expeditions to Southeast Asia.

1498 Da Gama, from Lisbon, Portugal, sails to India.

1549 Xavier, a Spanish Jesuit, goes to Japan as a missionary.

1594–97 Barents, a Dutch mariner, explores Arctic Ocean.

1725–29 Bering, from Denmark, crosses Siberia.

1734–42 Teams of explorers map Siberian coast and rivers.

1878–79 Nordenskjöld, from Finland, discovers the Northeast Passage.

Inuit igloo

AFRICA

Timbuktu

c.1490B.C. Egyptians sail to Punt.

c.600B.C. Phoenician fleet sails around Africa.

c.500B.C. Hanno, from Carthage in modern Tunisia, explores coast.

A.D.1480s Portuguese cross the Equator and sail around Cape of Good Hope.

1768–73 Bruce, from Scotland, searches for source of the River Nile and discovers Lake Tana.

▼ NAVIGATION
The first explorers had little to help them navigate, apart from the positions of the Sun, Moon, and stars, and had to stay close to land. The development of instruments like the magnetic compass, astrolabe, and quadrant made navigation easier and more exact.

the Pacific Ocean to the rich spice islands of Southeast Asia.

Explorers also set out seeking fame and fortune and for political advantage—to conquer new lands for their king and country. Many European explorers traveled out of religious conviction, attempting to convert other races to Christianity. But by the 18th century, it was scientific curiosity that sent Cook into the Pacific Ocean and Bates into the Amazon rainforest.

Today there are few places left on Earth that have not been fully explored. There are unexplored mountains in Tibet, and the ocean floor remains largely undiscovered, but now our attention has turned to the skies and space. Unmanned space probes explore the planets of our solar system and the wider reaches of our galaxy of stars, looking for life on other planets. Exploration has come a long way since those early sailing ships left the shores of Phoenicia and Egypt more than 3,500 years ago.

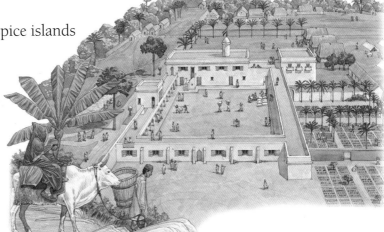

▲ TRADE
The Dutch East India Company was a powerful trading organization. By 1700 it had control of the valuable cinnamon, clove, and nutmeg trade in the East. It established trading posts throughout Asia and ruled what is now called Indonesia.

1795–1806 Park, from Scotland, explores the River Niger.

1841–73 Livingstone, from Scotland, explores southern and central Africa.

1844–45 Barth, from Germany, explores the Sahara Desert region.

1858-63 Englishman John Speke discovers the source of the River Nile.

1874–77 Stanley, from Wales, sails down Congo River.

Stanley's hat

AMERICA and the ARCTIC

A.D.980s–90s Vikings settle in Greenland and explore parts of North America.

1492 Columbus, from Italy, finds the West Indies.

1497 Cabot finds Newfoundland.

1502 Amerigo Vespucci, from Italy, explores South America.

1513 Balboa sights Pacific Ocean.

1519–33 Spanish conquer Aztecs.

1535–6 Cartier, from France, journeys up St. Lawrence River.

1603–15 Champlain explores Canada and founds Quebec.

1610–11 Englishman Henry Hudson searches for Northwest Passage.

1680–82 La Salle, from France, sails down Mississippi River.

1800s Several scientific expeditions explore the Amazon.

1804–06 Americans Lewis and Clark explore Louisiana Purchase.

1903–06 Amundsen, from Norway, finds the Northwest Passage.

1908 Peary, from the United States, reaches North Pole.

Lewis and Clark

AUSTRALASIA and the ANTARCTIC

c.1000B.C. Polynesians settle in Tonga and Samoa.

Boomerang

A.D.400 Polynesians reach Easter Island and Hawaii.

c.1000 Maoris settle in New Zealand.

1520–21 Magellan crosses Pacific on his round-the-world voyage.

1605 Jansz explores Queensland.

1642–43 Dutchman Tasman discovers New Zealand.

1770 Cook lands in Australia.

1828–62 Interior explored.

1911 Amundsen reaches South Pole.

Egyptians, Phoenicians, and Greeks

▲ BABOON
The Egyptians brought live baboons and cheetahs back from Punt, as well as leopard skins.

PEOPLE HAVE BEEN EXPLORING the world since ancient times. The earliest civilizations grew up in the Middle East thousands of years ago. Merchants began to trade with far-off cities so that they could get hold of goods that were not available in their own land. Gold, spices, and craftworks were bought and sold. The easiest way to make long journeys to other countries was by sea. The traders had no maps to guide them, so they had to discover the best routes for themselves. They soon learned about the winds and sea currents that would help their voyages and which seasons were best to travel in.

The ancient Egyptians lived along the banks of the River Nile. They had plenty of food and other goods, so traders did not venture very far. But eventually the traders wanted to find new markets, and this tempted them to explore farther afield. They started to sail ships out into the Mediterranean and the Red Sea.

In 1490B.C., Queen Hatshepsut of Egypt ordered a fleet to sail down the Red Sea in search of new lands. The fleet reached a place called Punt (modern Somalia or somewhere farther down the coast of East Africa). The sailors returned with ivory, ebony, spices, and myrrh trees—a present from the people of Punt. Other expeditions explored the interior of North Africa.

Phoenician sailors began to explore the Mediterranean Sea in about 1400B.C. The Phoenicians lived in cities along the coast of what is now Lebanon, at the eastern end of the Mediterranean. They were skilled seafarers and soon started to establish prosperous trading colonies throughout the region. One Phoenician fleet even sailed around Africa on behalf of an Egyptian pharaoh. In 500B.C. a man named Hanno sailed from Carthage, a Phoenician colony in North Africa, as far as modern Senegal, a journey of

▶ A PHOENICIAN SHIP
Phoenician ships were short, broad, and strong. They were built from cedar, which grew on the mountain slopes of Phoenicia. A single sail and oars powered the ship along.

SAILING THE MEDITERRANEAN

Phoenicia had little arable land, and so in 1400B.C. its people turned to the sea for a living. They became excellent seafarers, sailing great distances in search of new markets. They established colonies as far away as North Africa and Spain. Egyptians and Greeks also began to explore by sea.

◀ PHOENICIAN TRADERS
The Phoenicians traded grain, olive oil, glassware, purple cloth, cedar wood, and other goods throughout the Mediterranean area. They were somewhat like traveling shopkeepers.

▼ MUREX SHELL
One of the most precious items traded by the Phoenicians was purple cloth. The dye for the cloth was made from murex shells. Up to 6,000 shells were crushed to make 16 ounces of dye.

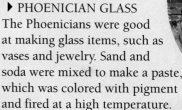

▶ PHOENICIAN GLASS
The Phoenicians were good at making glass items, such as vases and jewelry. Sand and soda were mixed to make a paste, which was colored with pigment and fired at a high temperature.

Single sail

Warehouse

▼ EGYPTIAN PORT
In Egypt, shallow-bottomed boats made of reeds, with a single sail, carried goods and passengers along the River Nile. After about 2700B.C. the Egyptians began to build wooden boats, which were stronger and could cross seas to foreign lands.

2,500 miles. Other Phoenician traders sailed to Britain, buying tin in Cornwall.

The Greeks also founded colonies throughout the Mediterranean. The Phoenicians were their great rivals, because they were so successful at trading by sea. Greek merchants wanted some of the business for themselves. In 330B.C., an explorer named Pytheas sailed to Britain, possibly to try to get access to the profitable tin trade.

▶ PYTHEAS
One of the most amazing voyages of ancient times was made by a Greek astronomer named Pytheas. In 330B.C. he set sail from Marseille in southern France, which was a Greek colony. He headed around Spain and then north to the British Isles, where he reported that the local people were friendly. Pytheas continued his voyage farther north to the land of Thule. Thule was probably Norway or Iceland. Pytheas noted that in Thule the sun never set. (In these countries it does not get dark in summer.)

Key Dates

- 1490B.C. Egyptians sail to Punt.

- 1400B.C. Phoenician traders explore the Mediterranean Sea and the eastern Atlantic Ocean.

- 1000B.C. First Phoenician colony established on Cyprus.

- c.800B.C. Greeks set up colonies in the eastern Mediterranean.

- 814B.C. Phoenicians found Carthage in North Africa.

- c.600B.C. Phoenician fleet sails around Africa.

- 500B.C. Hanno explores the coast of West Africa.

- 330B.C. Pytheas sails to Thule.

Europe and Asia

▲ SILKWORM
A silkworm feeds on a mulberry leaf. The Chinese began cultivating silkworms for silk over 4,500 years ago.

IN ANCIENT TIMES there was not much contact between Europe and Asia. In Europe the flourishing trading empires of the Phoenicians and Greeks were centered on the Mediterranean Sea. In eastern Asia the Chinese had their own trading centers. In between the two continents were the deserts, mountains, and arid plateaus of central Asia.

The Chinese were famous for making beautiful silk fabric. A few hardy traders made the long journey between Europe and China along a route known as the Silk Road. They bought bales of silk from Chinese merchants to take back with them. There are records of Chinese silk being sold in the Greek city of Athens as early as 550 B.C.

Two hundred years later, King Alexander of Macedon (later known as Alexander the Great) invaded the huge Persian Empire, which extended into central Asia. Many scholars and historians went with him. They began to explore the vast regions that Alexander had conquered, and learned a lot about them.

When Alexander died his empire broke up. But links between Europe and Asia became stronger over the next century. The empires of different rulers lay all along the Silk Road. The Romans controlled Europe, the Parthians ruled Persia, and the Kushans dominated central Asia. In China the country became united for the first time under the first Ch'in emperor in 221 B.C. These four empires spanned the length of the Silk Road, and for more than 400 years there was uninterrupted trade between East and West. Few Roman merchants visited China, but a wide variety of goods flowed along the Silk Road in both directions.

There was also a thriving sea trade across the Indian Ocean between Egypt and India, and from there on to China. This too helped to increase international trade and contacts.

▶ TRADERS
The Silk Road was a busy route. Merchants from Europe, the Middle East, central Asia, and China used it on trips to buy and sell goods. However, not many of them ever traveled along its entire length.

FROM WEST TO EAST
The major trade route between China and Europe was known as the Silk Road, because Chinese silk was brought along it by traders returning to Europe. In exchange, China received gold and silver, cotton, and a wide variety of fruits and other produce.

▼ ALEXANDER THE GREAT
Alexander was only 20 when he succeeded his father as king of Macedon in 336 B.C. By the time of his death, 13 years later, he had conquered an empire that stretched from the Adriatic Sea in southern Europe to the mouth of the River Indus in India.

◀ BEASTS OF BURDEN
Donkeys, horses, and two-humped Bactrian camels were all used on the Silk Road. They worked hard carrying the traders and their cargoes.

▲ JADE
Jade was the most precious substance known to the Chinese. They carved it into elaborate and intricate ornaments and utensils, such as this brush-washer.

The Silk Road was also important in linking the different Asian empires together. Buddhist monks brought their religion from India into China in about A.D.100. Chinese explorers journeyed into neighboring countries, which helped to strengthen religious and trading ties between them. Chang Ch'ien, a court official, traveled into central Asia in 138B.C. A monk named Fa Hsien visited India and Sri Lanka in A.D.399. However, by A.D.400 these ties had weakened. Civil war

▲ THE SILK ROAD
The Silk Road started in the Chinese capital of Loyang and ran westward across northern China and central Asia to Ctesiphon on the River Tigris in southwest Asia. It later continued to the Mediterranean. It was not a single road, but a series of well-marked routes. Traders using them were fairly safe from attacks by robbers.

broke out in China, and barbarian invaders and nomads from central Asia overran the Silk Road. By A.D.450 the links between East and West were broken.

▶ CARAVANSERAI
Traders on the Silk Road stopped each night in one of the many caravanserais, or inns, that lay along the route. Here they relaxed, had a meal, and exchanged information and gossip with their fellow traders. Their animals were fed and had a good rest before the next day's journey.

Key Dates

- c.500B.C. Silk Road established for trade from China to Europe.

- 334B.C. Alexander of Macedon conquers Persian Empire.

- 221B.C. China united.

- 138B.C. Chang Ch'ien travels from China into central Asia.

- A.D.100 Buddhism reaches China.

- A.D.166 Roman traders in China.

- A.D.220 After lengthy civil war China splits into three parts.

- A.D.399 Fa Hsien travels from China to India and Sri Lanka to study Buddhism.

The Invasion of Europe

THE CITY OF ROME started off as a small cluster of villages in the hills around the River Tiber in central Italy. By 500B.C. it had grown into the most powerful city in Italy. Rome declared war on its main rival, the Phoenician city of Carthage. Carthage was defeated, and the Romans built an empire that spanned the Mediterranean. By the reign of Emperor Trajan (A.D.98–117), the Roman Empire stretched from Portugal to Mesopotamia, and from the Sahara Desert to the border between Scotland and England.

The long eastern frontier of the Romans' vast empire was easy to invade. In A.D.300, the Huns, from the vast steppes of central Asia, began to head westward into southeast Europe, in search of new pastures. This pushed the Germanic tribes living there (including the Goths, Visigoths, Vandals, Alans, and Franks) across the Roman frontier.

At first the various tribes lived peacefully in the Roman Empire. But in A.D.378 fighting broke out, and the Visigoths defeated the powerful Roman army in the Balkans. From there the Visigoths moved farther into the Roman Empire. They successfully attacked Rome in A.D.410 and continued westward to settle in Spain. The Franks and

▲ GOTHIC ART
This illuminated manuscript from the 1100s is by the Goths. They were the first Germanic people to become Christians. Many years later an ornate style of art developed, based on original Gothic designs.

▼ ROME DESTROYED
In AD410 the Visigoths captured and plundered Rome, killing many of its inhabitants. The Vandals did the same in AD455. But Rome continued as a thriving city until AD546, when the Ostrogoths captured it and expelled its entire population, leaving it in ruins.

THE DARK AGES

The period after the fall of the Roman Empire is often called the Dark Ages. This is because Europe became a poorer place. People managed to grow enough food, but trade and commerce declined rapidly. Europe seemed to be taking a step backward from the great culture and prosperity enjoyed by the Romans. However, learning and scholarship continued in monasteries everywhere. Christianity became the main religion of Europe, and the new rulers of Europe soon developed cultures of their own.

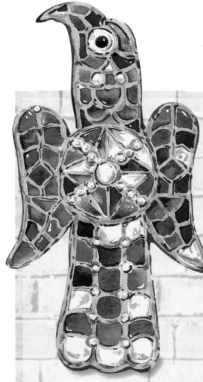

▲ ENAMELED BROOCH
Many of the barbarian invaders were skilled craftworkers, as can be seen from this brooch.

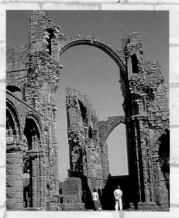

▸ LINDISFARNE
In monasteries such as Lindisfarne Priory, in northeast England, monks kept education alive during the times known as the Dark Ages.

▲ MAUSOLEUM
The barbarian invaders of Europe soon adopted Roman customs. This mausoleum was built in the Roman style in A.D.526 in Ravenna, northern Italy, as the burial place of Theodoric, an Ostrogoth chief.

Vandals crossed the River Rhine and invaded Gaul (France). The Vandals kept going south until they reached North Africa. Finally the Huns, led by Attila, arrived in Europe. The Romans managed to defeat Attila in A.D.453 with the help of friendly Germanic tribes, but by then their empire was weak and exhausted.

In A.D.476 the last Roman emperor was removed from power. Rival invading tribes fought over the remains of the Roman Empire. The Romans called the invaders barbarians, but many were educated people looking for a safer land to live in.

The old Roman Empire was swept away, but the tribes of Europe remained disunited for several hundred years. Then in A.D.800 Charlemagne, a Frankish king from northern Europe, was crowned "Holy Roman Emperor" by the pope in Rome. By that time Christianity was the main religion across Europe. Between them, the pope and Charlemagne brought some unity to the peoples of western Europe.

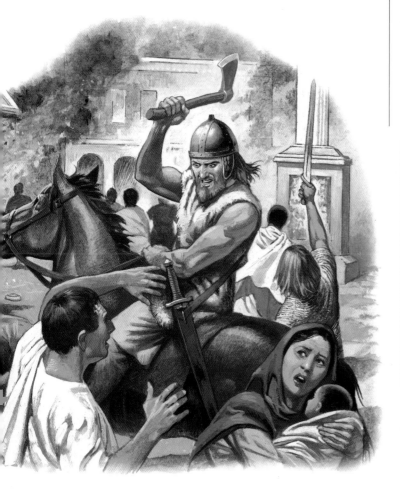

▲ ROMAN RUINS

After the collapse of the Roman Empire many of its impressive buildings, such as this forum, fell into disuse. The stone was removed to construct new buildings, and the roofs were left to rot and fall in.

▲ CHARLEMAGNE

In A.D.768 the Frankish leader Charlemagne began to conquer a vast empire that included modern France, Germany, the Low Countries, and Italy. The new empire reunited western Europe for the first time since the fall of the Roman Empire.

Key Dates

- 264–146B.C. Rome overthrows Carthage after three wars.

- A.D.300s Germanic tribes begin to enter Roman Empire.

- A.D.378 Visigoths defeat Roman army in the Balkans.

- A.D.410 Visigoths ransack Rome.

- A.D.455 Vandals plunder Rome.

- A.D.476 Roman emperor deposed.

- A.D.546 Ostrogoths destroy Rome.

- A.D.768 Charlemagne, Frankish leader, begins to reunite Europe.

- A.D.800 Charlemagne is crowned emperor by the pope in Rome.

The Vikings

▲ BROOCH
Lavishly decorated clasps and brooches made of bronze, silver, and gold were used to hold clothes in place.

T HE VIKINGS SEEMED to come from nowhere. Setting out from Norway and Denmark, they suddenly became a frightening force that dominated the northern seas, from the Atlantic Ocean to the Black Sea. They struck terror into all those they met on land. The records kept by Christian monks describe them as ruthless fighters who plundered towns and slaughtered all the inhabitants. Few towns managed to hold off these ferocious invaders.

The name "Viking" means "men of the creek," and they came from the fjords and lowlands of Scandinavia, in the north of Europe. Although the Vikings have a reputation for cruelty, they were a talented people. They were skilled shipbuilders and navigators and excellent engineers and craftworkers. They had a rich tradition of myths and legends and had worked out a fair system of rules for the way their people lived.

In about A.D.790, parties of Vikings began to leave their homeland, launching their boats into the open sea. No one is quite sure why they began to do this. Some

▼ VIKING SAILORS
Much of the Vikings' homeland was mountainous, with few roads. They used their boats to travel the fjords and the open seas.

historians believe that overcrowding in the country drove out the younger sons, who had nothing to inherit from their fathers. Or perhaps the climate was getting colder and harvests often failed, leading people to search for new sources of food.

Vikings from Norway and Denmark crossed the North Sea to raid Britain, Ireland, and northern France. They ventured across the North Atlantic to Iceland, Greenland, and the east coast of North America. Vikings from Sweden preferred trading with other

THE VIKING WAY OF LIFE

There were three classes of Vikings—slaves, who did most of the work, freemen, and nobles, who were the rulers. Nobles had to obey rules made by the Thing, a local assembly where freemen could discuss these rules. But by about 1050, powerful kings ruled most Viking lands. The Things were no longer so important, and their role gradually declined.

◄ CLOTHES
Clothes were made from wool or flax spun on a vertical loom. Women wore a long dress with a shorter tunic on top. Men typically wore trousers, a shirt, a tunic, and a cloak.

▶ LEIF ERIKSSON
Vikings living in the colony of Greenland heard stories of a flat land to their west covered with trees. In A.D.992 Leif Eriksson set out due west, and found what was probably Baffin Island. He then sailed south past Labrador and Newfoundland, in eastern Canada, to a place he named Vinland, the "land of wine," as he found so many shrubs and wild berries there.

◄ RUNES
The Vikings used an alphabet system based on runes, which were usually carved in wood or on pieces of stone. Calendars, bills, accounts, and even love messages were all written in runic script.

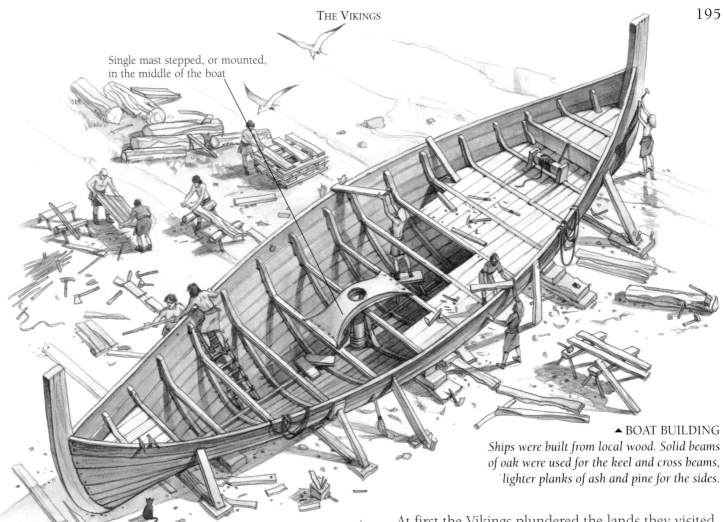

Single mast stepped, or mounted, in the middle of the boat

▲ BOAT BUILDING
Ships were built from local wood. Solid beams of oak were used for the keel and cross beams, lighter planks of ash and pine for the sides.

countries to conquering them. They sailed east, across the Baltic Sea and down the rivers of Russia to the Black Sea and the Mediterranean. They even reached the city of Baghdad on the river Tigris in modern Iraq.

At first the Vikings plundered the lands they visited, taking their booty home. But gradually they started to establish trading posts in places such as Dublin in Ireland and Kiev in Ukraine. Soon they began to marry the local people and settle down. Many converted to Christianity. The Viking raids were over.

Viking routes A.D.800–1100
Eric the Red A.D.982
Leif Eriksson A.D.992

0   Kilometers   3200
0   Miles   2000

▲ VIKING EXPEDITIONS
Viking traders from Sweden sailed down the rivers of Russia. Others sailed around the Atlantic coast into the Mediterranean. Eric the Red was expelled from the Viking colony on Iceland and sailed to Greenland, and Leif Eriksson voyaged to Vinland.

Key Dates

- A.D.793 Vikings attack Lindisfarne Priory in northeast England. It is their first major raid on England.

- A.D.815 Vikings from Norway settle in Iceland.

- A.D.841 Foundation of Dublin.

- A.D.855 Vikings sail up the river Seine in France and raid Paris.

- A.D.911 Vikings settle in Normandy, France.

- A.D.982 Eric the Red begins his epic voyage to Greenland.

- A.D.992 Leif Eriksson leaves Greenland and sails to Vinland.

The Polynesians

▲ PELE GOD
▲ PELE GOD
Polynesians made statues, as here, of dead ancestors, as they thought their spirits became gods.

THE ISLANDS OF THE South Pacific were uninhabited until about 3,000 years ago. Then the first Polynesians arrived to live there. We do not know much about these people. Historians think that they originally came from Asia or America.

Over the next 2,000 years the Polynesians slowly spread out across the vast South Pacific Ocean. They sailed north to Hawaii, east to Easter Island, and, finally, south to New Zealand. They were probably the greatest explorers and navigators in history. When Europeans first visited the region in the 1500s, they got a surprise. They could not believe that the Polynesians, who they thought were a very primitive people, could have developed such advanced skills.

The immense Pacific Ocean is scattered with islands, but these make up only a minute part of its total area and lie hundreds of miles apart from each other. The rest is open sea, and it is easy to sail for days without sighting any land. The Polynesians did not have any maps or modern navigation equipment, but they successfully explored the entire ocean in their sturdy canoes. They settled on almost every island, finding them by following migrating birds and by watching changes in wind direction and wave pattern.

The Polynesians gradually built up a detailed knowledge of where each island was and how they could find it again in the future, using the Sun, Moon, and stars as navigation aids. They gave each island its own "on top" star. Sailors knew that when this was directly over their boat, they were on the same latitude as the island. Using the position of the Sun, they sailed due east or west until they reached land. Sirius, for example, was the "on top" star for Tahiti.

All this information was passed down

▶ GIANT STATUES
Easter Islanders erected 600 giant carved statues across their small island between AD 1000 and 1600. No one knows what these statues were for or how the islanders managed to move and erect the huge stones.

ASIAN OR AMERICAN?
Some historians think that the Polynesians originally came from Southeast Asia, but there are many similarities between the cultures of Polynesia and Peru. One modern explorer from Norway named Thor Heyerdahl set out to prove that Polynesians could have come from South America. He built a raft like those used by early settlers and sailed from Peru to the South Pacific.

▼ THOR HEYERDAHL
Thor Heyerdahl was born in 1914 and studied zoology and geography at college. He became fascinated by Polynesia and lived for two years in Tahiti.

◀ *KON-TIKI*
Thor Heyerdahl's raft was called *Kon-Tiki* after the Peruvian sun god. The god was believed to have migrated to the Pacific islands. The raft measured 45 feet long and 18 feet wide and was made of balsa wood and bamboo.

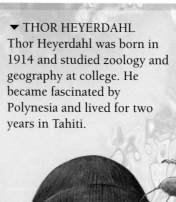

▲ SWEET POTATOES
South Pacific islanders ate sweet potatoes. The plant comes from the Americas, and Heyerdahl thought it might have been taken to Polynesia by settlers from South America.

▼ POLYNESIAN BOAT
Polynesian canoes were up to 100 feet long. They were built with two hulls or a single hull and an outrigger. The sails were made from coconut-palm leaf matting sewn together.

Canoe steered by single oar

Main hull

Outrigger

▲ PACIFIC ISLANDS
There are about 20,000 islands in the Pacific Ocean. Most are either high volcanic peaks or low coral reefs. Apart from New Zealand, the vast majority are small, some only a few miles across.

through the generations and recorded on a chart made of palm sticks tied together with coconut fiber. The framework of sticks represented distance, and shells threaded on the sticks showed where the islands were.

The Polynesians used these simple but effective charts to make accurate voyages across vast expanses of ocean. They took colonists and supplies to newly discovered islands and brought back fish and other goods.

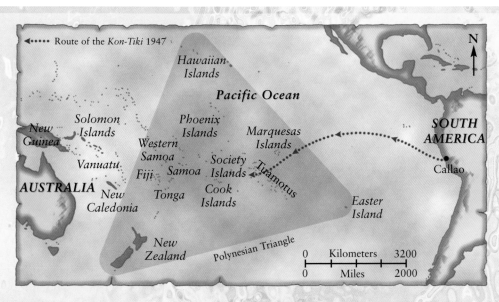

Route of the *Kon-Tiki* 1947

Hawaiian Islands

Pacific Ocean

New Guinea

Solomon Islands

Phoenix Islands

Marquesas Islands

SOUTH AMERICA

Western Samoa

Society Islands

Tuamotus

Callao

Vanuatu

Fiji   Samoa

AUSTRALIA   New Caledonia

Tonga

Cook Islands

Easter Island

New Zealand

Polynesian Triangle

N

0   Kilometers   3200
0   Miles   2000

▲ THOR HEYERDAHL'S VOYAGE
In 1947 *Kon-Tiki* set sail from Peru. It steered westward, making use of the winds and sea currents. After a voyage of 4,290 miles, lasting 101 days, Thor Heyerdahl reached the Tuamotu archipelago in the South Pacific.

Key Dates

- 1000 B.C. Polynesians begin to settle in Tonga and Samoa.

- 150 B.C. Settlers leave Samoa for Marquesas Islands.

- A.D. 400 Polynesians reach Easter Island in the east and the Hawaiian Islands in the north.

- 1000 Polynesian Maoris settle in New Zealand.

- 1000–1600 Statues built on Easter Island.

- 1947 Thor Heyerdahl's *Kon-Tiki* expedition from Peru to the South Pacific.

Crossing the Deserts

IN A.D.622 ARABIA GAVE birth to a new religion called Islam, which soon became the main religion there. Islam was founded by the Prophet Muhammad, who died in A.D.632. Within a few years an Islamic Empire stretched from the Atlantic Ocean across North Africa and the Middle East to the borders of India. Much of the Islamic world was desert, including the Sahara Desert in North Africa, which is the biggest in the world.

▲ THE DESERT
The deserts of North Africa and Arabia are a mixture of rocky plains, sand dunes, and high mountains.

The Arabs dominated the Islamic Empire, conquering other lands. Soldiers and missionaries spread Islam to all the people they conquered. The Arabs were great travelers. Merchants and traders followed the soldiers into the new lands in search of markets to exploit and goods to trade. Scholars and scientists traveled to increase their knowledge of the world. Every Muslim (a believer in Islam) also made a once-in-a-lifetime pilgrimage to the holy city of Mecca in Arabia. As a result, towns and cities were bustling with travelers stopping to rest for the night after a long day's journey. Markets and public places were full of people telling stories about faraway cities and strange lands they had visited.

▲ MUSLIM TRAVEL
Muslim travelers felt at home wherever they went in the Islamic world, since everyone spoke the common language of Arabic and all were followers of Islam. Travelers got a warm welcome at every town.

MUSLIM TRAVELERS

There are many reasons why the Muslims were great travelers. One was because of Islam. It was the duty of all Muslims to make a pilgrimage to the holy city of Mecca. People also traveled on business or because they were curious about other places.

▲ MUSLIM PRAYER CASE
Muslims carried verses from their holy book, the Koran, in prayer cases. These were often carved and decorated.

◀ SALT
Salt occurs naturally throughout the Sahara Desert, and was much prized as a food preservative. Camel trains were used to bring the mineral to the Mediterranean for shipment to Europe.

▼ IBN BATTUTA
Ibn Battuta was born into a wealthy, educated family in Tangier, North Africa, in 1304. After a pilgrimage to Mecca in 1325, he was inspired to devote his life to travel. After his final journey in 1352–53, he recorded his adventures in a book called the *Rihlah*, which means "Travels." He died in 1368.

◀ ARAB DHOW
The main type of ship used by the Arabs for their travels was the dhow. It had one or two masts and a triangular sail bent on to a spar. This was called a lateen sail.

▲ SHIP OF THE DESERT
Camels can travel for many days without food or water. Fat stored in their humps gives them energy when food is scarce.

Many Muslims left records of their travels. One of them, Ibn Battuta, was the greatest traveler of his age. The geographer Al Idrisi (1100–65) used his explorations to produce a book on geography and two large-scale maps of the world. Al Idrisi even sent out scientific expeditions to explore northern Europe and other areas unfamiliar to the Arabs.

At first Arabs avoided the Indian Ocean, calling it the "Sea of Darkness." But then they developed the dhow, a versatile ship that could carry large cargoes, but which needed only a small crew. Astrolabes, quadrants, and other devices were used to navigate. At that time, most European people thought that the world was flat and that it was unsafe to venture far beyond land. The Arabs were sailing across the Indian Ocean to purchase silks and spices from India, Indonesia, and China, and traveling vast distances as traders, pilgrims, or adventurers.

▼ THE TRAVELS OF IBN BATTUTA
Ibn Battuta spent a total of 28 years traveling to find out more about the world. He explored the entire Islamic Empire, as well as much of Europe, Southeast Asia, and China. He covered a total distance of 74,970 miles.

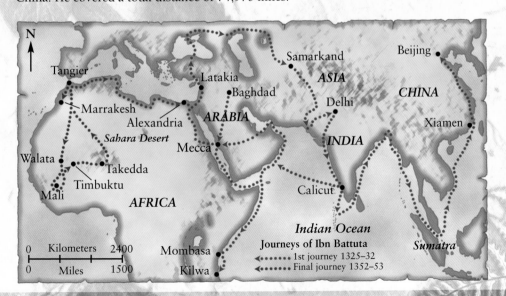

Journeys of Ibn Battuta
•••••• 1st journey 1325–32
•••••• Final journey 1352–53

Key Dates

- A.D.622 Muhammad and his followers flee persecution in Mecca and go to Medina, starting the Islamic religion.

- A.D.632 Death of Muhammad.

- A.D.634–50 Muslims conquer Middle East.

- A.D.650 The Koran (the sacred book of Islam) is written.

- A.D.712 Islamic Empire extends east to Spain and west to India.

- 1200s The dhow sailing boat is developed.

- 1325–53 Ibn Battuta travels around the Islamic world.

The Chinese Empire

▲ PORCELAIN
The Chinese invented a new type of pottery called porcelain. It is very fine and hard, and light can shine through it.

DURING THE 1200s, a new threat emerged from the empty, hostile grasslands or steppes of central Asia. It was the Mongols, a nomadic people who were skilled horsemen and warriors. They conquered most of Asia and eastern Europe in a series of brilliant military campaigns led by their ruler, Genghis Khan, and his successors. Their empire stretched from the eastern frontier of Germany to Korea, and from the Arctic Circle to the Persian Gulf. It was the biggest empire the world had ever seen. Although the Mongols had a reputation for extreme violence, they kept strict law and order throughout their empire and encouraged trade. The main trade link between Europe and Asia—the Silk Road—had fallen into disuse after the collapse of the Roman Empire and the Han dynasty in China. The Silk Road was now in the Mongol Empire. The Mongols made sure that the road was safe to use.

Two Venetian merchants, Niccolò and Maffeo Polo, were among the first traders to travel its entire length. The Mongol ruler of China, Kublai Khan, welcomed

them to his court, as he was fascinated by the foreigners and the mysterious lands they came from. When the Polos returned home, they promised him that they would serve as his envoys to the pope in Rome and would arrange for 100 theologians to go to China to discuss Christianity with Mongol philosophers. Kublai Khan gave them a golden tablet inscribed with the imperial seal to guarantee them good treatment and hospitality while in Mongol territory.

When the Polo brothers returned to China, they took Niccolò's son Marco with them. He served Kublai

▲ VENICE
The port of Venice in Italy was the richest city in Europe in the 1200s. It controlled much of the trade in the Mediterranean. It was from here that the Polo brothers set out on their travels.

CHINESE VOYAGES

In 1368, nearly a century after Marco Polo's amazing reports of the court of Kublai Khan, the Mongols were thrown out of China. To try to restore China's prestige in Asia, the new Ming dynasty sent Admiral Zheng He (1371–1433) on a series of seven diplomatic journeys through the whole region.

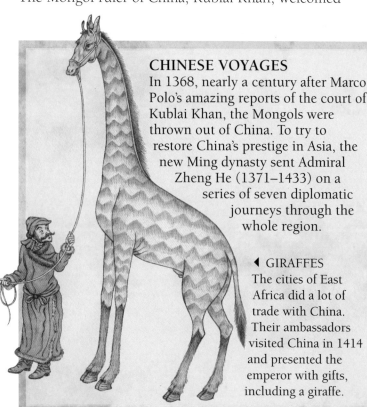

◀ GIRAFFES
The cities of East Africa did a lot of trade with China. Their ambassadors visited China in 1414 and presented the emperor with gifts, including a giraffe.

▲ CHINESE JUNKS
Zheng He commanded a fleet of ocean-going junks. These were two-masted ships that could carry large cargoes. Some junks were five times larger than European ships of the time.

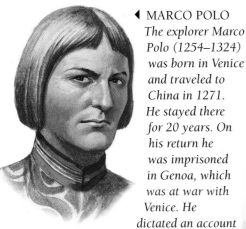

◀ MARCO POLO
The explorer Marco Polo (1254–1324) was born in Venice and traveled to China in 1271. He stayed there for 20 years. On his return he was imprisoned in Genoa, which was at war with Venice. He dictated an account of his travels to a fellow prisoner. Il milione (The Travels) was read throughout Europe.

Khan for the next 20 years and traveled throughout eastern Asia. When Marco Polo returned to Europe, he wrote a book about his epic journeys. He described the fabulous court of Kublai Khan, and he praised the artistic and technological achievements of Mongol China. However, some modern scholars believe that Marco Polo did not go to China but wrote his book after reading other people's reports.

▲ KUBLAI KHAN
The Mongol ruler of China, Kublai Khan, was a highly intelligent and civilized man. His summer palace at Shangdu, where he welcomed the Polos to China, and his court in Cambaluc (Beijing) were both magnificent buildings.

▼ MARCO POLO'S ROUTE
In 1271 the Polo family set out from Europe along the Silk Road, taking over three years to reach China. There they stayed for 20 years, while Marco traveled around the vast Mongol Empire. They returned to Europe across the Indian Ocean in 1295.

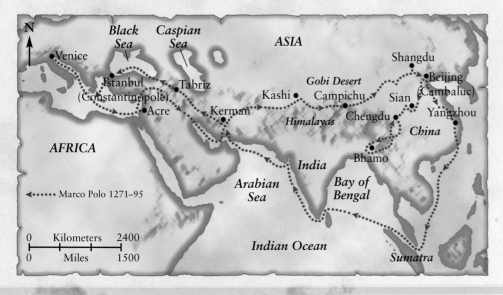

N

Venice • Black Sea • Caspian Sea • ASIA
Shangdu
Istanbul (Constantinople) • Tabriz • Gobi Desert • Beijing (Cambaluc)
Acre • Kashi • Campichu • Sian
Kerman • Himalayas • Chengdu • Yangzhou
AFRICA • China
India • Bhamo
Marco Polo 1271–95 • Arabian Sea • Bay of Bengal

0 Kilometers 2400
0 Miles 1500

Indian Ocean • Sumatra

Key Dates

- 1211 Genghis Khan begins invasion of China.

- 1234 Mongols overrun northern China.

- 1260–94 Mongol leader Kublai Khan rules China.

- 1261–69 Polo brothers travel to China.

- 1271–95 Marco Polo travels throughout the Mongol Empire.

- 1368 Mongols thrown out of China by the Ming dynasty.

- 1405–33 Zheng He leads seven expeditions to Southeast Asia and Indian Ocean.

Travelers in Europe

▲ CITY OF DANZIG
The ship on Danzig's official seal shows membership of the Hanseatic League, a network of trading cities in northern Europe.

TODAY WE KNOW OF Europe as a busy place with a huge population. However, a thousand years ago Europe was a very different place indeed.

In the year 1000 the total population of western Europe was fewer than 30 million, which is about half that of modern France. Only a handful of cities, including Paris, Milan, and Florence, had more than 40,000 people. Most had fewer than 10,000 inhabitants. Roads were rough and uneven, and much of the countryside was covered in thick forests. Bandits lay in wait to rob travelers. Yet despite these problems, a surprising number of people ran the risk of getting lost or being robbed and took to the roads.

Pilgrims journeyed in great numbers to holy sites, such as the shrine of St. James in Santiago de Compostela, northern Spain. Some went even farther afield, to Jerusalem in the Middle East. Armies of Crusaders assembled to reconquer the Holy Land from its Muslim occupiers. National armies marched off to fight wars on behalf of their kings. Merchants and traders traveled from town to town, buying and selling goods at the increasing number of trade fairs held in northern France, Germany, and Flanders (Belgium). Government and church administrators moved from town to town on official business. Scholars often passed

▼ PILGRIMAGES
Pilgrims traveled to the great religious shrines in large groups, telling each other stories and singing songs to pass the time.

THE CRUSADES
Between 1095 and 1444, armies of Christian knights went to Palestine in the Muslim Empire. They intended to secure the Christian holy places against Muslim control. The First Crusade successfully captured Jerusalem. In 1291, the last Crusader stronghold was lost. Later Crusades all ended in failure.

◀ THE CRUSADERS
Crusading knights and soldiers were inspired by religious devotion. They also followed a code of conduct called chivalry, which meant that they pledged to be brave and loyal to their lord and to protect women.

▲ RICHARD I
Many kings and princes joined the Crusades. Richard I of England (ruled 1289–99) took part in the Third Crusade.

▼ HEIDELBERG
Heidelberg and other fortified towns throughout Germany were good centers for recruiting men for the Crusades. All types of people went, commoners and knights, to spread Christianity through the Holy Land.

from one university to another for their studies. Craftworkers and builders made their way to the cities where new cathedrals were being built.

Most people traveled on foot or, if they were rich, on horseback, but progress was slow, and it could take up to a week to travel 100 miles. Every night they stopped at village inns. Yet travelers were a small minority of the population. The vast majority of people never left the place where they were born. For them, the next town was like a foreign land.

▲ HERRING
The coastal cities of northern Europe, especially Amsterdam and Lübeck, grew rich from fishing. Salted herring and other fish were sent to markets in England and Flanders in exchange for wool, cloth, pewter, and other goods.

◄ MARKETS
Every town had a regular market, where local agricultural produce was bought and sold. Some of these markets developed into large commercial trade fairs. Merchants from all over Europe would come to trade in goods from Europe, the Arab world, and Asia.

▼ KRAK DES CHEVALIERS
The Crusaders built castles throughout Palestine to secure their conquests against Muslim invaders. The most impressive was Krak des Chevaliers, which is in present-day Syria. It eventually surrendered to Muslim armies in 1271.

Key Dates

- 1095 Pope Urban II calls for a Crusade to defend the Church.

- 1099 Crusaders capture Jerusalem and set up Crusader kingdoms throughout Palestine.

- 1187 Muslim leader Saladin retakes Jerusalem and overruns most of the Crusader kingdoms.

- 1189–92 Third Crusade recaptures Acre from Saladin.

- 1241 Hamburg and Lübeck set up the Hanseatic League.

- 1291 Acre, the last Crusader stronghold in Palestine, is lost.

- 1444 Final Crusade.

The Portuguese

▲ DA GAMA
In May 1498 the Portuguese navigator Vasco da Gama (1460–1524) became the first European to reach India by sea.

PORTUGAL IS ON THE EXTREME west of Europe, facing the Atlantic Ocean. The Portuguese relied on the sea to give them a living. Traditionally, they had fished and traded northward along the Atlantic coast with France and Britain. But during the 1400s they turned their attention south and started looking at Africa.

The Portuguese wanted to explore Africa for two main reasons. They aimed to convert the Moors (the Muslim people of North Africa) to Christianity. They were also going to search for gold and other riches. To do this they needed better ships than the inshore, open boats they usually sailed. They developed the caravel, which was able to withstand the storms and strong currents out at sea.

Caravels allowed the Portuguese to venture farther and farther from their own shores. Expeditions boldly set off down the African coast, erecting *padrãoes*, or stone pillars with a Christian cross on the top, to mark their progress. By 1441 they had reached Cape Blanc in what is now Mauritania. By 1475 they had sailed

▲ CARAVEL
The development of the small but sturdy caravel enabled the Portuguese to leave coastal waters and venture out into the open seas. A caravel was about 65 feet long and held a crew of 25.

around West Africa and along the coast to the Gold Coast (Ghana) and Cameroon.

By now the Portuguese had an extra reason to voyage south. In 1453 the Ottoman Turks had captured the Christian city of Constantinople, which was the gateway to Asia, and closed the Silk Road to China. Europeans needed to find a new way to get to the wealth of the East. In 1482 Diego Cāo was the first

NAVIGATION
The first sailors navigated by sailing along the coast from one landmark to the next. Once out of sight of land, they could not do this! Portuguese sailors learned how to use the positions of the Sun and stars to calculate where they were. With the aid of compasses, astrolabes, quadrants, sand glasses, and nocturnals, they were able to navigate over long distances with increasing accuracy.

◀ PRINCE HENRY "THE NAVIGATOR"
Prince Henry (1394–1460) was the son of King John I of Portugal. He was keenly interested in the sea and supported many voyages of exploration. He set up a school of navigation, astronomy, and cartography (mapmaking) to educate captains and pilots. These skills enabled Portuguese sailors to explore the coast of Africa.

▶ SAND GLASS
Sailors told the time with a sand glass. The sand took 30 minutes to run to the bottom and it was then turned over. To calculate the ship's speed, they floated a knotted rope beside the ship, and worked out how long it took to pass each knot.

▲ NOCTURNAL
The old way of telling the time, by the position of the Sun, did not work at night. The development of the nocturnal during the 1550s solved this problem. By lining it up with the Pole Star and two stars close to it, sailors could tell the time to within ten minutes.

European to cross the Equator. On his second voyage in 1485–86 he sailed as far south as the Namib Desert. He thought that the African coast was endless and that there was no way round it toward Asia. But in 1487–88 Bartolomeu Dias proved him wrong when he sailed around the stormy Cape of Good Hope into the Indian Ocean. He was the first Portuguese explorer to enter these waters. Although Dias wanted to go on, his exhausted crew made him turn back. Ten years later Vasco da Gama achieved the Portuguese dream. He rounded the tip of Africa with a fleet of four ships. After sailing up the east coast, he headed across the Indian Ocean. In May 1498 he arrived in the busy trading port of Calicut in the south of India. He had discovered a new route to Asia.

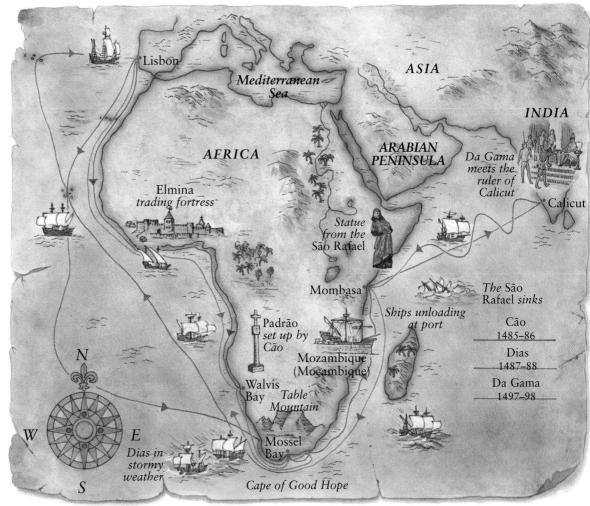

▲ THE ROUTE TO INDIA

By slowly mapping the coast of Africa, the Portuguese discovered a route that took them around the Cape of Good Hope to East Africa and then, using the westerly winds, across the ocean to India. Once the coast was mapped, later voyages could take a more direct route.

▶ USING A COMPASS

The magnetic compass was developed by both the Chinese and the Arabs. It was first used in Europe during the 1200s. By lining up the compass with the magnetic North Pole, sailors could tell which direction they were sailing in. However, early compasses were often unreliable and were easily affected by other iron objects on board ship. As a result, many ships headed off in the wrong direction. By the time of Henry the Navigator in the 1400s, compasses were much improved.

Key Dates

- 1419 Prince Henry establishes a school of navigation.

- 1420s First voyages south to southern Morocco.

- 1475 Portuguese sailors map the African coast from Morocco to Cameroon.

- 1482 Diego Cão crosses over the Equator.

- 1485–86 Diego Cão sails south to Namibia.

- 1487–88 Bartolomeu Dias sails around Cape of Good Hope.

- 1497–98 Vasco da Gama sails around Africa to India.

Christopher Columbus

▲ COLUMBUS
Christopher Columbus (1451–1506) was born in the Italian port of Genoa. He was named after St. Christopher, the patron saint of travelers. His discoveries included Cuba and the Bahamas.

FOR CENTURIES EUROPEANS believed that the world consisted of just three continents—Europe, Africa, and Asia. They thought that the whole of the rest of the world was covered by sea.

The traditional route to Asia had always been overland along the Silk Road. During the 1400s, the Portuguese discovered a way of getting there by sea, sailing south and east around the coast of Africa. Then an Italian named Christopher Columbus worked out that it should be possible to get to Asia by sailing west, across the great Atlantic Ocean.

Columbus devoted his life to finding this sea route to the riches of Asia. At first, people thought that it was a stupid idea, and Columbus could not get any support. But in 1492 Queen Isabella of Spain agreed to give him money to make the voyage on behalf of Spain. He set out with three ships in August 1492, and after 36 days landed in what we now call the Bahamas. Sailing southeast, he passed Cuba and Hispaniola (present-day Haiti) before returning home in triumph in March 1493.

▼ LANDING IN AMERICA
When Columbus and his crew landed on Watling Island in the Bahamas, he claimed the island for Spain and renamed it San Salvador "in honor of God who guided us and saved us from many perils."

Columbus was convinced that he had found a new route to Asia. Although he was disappointed that the new lands were not full of gold, he set off again later in the year to confirm the discoveries of his first voyage.

Columbus made four voyages west across the Atlantic, establishing Spanish colonies on the islands he passed and claiming the region for Spain. Right up to

THE NEW WORLD?
The lands visited by Columbus disappointed him, for he did not find the walled cities and fabulous wealth of China and Japan that he expected. Yet he remained convinced that he had sailed to Asia and never realized that what he had discovered was a continent previously unknown to Europeans.

◄ FERDINAND AND ISABELLA
When Ferdinand of Aragon married Isabella of Castile in 1469, Spain became a united country for the first time since the Roman Empire. Isabella sponsored Columbus's first voyage.

◄ NATIVE AMERICANS
The Arawak peoples of the West Indies lived off the abundant fruits and berries of the islands. They lived in shelters that they built out of palm leaves and branches. Most people did not wear anything, although some wore clothes for ceremonies.

▼ TOBACCO
While in Cuba, Columbus saw the Arawak people roll the dried leaves of the tobacco plant into a tube, set light to it, and smoke it. Smoking soon became a popular pastime throughout Europe. Below you can see tobacco leaves being dried in a shed.

▲ COCONUT PALMS
During his travels, Columbus saw many crops unknown to Europeans, including coconuts, pineapples, potatoes, and corn.

▼ THE *SANTA MARIA*
Columbus's flagship was the Santa Maria, a three-masted, square-rigged cargo ship capable of holding up to 40 crew. The other two ships, the Niña and Pinta, were much smaller.

his death in 1506, he remained convinced that he had sailed to Asia, although he failed to find proof. Because he had sailed west, the new islands he had come across became known as the West Indies.

Few people accepted his claims. In 1502 Amerigo Vespucci (1451–1512) returned to Europe from an expedition down the east coast of South America. He was certain that the lands were not part of Asia but part of a continent unknown to Europeans. He called it *Mundus Novus*—the New World. In 1507 a German geographer, Martin Waldseemüller, renamed it America in honor of Amerigo Vespucci. What Columbus had actually discovered was of far greater importance than a lengthy sea route to Asia. By sailing west, he had stumbled upon the American continent. As a result, within a few years the history of both America and Europe was completely transformed.

▼ THE VOYAGES OF COLUMBUS
Over the course of four voyages, Columbus sailed around most of the Caribbean islands and explored the coasts of South and Central America, believing that he had discovered a new route to Asia.

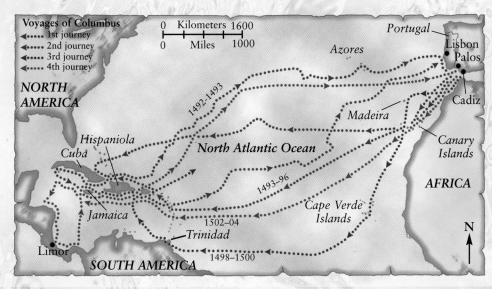

Key Dates

- 1492–93 Columbus makes his first voyage to the West Indies, finding the Bahamas, Cuba, and Hispaniola.

- 1493–96 His second voyage takes him throughout the West Indies. He builds settlements on Hispaniola and explores Jamaica.

- 1498–1500 On the third voyage he sails between Trinidad and South America and is the first European to land in South America.

- 1502–04 Fourth voyage, along the coast of Central America.

Conquering the New World

▲ KNIFE
The Aztecs were skilled craftworkers. They used wood inlaid with gems and pieces of shell and turquoise to make the handle of this sacrificial knife. This knife was given as a gift to Hernán Cortés.

IN THE YEARS AFTER THE HISTORIC voyages of Columbus a wave of Spanish explorers descended on Central and South America. They were searching for treasure.

Vasco de Balboa (1475–1519) was one of these adventurers. He was a colonist living in Hispaniola (Haiti), who fled to Central America to escape his debts. In September 1513 he set off into the interior of the country in search of gold. Twenty-seven days later he gazed westward across a vast sea, becoming the first European to look at the eastern shore of the Pacific Ocean.

In November 1518 a second expedition left the Spanish colony of Santiago in Cuba, bound for Mexico. Previous expeditions had reported that there were vast temples and huge amounts of gold there. The 11 ships and 780 men were commanded by Hernán Cortés, a Spanish lawyer who had gone to the West Indies to seek his fortune. Cortés sailed along the coast for some months, raiding local towns and gaining valuable intelligence, then set off inland to the Aztec capital of Tenochtitlán.

Although the Aztecs were immensely skilled people, they were no match for the Spanish. The Aztecs had no gunpowder, and horses were unknown in the Americas. Cortés enlisted the help of the Aztecs' many enemies, then entered the city and captured its ruler, Montezuma. Cortés finally secured Tenochtitlán in August 1521, with only 400 men. The mighty Aztec Empire now became the province of New Spain.

Soon, rumors began to circulate about another rich empire, this time in South America. In 1530 Francisco Pizarro set out to conquer it with only 168 soldiers. The Inca Empire he found was weakened by civil war and an epidemic (probably smallpox). Once again, the Spanish soldiers overwhelmed the enemy. By 1532 the vast Inca Empire was defeated and its huge reserves of gold and silver were now under Spanish control.

◄ MONTEZUMA'S HEADDRESS
The Aztecs and Incas hunted tropical birds for their feathers. The quetzal's bright green feathers were highly prized and used in the headdress of Montezuma, the last Aztec ruler.

THE INCAS

The Incas were a hill tribe from Peru. Over the course of 300 years, they came to dominate the whole of the Andes mountains. By 1500 their empire stretched nearly 2,500 miles. Although they had no wheeled transportation, they built a huge network of roads and large cities of stone. They seem to have had no alphabet, so could not read or write. Despite this, their civilization was as advanced as any in Europe. The Incas were overthrown by Pizarro's small army.

▲ PIZARRO
The Spaniard Francisco Pizarro (1475–1541) went to the Americas to seek his fortune. He was spectacularly successful, crushing the powerful Inca Empire.

▶ QUIPU
Special officials kept records of taxation, population figures, and other statistics on quipus. A quipu is a series of vertical knotted strings, of varying length and color, that hang from a horizontal cord. The length and color of each string, its position, and the type of knot record the information.

◄ GOLD LLAMA
Llamas were valued by the Incas for their meat and wool and as beasts of burden. Gold figurines were made to show their importance.

◀ TENOCHTITLAN
The Aztecs' capital city had a population of 200,000, more than in any Spanish city, yet Cortés and his 400 men managed to capture it using trickery and deceit.

Cortés, Pizarro, and the other adventurers were *conquistadores,* which means conquerors in Spanish. The conquistadores were brutal and often dishonest. They went in search of wealth and to convert everyone they met to Christianity. Their conquests stretched the length of the Americas, from Mexico to Chile. Within 50 years of the expedition by Columbus, the Americas were under European control.

▶ MACHU PICCHU
The Incas established the city of Machu Picchu in a strategic position, protected by the steep slopes of the Andes Mountains. It was built of stone blocks fitted together without mortar. Temples, ceremonial places, and houses made up the 143 buildings. The city was so remote that the Spanish failed to discover it, and it was forgotten until an American explorer found it in 1911. It is located in south Peru.

Key Dates

- 1100s Incas start to dominate central Peru.

- 1325 Aztecs found the city of Tenochtitlán.

- 1430 Incas begin to expand north along the Andes.

- 1450s Incas build Machu Picchu.

- 1500 Aztec and Inca empires at their greatest extent and power.

- 1513 Vasco de Balboa first sees Pacific Ocean.

- 1521 Spanish capture Tenochtitlán and take over the Aztec Empire.

- 1532 Inca Empire conquered and under Spanish control.

Around the World

▲ FERDINAND MAGELLAN
Magellan (1480–1521) was a Portuguese sailor who quarreled with the Portuguese king and left the country in 1514 to work for the King of Spain. His round-the-world fleet sailed under the Spanish flag.

EUROPEAN NATIONS WERE entranced by stories about the vast wealth of Asia. Travelers and merchants told of treasures in India, China, Japan, and the spice-rich islands off their coasts. Throughout the 1500s sailors made epic voyages to seek out new routes to this wealth.

After the voyages of the Portuguese to the Indian Ocean and Columbus to America, Spain and Portugal made the Treaty of Tordesillas in 1494. The two countries divided the undiscovered world between them. They drew a line on a map and agreed that everything to the west of it was the property of Spain and everything to the east belonged to Portugal. South America was cut in half by the line.

Spanish explorers still wanted to find a new route to Asia by going west, as Columbus had tried to do. Columbus had discovered America when he went west, although he thought it was Asia. His successors had to find a way around America in order to get to Asia. In 1519 Ferdinand Magellan left Spain with five ships and 260 men to find a route to the rich Spice Islands (the

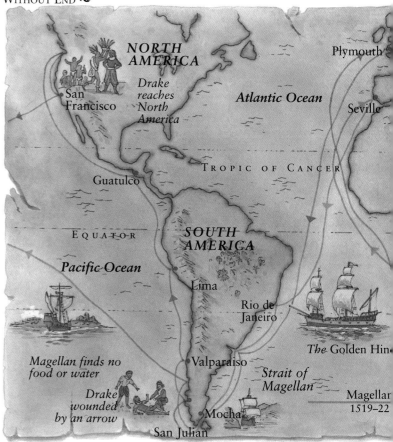

Moluccas, now part of Indonesia). In 1520 he sailed through the straits at the tip of South America and into the Pacific Ocean. He sailed northwest and in 1521 reached the Philippine Islands.

Magellan never reached the Spice Islands, because he was killed in a skirmish in April 1521. But one of his ships managed to get there. The *Victoria* was captained

PRIVATEERS AND PIRATES

Treasure ships heading for Spain laden with riches were soon noticed by Spain's main enemies, France and England. In wartime, both nations allowed privately owned ships (known as privateers) to attack Spanish ships and keep the booty. However, privateers often attacked in peacetime. Illegal pirate ships also joined in. Spain considered everyone who attacked one of its ships to be a pirate.

▲ JOLLY ROGER
During the 1600s, pirate ships began to fly the Jolly Roger—a black flag with a skull and crossbones on it— to show other ships their hostile intent. Each pirate ship had its own flag, but the most feared was the plain red flag, which meant death to every sailor who resisted a pirate takeover.

▼ DOUBLOONS
The Spanish mined precious gold and silver in the Americas. Some was made into coins to take to Spain. Gold was minted into doubloons, silver into pieces of eight.

▶ PIRATES
Pirates faced death if they were captured. Escaped slaves and convicts often became pirates. When they were attacked by a pirate ship, sailors often joined the pirates, hoping to get rich.

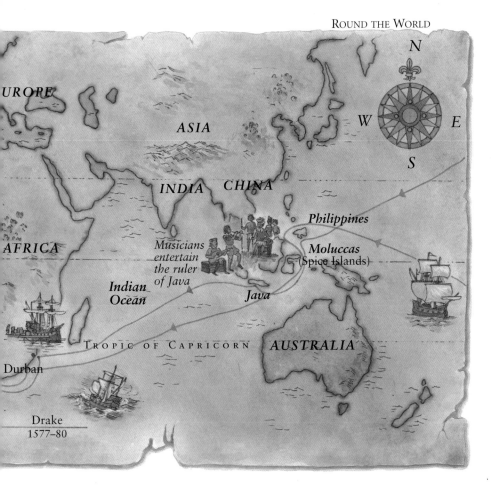

Durban

Drake
1577–80

◀ AROUND THE WORLD
Both Magellan and Drake sailed in a westerly direction. From Europe their voyages took them to the south Atlantic Ocean, around Cape Horn, across the Pacific and Indian oceans, then back via the Cape of Good Hope and Atlantic.

▲ THE *GOLDEN HIND*
Francis Drake's flagship, the Golden Hind, *was originally called the* Pelican. *It had three masts and was the largest of the five ships in the fleet.*

by Juan de Elcano (1476–1526). When the crew reached the Spice Islands they loaded the ship with spices and headed home across the Indian Ocean.

In trying to find a westerly route to the Spice Islands, Magellan and his sailors had inadvertently become the first people to circumnavigate the Earth. Others followed Magellan. Francis Drake (1543–96)

was an English seafarer and pirate with a successful record of raiding Spanish ships. In 1577 he set off to explore the Pacific Ocean, attacking Spanish treasure ships and collecting their gold as he went. In the Spice Islands he bought about 6 tons of valuable cloves. When he returned to England, this treasure was worth about $16 million in today's money.

▶ SPICES
Spices were highly valued in Europe for flavoring meat after it had been salted to preserve it, as well as for adding flavor to other foods and drinks. Cloves, nutmeg, cinnamon, pepper, and other spices all grew wild in the Far East. They had also been cultivated for centuries and were sold in markets as they are today.

cloves

cinnamon

Key Dates

- 1519–21 Magellan sails from Spain to the Philippines across the Pacific Ocean.

- 1521–22 Juan de Elcano completes the first circumnavigation of the world.

- 1520s First treasure ships bring Aztec gold back to Spain.

- 1545 Silver discovered in vast Potosí mine in Bolivia. It was the world's biggest single source of silver for the next 100 years.

- 1545 Major silver mine opened in Zacatecas, Mexico.

- 1577–80 Drake is the second person to sail around the world.

Into Canada

▲ JOHN CABOT
The adventurer John Cabot (1450–99) was probably born in Genoa in Italy. He traded in spices with the Arabs before moving to England.

IN ABOUT 1494 AN ITALIAN merchant named John Cabot arrived in England. Like Columbus, he planned to sail west across the Atlantic in search of the Spice Islands of eastern Asia. However, he proposed to make the voyage at a more northerly latitude, making the journey shorter. Cabot needed to find someone to finance his trip. After rejection by the kings of both Spain and Portugal, Cabot took his idea to King Henry VII of England. Henry had previously refused to sponsor Columbus. This time he was aware of the riches of the New World and was eager to support Cabot so that he could profit from any discoveries.

In May 1497 Cabot set sail from Bristol on board the *Matthew*. A month later he landed in Newfoundland, off the east coast of Canada, which he claimed for England. He had not found Asia, nor had he found wealth, but he had discovered rich fishing grounds and lands not yet claimed by Spain.

The French set out to explore these new lands. In 1534 Jacques Cartier (1491–1557) sailed from St. Malo. Like Cabot, he too was searching for a new, northerly route to Asia. He sailed around the mouth of the great St. Lawrence River, and the following year he returned to sail up it to present-day Montreal. He struck up good relations with the Huron Indians who lived there, who told him about the riches of the kingdom of Saguenay, farther west up the St. Lawrence. In 1541 Cartier decided to return to find Saguenay. But not surprisingly he failed to do so, because Saguenay was an imaginary place. The Hurons had made up the story about this marvelous

◀ MONTREAL
When Cartier sailed up the St. Lawrence River in 1535, he got as far as the wooden-walled Huron village of Hochelaga. Cartier climbed the hill behind it, naming it Mont Réal (Mount Royal), the present-day Montreal.

NATIVE AMERICANS
Numerous tribes of Native Americans lived in the woods and plains of the St. Lawrence valley. Five of the main tribes—the Mohawk, Onondaga, Seneca, Oneida, and Cayuga—joined together to form the Iroquois League in the early 1600s to protect themselves from other powerful tribes in the area.

▼ FUR TRADE
The rivers and woods of Canada teemed with wildlife, providing furs for clothing and meat for food. Animal pelts, particularly from the seal, otter, and beaver, were prized by the Europeans. They traded guns and other goods to obtain the skins from the Native Americans.

◀ A HURON BRAVE
The Hurons welcomed the French to North America, trading furs and other goods with them and acting as guides and advisers. They also enlisted the French to help fight their wars with the Iroquois, who were their deadly enemies.

▲ A SCALP
Fierce warfare between the different tribes was common. The most important trophy a brave could win in battle was the scalp of his opponent. Skin and hair were removed in one piece and then displayed on a wooden frame.

▶ QUEBEC

When Champlain visited Canada in 1608, he built a wooden fort on a hill overlooking the St. Lawrence River at a point where it narrowed considerably. The Native Americans called the place Kebec, and today it is known as Quebec.

Balcony for strategic lookout

Cannon positioned for quick firing

Bridge for crossing the St. Lawrence

Fort built of wood

kingdom, full of treasures, to please their French visitors!

Fur traders and fishermen followed Cartier's route up the St. Lawrence. But it was not until the next century that the French abandoned their search for a new route to Asia and began to settle in Canada. Samuel de Champlain (1567–1635) explored the east coast of North America and went inland as far as the Great Lakes. In 1608 he founded the city of Quebec, the first permanent French settlement in North America. The continent was now open for European colonization.

▼ EXPLORING CANADA

After John Cabot's exploratory voyage in 1497, the Frenchmen Jacques Cartier and Samuel de Champlain explored the valley of the St. Lawrence River and claimed the region for France. Champlain founded the city of Quebec.

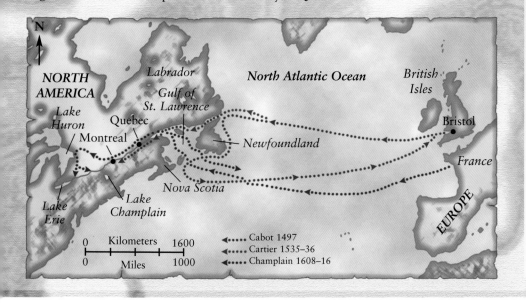

NORTH AMERICA
Labrador
Gulf of St. Lawrence
Lake Huron
Quebec
Montreal
Newfoundland
Nova Scotia
Lake Erie
Lake Champlain
North Atlantic Ocean
British Isles
Bristol
France
EUROPE

| 0 | Kilometers | 1600 |
| 0 | Miles | 1000 |

◄···· Cabot 1497
◄···· Cartier 1535–36
◄···· Champlain 1608–16

Key Dates

- 1497 John Cabot claims Newfoundland for England.

- 1534 Jacques Cartier explores St. Lawrence estuary in Canada.

- 1535–36 Cartier sails up St. Lawrence as far as Montreal.

- 1603 Champlain sails up the St. Lawrence to Montreal.

- 1604 Champlain explores from Nova Scotia to Cape Cod.

- 1608–09 Champlain founds settlement of Quebec.

- 1615 Champlain explores Lakes Huron and Ontario.

The Northwest Passage

▲ POLAR BEARS
Polar bears were a constant threat to Arctic explorers, although their meat was a useful supplement to rations.

WHEN SPAIN AND Portugal divided up the undiscovered world between them in 1494, other European nations were prevented from sailing to Asia around the south of Africa or America. The Pope had split the world between Spain and Portugal, whose ships stopped British and Dutch traders from sailing south across the Atlantic. The only way left for the British and Dutch was to sail around the top of the world. For more than 300 years, explorers had tried to find a route through the Arctic Ocean, either around Canada, or around Siberia. Their efforts, however, proved fruitless.

In 1576 Queen Elizabeth I of England sent Martin Frobisher off to find a northwest passage to China. He reached Baffin Island, then returned home with rocks of gold. These turned out to be iron pyrites, or "fool's gold," and had no value.

The Englishman Henry Hudson was an experienced navigator who discovered a big river on the east coast of America in 1609. It was named the Hudson River after him. But he could not find a northwest passage either.

In 1610 he sailed his ship *Discovery* around northern Canada before heading south toward what he hoped would be the Pacific Ocean. In fact it turned out to be the vast but landlocked bay now called Hudson Bay. His crew refused to continue and mutinied, setting Hudson and the loyal members of his crew adrift in an open boat.

Over the next two centuries, a number of expeditions mapped the north coast of Canada but failed to make much headway through the maze of Arctic islands. Interest in the project faded. Then in 1817 the British government offered a prize of £20,000 to whoever could find a northwest passage. Many explorers set out but failed to find it. In 1844 the British Royal Navy organized a big expedition led by

▲ THE ARCTIC
The seas to the north of Canada are filled with islands. Between them are narrow channels which freeze solid every winter and are full of floating pack ice and icebergs during the short summer.

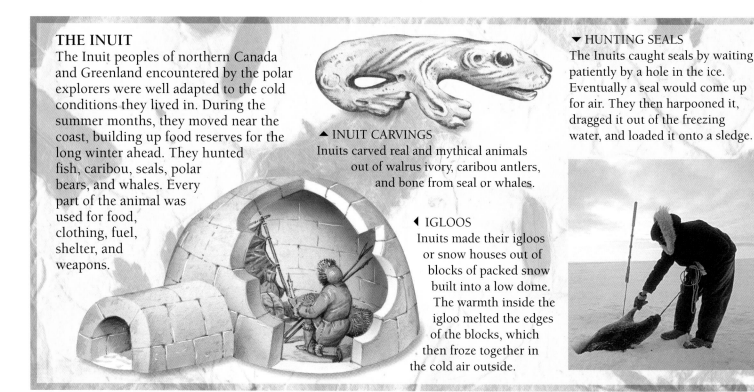

THE INUIT
The Inuit peoples of northern Canada and Greenland encountered by the polar explorers were well adapted to the cold conditions they lived in. During the summer months, they moved near the coast, building up food reserves for the long winter ahead. They hunted fish, caribou, seals, polar bears, and whales. Every part of the animal was used for food, clothing, fuel, shelter, and weapons.

▲ INUIT CARVINGS
Inuits carved real and mythical animals out of walrus ivory, caribou antlers, and bone from seal or whales.

◀ IGLOOS
Inuits made their igloos or snow houses out of blocks of packed snow built into a low dome. The warmth inside the igloo melted the edges of the blocks, which then froze together in the cold air outside.

▼ HUNTING SEALS
The Inuits caught seals by waiting patiently by a hole in the ice. Eventually a seal would come up for air. They then harpooned it, dragged it out of the freezing water, and loaded it onto a sledge.

◄ MUTINY
In June 1611 the crew of Hudson's ship Discovery *mutinied in Hudson Bay. They put Hudson, his son and his loyal crew in an open boat with no oars. They were left to die.*

John Franklin. But he fell victim to the extreme cold and died in 1847, along with all his men.

Over the next decade, more than 40 expeditions went to look for Franklin. In 1859 the last message he left was found on King William Island. Some of those ships found the Northwest Passage, although none sailed through it. It was not until 1906 that the Norwegian polar explorer Roald Amundsen sailed from east to west along the north coast of Canada to the Pacific Ocean. By then, Spain and Portugal no longer controlled the southern seas, and the Panama and Suez canals were open for international shipping. The Northwest Passage was now just a long stretch of icy, treacherous water and of no commercial or political interest whatsoever.

▼ THE NORTHWEST PASSAGE

It took more than 300 years for explorers to navigate the Northwest Passage, and many died in the attempt. Finally, Roald Amundsen succeeded in 1906. By that time, there were easier ways of getting to Asia.

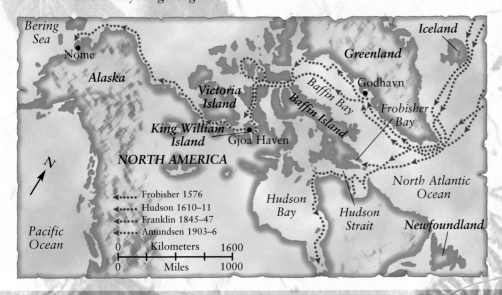

Frobisher 1576
Hudson 1610–11
Franklin 1845–47
Amundsen 1903–6

Key Dates

- 1576 Martin Frobisher lands on Baffin Island and returns to England with rocks that he thinks are gold.

- 1610–11 Henry Hudson explores the vast, inland Hudson Bay, but his crew mutiny and return home without him.

- 1845–47 John Franklin tries to find a northwest passage but perishes in the attempt.

- 1903–06 Norwegian Roald Amundsen makes the first successful voyage along the Northwest Passage.

The Northeast Passage

▲ SEALS
Siberian peoples and explorers seeking the Northeast Passage, hunted seals for food. Their skins also had many uses.

WHILE ENGLISH SAILORS concentrated on finding a northwest passage around the north of Canada, the Dutch were seeking a northeast passage to the north of Russia and Siberia. The Dutch were good sailors, and their fishing and whaling fleets regularly sailed in the Arctic Ocean, but even so they were unsure whether a northeast passage really did exist.

The Dutch followed in the wake of the Englishman Hugh Willoughby (1510–54), who had succeeded in sailing as far as the large island of Novaya Zemlya. But on his return journey, he perished in the pack ice off Murmansk on the Kola Peninsula.

In 1594 the Dutch mariner Willem Barents (1550–97) set sail on the first of his expeditions to find the Northeast Passage. He too was unsuccessful, although on his third voyage in 1596 he discovered Bear Island, which got its name after his crew had a fight with a polar bear. He also found the rich fishing grounds of the Spitsbergen archipelago, which was to become hugely profitable for Dutch hunters of whales, seals, and walruses. Then Barents's ship became trapped and damaged by the winter pack ice. He set off to row

▲ SIBERIA
The northern coast of Siberia lies inside the Arctic Circle. Here the temperature barely reaches above freezing point in summer and drops far below it in winter. Little grows in such an inhospitable landscape, although animals such as reindeer live there.

and sail the 1,590 miles to Kola, but died of starvation at sea. His crew survived and managed to return home once the ship was free.

After the failure of Barents's trip, there were no more expeditions until the Russian explorer Semyon Dezhnev (1605–72) sailed around the eastern tip of Siberia into the Pacific Ocean, proving that Asia and America were not joined. This knowledge did not reach Europe for

THE ARCTIC OCEAN
Although the waters north of Siberia do not freeze over as much as those north of Canada, the Arctic Ocean is still a harsh place. The ice-free summer months are short, and ships risk being caught and trapped in pack ice during the winter, which can last for up to nine months.

◀ THE *VEGA*
The 300-ton *Vega* was built in Germany as a whaling ship. It was constructed of oak with an outer skin of tougher wood to protect it against the ice. The ship had sails and a powerful steam engine. Nils Nordenskjöld made the first successful transit of the Northeast Passage in it during 1878–79.

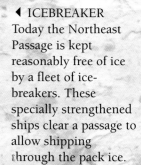

◀ ICEBREAKER
Today the Northeast Passage is kept reasonably free of ice by a fleet of ice-breakers. These specially strengthened ships clear a passage to allow shipping through the pack ice.

▶ WHALES
The first people to explore the Arctic Ocean were whalers (whale hunters) from ports in northern Europe. They sailed the ocean in reinforced ships. Whales were caught for their meat, blubber, and bone.

Icicles hanging on the bunk beds

Chimney to escape through if snow blocked the door

Turkish bath made of a barrel

◀ AN ARCTIC SHELTER
In the winter of 1596 the ship of Barents and his crew of 20 men was trapped by ice in the Arctic. The men survived by building a hut out of driftwood. It measured 33 feet x 20 feet and contained a fireplace, with a chimney to escape through if the hut was buried by snow. It even had a primitive Turkish bath made out of a barrel.

many years, and the Arctic Ocean was mainly left to the Siberians to fish. It was not until the late 1800s that there was interest in the Northeast Passage again, when Russia and other European countries realized that the great rivers and forests of Siberia might be a rich hunting ground. In 1878 the Finnish polar explorer Nils Nordenskjöld (1832–1901) set out from southern Sweden on board his ship, the *Vega*. Keeping close to the Siberian coast, he voyaged east until ice near the Bering Strait blocked his way. The following July he sailed into the Pacific Ocean. The quest was over and the Northeast Passage was now open for commerce.

▲ THE NORTHEAST PASSAGE
For more than 300 years, explorers sailed northeast from Europe in the hope of finding a way along the top of Siberia and around into the Pacific Ocean. They were looking for an easy way to the riches of Asia.

Key Dates

- 1554 Hugh Willoughby reaches Novaya Zemlya.

- 1594 Barents sails into Kara Sea east of Novaya Zemlya.

- 1595 Barents's second voyage ends in failure in the Kara Sea.

- 1596 Barents discovers Bear Island and the rich fishing grounds of Spitsbergen.

- 1597 Barents dies on the sea that now bears his name.

- 1648 Semyon Dezhnev sails around eastern tip of Siberia.

- 1878–79 Nils Nordenskjöld navigates the Northeast Passage.

Exploring Asia

▲ PETER THE GREAT
Peter I (Peter the Great) was Czar of Russia from 1682 to 1725. Under him, the backward country was transformed into a great European power.

At the start of the 1700s Russia had a dynamic ruler, Czar Peter I. He built up a big navy and army, reorganized the government, and constructed the country's new capital of St. Petersburg. In previous years Russia had extended its territory right across Siberia to the shores of the Pacific Ocean. However, few Russians had any idea what their new land contained, or whether it was joined to America, so Peter the Great decided to find out.

Vitus Bering (1681–1741) was born in Denmark. He was a superb administrator, and Peter invited him to help modernize the Russian navy. In 1724 Peter appointed him to lead a large expedition across Siberia. The expedition left St. Petersburg in 1725 and reached the Pacific Ocean two years later. There Bering and his men built a ship, the *St. Gabriel*, and sailed up the coast and into the Arctic Ocean. From what he saw, Bering was satisfied that Siberia and America were not linked. He returned to St. Petersburg in 1730. In 1732 Bering was put in charge of a huge new undertaking. The Great Northern Expedition consisted of more than 3,000 men, including 30 scientists and 5 surveyors, with 13 ships and 9 wagonloads of scientific instruments. Its task was to explore the entire northern coast of Siberia as well as the seas to its east.

Over the next ten years five teams mapped the northern coast and the great rivers that flowed north through the country toward it. Bering concentrated on the seas beyond Siberia. This time he sailed across the Pacific to Alaska, returning to the Kamchatka Peninsula along the string of islands called the Aleutian Islands.

▲ CROSSING SIBERIA
Travelers in Siberia used teams of trained reindeer or huskies to pull sledges bearing food and other provisions. People sometimes wore wide snowshoes to stop themselves from sinking into the snow.

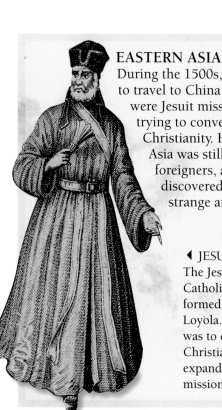

EASTERN ASIA

During the 1500s, Europeans began to travel to China and Japan. Most were Jesuit missionaries, who were trying to convert people to Christianity. However, eastern Asia was still mainly closed to foreigners, and little was discovered about these strange and distant lands.

◀ JESUIT PRIEST
The Jesuits are a Roman Catholic religious order formed in 1534 by Ignatius Loyola. Their first main aim was to convert Muslims to Christianity, but they soon expanded their work, opening missions in India and China.

▲ FRANCIS XAVIER
Francis Xavier (1506–52) was a Spanish Jesuit who traveled around India before visiting Japan in 1549. He admired Japanese people for their sense of honor, and he made many converts.

▶ PRAYER WHEEL
Siddhartha Gautama was an Indian prince who became known as the Buddha. The religion of Buddhism is based on his teachings. From about 400 B.C. it began to spread throughout eastern Asia. Many Tibetan Buddhists use a prayer wheel for saying their prayers.

▲ HUNTERS' PREY
The Siberian tiger lives in southeast Siberia, near the border with China. Its pelt (skin) was much prized by fur trappers.

▶ DEATH OF BERING
In 1741 Bering started the voyage back from the Aleutian Islands off Alaska. He reached an island near the Kamchatka Peninsula, where he died of scurvy and exposure. The island is now named after him.

Bering died in 1741, before the expedition was finished, but he achieved a great deal. His team had mapped Siberia and opened up both Siberia and Alaska to Russian fur traders. By 1800 Alaska was part of the Russian Empire. Although Semyon Dezhnev had discovered a century earlier that Siberia and America were separated by sea, he left no records, and few people were aware of his work. Bering confirmed these findings, so in his honor, the strait between the two continents is named the Bering Strait.

▶ LHASA
In Tibet, the isolated city of Lhasa was the center of Tibetan Buddhism. In 1658 the German Jesuit John Grueber (1623–80) and the Belgian Albert d'Orville (1621–62) set out from China to find an overland route to India so as to avoid hostile Dutch ships on the sea route. In 1661 they entered Lhasa— the first Europeans to set eyes on the mystical city with its palaces and great temple complexes.

Key Dates

- 1549 Francis Xavier in Japan.

- 1661 Grueber and d'Orville visit Lhasa in Tibet.

- 1725–29 Bering crosses Siberia and explores the sea between Siberia and Alaska.

- 1732 Bering organizes Great Northern Expedition.

- 1734–41 Bering crosses Siberia and explores coast of Alaska.

- 1734–42 Five teams of explorers map the northern Siberian coast and the Ob, Yenisei, and Lena rivers.

Advancing into America

▲ JEFFERSON
In 1803 President Thomas Jefferson bought the Louisiana territory from France, more than doubling the size of the U.S.

TWO HUNDRED years after Columbus landed in the West Indies, Europeans still knew surprisingly little about the enormous American continent to the north. The Spanish explored Florida and the Gulf of Mexico, the English established colonies on the east coast, and the French sailed up the St Lawrence River and settled in Canada. But the vast lands that lay in between remained a mystery.

In 1541 the Spaniard Hernando de Soto set out to explore Florida and became the first European to set eyes on the wide southern reaches of the Mississippi River. Unfortunately he died soon afterwards and the Spanish failed to explore further. More than a century later, hundreds of kilometres to the north, Louis Jolliet (1645–1700) and the French Jesuit missionary Father Jacques Marquette (1637–75) discovered a route to the Mississippi River from the Great Lakes. They explored the river as far south as Arkansas. However, it was another Frenchman, Robert de La Salle (1643–87), who became the first European to sail down the river to its mouth on the Gulf of Mexico. He claimed the land in

▶ SACAJAWEA
In 1804 Lewis and Clark were joined by Sacajawea, a member of the Shoshone tribe. She spoke many native languages and acted as the interpreter on the expedition.

this area for his country, naming it Louisiana after the French king, Louis XIV.

Over the next century, European influence in North America changed considerably. The Spanish still controlled Mexico and Florida, but in 1760 the English had thrown the French out of Canada. Most importantly, the English colonists rebelled against their own country and set up an independent United States which stretched from the Atlantic coast to the east side of the Mississippi River. West of the Mississippi lay the huge Louisiana territory, which in 1803 the United States purchased from France.

U.S. President Thomas Jefferson wanted to find out more about this vast new Louisiana Purchase, as it was known. In 1804 he sent two men to explore it. They were his personal secretary, Meriwether Lewis (1774–1809), and William Clark (1770–1838), a former

THE NEW CONTINENT

The Spanish were the first Europeans to explore North America, moving northward from their empire in Mexico. Pánfilo de Narváez (1470–1528) explored the Gulf of Mexico, while Hernando de Soto (1500–42) became the first European to see the Mississippi River in 1541. These were the first of many people to push across this huge new continent.

▲ CABEZA DE VACA
Alvar Núñez Cabeza de Vaca (1490–1556) sailed with De Narváez around the Gulf of Mexico. The fleet was wrecked off Texas in November 1528, but Cabeza de Vaca was saved by Yaqui tribesmen. He stayed with them for five years, then set out on foot through Texas and across the Rio Grande into Mexico, reaching the safety of Mexico City in 1536.

▶ THE MISSISSIPPI RIVER
The mighty Mississippi River flows south through the United States to the Gulf of Mexico. The discovery of its northern reaches by Jolliet and Marquette opened up America to European explorers and settlers.

◀ BISON
For 350 years European settlers hunted the bison herds of the plains almost to extinction, wiping out the Native Americans' main source of food and clothing.

army officer. Over the course of two years, they traveled from St. Louis up the Missouri River, over the Rockies, and down the Columbia River to the Pacific coast, before returning to St. Louis.

The success of the expedition convinced the U.S. government that Louisiana was suitable for people to live in. Within a generation, settlers were pouring across the Mississippi to start a new life on the Great Plains and the Pacific coast. The expansion of the United States across the continent was gaining momentum.

▲ SHOOTING RAPIDS
Lewis and Clark used canoes to navigate the dangerous Missouri, Columbia, and Yellowstone rivers.

▶ GRIZZLY BEARS
Bears were a menace to the expedition. One chased six men from Lewis and Clark's party into the Missouri River.

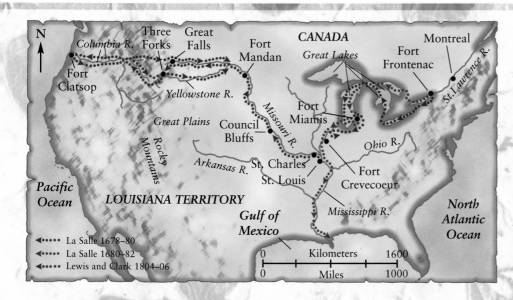

Key Dates

- 1527–28 De Narváez explores the Gulf of Mexico.
- 1528–36 De Vaca explores Texas.
- 1541 De Soto is first European to see the Mississippi.
- 1672 Marquette and Jolliet explore the upper Mississippi.
- 1678–80 La Salle explores the Great Lakes.
- 1680–82 La Salle sails down Mississippi to Gulf of Mexico and claims the region for France.
- 1804–6 Lewis and Clark explore the Missouri River and routes to the Pacific.

▲ SPREADING OUT ACROSS AMERICA
Robert de la Salle's two voyages around the Great Lakes and down the Mississippi River and the expedition of Lewis and Clark up the Missouri River did much to open up North America to traders and eventually to settlers.

Across the Pacific

▲ ABEL TASMAN
The two voyages of Abel Tasman did much to map the uncharted lands of the southern oceans.

EVER SINCE THE time of the ancient Greeks, people in Europe had imagined that there was a great continent lying on the other side of the world. They reasoned that since there was a Eurasian continent in the northern hemisphere, there must be a similarly large continent in the southern hemisphere, in order to balance the world! The only problem was that no one had ever managed to discover where this southern continent actually was.

Several sailors employed by a trading organization, the Dutch East India Company, stumbled across unknown land during their voyages. In 1605 Willem Jansz (1570–1629) sailed south from New Guinea and found the northern tip of Australia. In 1615 Dirk Hartog (1580–1630), traveling to Indonesia, sailed too far east and landed in Western Australia. Both sailors reported that this new land was too poor to bother with. So the Dutch East India Company took no further action, as it was interested in trade, not exploration.

In 1642 the company changed its mind and began to search for Terra Australis Incognita, or "unknown southern land." In 1642–43 Abel Tasman (1603–59)

▲ TASMANIA
When Tasman landed on a new island in November 1642, he named it Van Diemen's Land, after the governor-general of Batavia in the East Indies. It was later renamed Tasmania, after Tasman.

sailed around the Indian and Pacific oceans in a huge circle without discovering a southern continent, although he did find the island later named after him—Tasmania—and New Zealand. In 1643–44 he explored the Australian coastline that Jansz and Hartog had found. Tasman thought that the land to the south of

THE SOUTH PACIFIC

Although both Magellan and Drake crossed the Pacific, their routes took them north of the many island groups. During the following centuries these islands were gradually reached by Europeans: Alvaro de Mendaña (1541–95) reached Tuvalu and the Solomon Islands; Pedro Quirós (1565–1614) got to Vanuatu; and Tasman saw Fiji and Tonga. Louis Bougainville (1729–1811) mapped the region but did not reach eastern Australia because the Great Barrier Reef was in the way.

◀ THE GREAT BARRIER REEF
This 1,200 mile-long coral reef runs along the coast of north-east Australia. It is made up of the skeletons of millions of tiny sea creatures and is home to lots of marine life. It prevented Bougainville and other explorers from landing in Australia.

◀ THE SOLOMON ISLANDS
The first South Pacific islands to be explored by Europeans were the Solomon Islands, off the coast of New Guinea, which were found by De Mendaña in 1568. Over the next 200 years the rest of the islands in the region were slowly explored and mapped by visiting Europeans.

▶ BOUGAINVILLEA
On his round-the-world voyage Louis Bougainville took a botanist with him. One of the plants they brought back to Europe was a flowering climber now named bougainvillea in his honor.

▶ DUTCH EAST INDIA COMPANY
In 1602 the Dutch set up a company to coordinate their trading activities in the East Indies. They established trading posts, like the one pictured here, in India, China, and Japan, soon controlling the local spice trade.

New Guinea was not part of a southern continent, but he did not find out whether it was connected to New Guinea or whether it was an island.

Strangely enough, Luis Torres (c.1570–1613) had already proved that New Guinea was an island. In 1607 he sailed right around New Guinea through the strait that now bears his name, showing that it was an island. Therefore the land to its south, Australia, could not be attached to it. However, Tasman did not realize the significance of this discovery, so the mystery concerning the great southern continent, and the unnamed land that lay above it, remained unsolved.

▼ TASMAN AND BOUGAINVILLE
Neither Abel Tasman nor Louis Bougainville actually landed in Australia, although both did much to increase knowledge of the continent. Bougainville's voyage around the world established a French presence in the South Pacific.

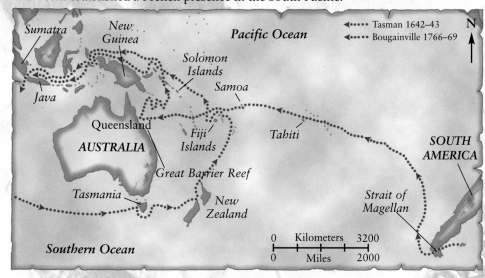

Key Dates

- 1567–69 De Mendaña discovers the Solomon Islands.

- 1602 Dutch East India Company is established.

- 1605 Willem Jansz explores Queensland.

- 1615 Dirk Hartog discovers Western Australia.

- 1642–43 Tasman discovers Tasmania and sees New Zealand and the Fiji Islands.

- 1643–44 Tasman maps north coast of Australia.

- 1766–69 Louis Bougainville circumnavigates the world.

Captain Cook

▲ CAPTAIN COOK
James Cook (1728–79) sailed in the merchant navy for ten years and became an experienced navigator and seaman before he joined the British Royal Navy in 1755.

B Y THE 18TH CENTURY Europeans were still not sure of the shape and size of the strange land—*Terra Australis Incognita*—in the southern hemisphere. They did not even know for sure whether this mysterious new continent actually existed. By now, the British had overtaken the Dutch as the major trading nation in the world, and their Royal Navy ruled the waves. In 1768 the British Navy sent an expedition to the South Seas to search for the southern continent. James Cook was the ideal choice to lead it—he was an expert in navigation and an experienced seaman, having spent more than ten years on merchant ships.

Cook set sail from Plymouth, England, in August 1768. In April 1769 he reached Tahiti, where he and his crew were impressed by the warm climate and the beautiful plants and wildlife. Then he sailed southwest to New Zealand, the west coast of which had been discovered by Tasman. By steering a course in the shape of a figure eight, he found that New Zealand was two islands, not one. Cook continued west, landing at a place that is now called Botany Bay, in Australia, which he claimed for Britain. He then sailed up the coast until he got to the Great Barrier Reef, where his ship, the *Endeavour,* ran aground and had to be repaired. He then went through the Torres Strait and home to England across the Indian and Atlantic oceans. Cook made two more voyages to the South Seas. His second trip, in 1772–75, took him toward the South Pole, which was where Cook thought the southern continent lay.

▼ BAY OF ISLANDS, NEW ZEALAND
Cook visited many fine harbors on his voyages to New Zealand. The Bay of Islands, shown below, is on New Zealand's North Island.

THE SOUTH SEAS
Everywhere Cook went he was greeted with strange and wonderful sights. He found many animals and plants previously unknown to Europeans and met many different people. Although the Polynesians were mainly friendly, the Maoris of New Zealand were somewhat more suspicious.

▼ MAORI CANOES
The Maoris were skilled seamen. They greeted Cook on his arrival in New Zealand with a fleet of intricately decorated and carved canoes that were able to carry up to 100 warriors.

▲ KANGAROOS
Cook's crew were the first Europeans to see a kangaroo, but they could not decide what type of animal it was. In the end they decided that it was "some kind of stag."

▶ LIME
During long voyages, most sailors developed scurvy, a disease caused by a lack of vitamin C in their diet. Cook solved this problem by feeding the crew with vitamin C-rich pickled cabbage, vegetables, and limes.

◀ HONEYSUCKLE
Sydney Parkinson was an illustrator who went on the voyage. He drew many of the exotic plants that he saw on the journey. One was a type of honeysuckle.

His final voyage, in 1776–79, took him north in a search for an inlet into the Arctic Ocean.

Cook met a tragic end when he was killed in Hawaii after a scuffle broke out on the beach. But in his three voyages, Cook finally proved that Australia and New Zealand were separate islands and not part of a larger southern continent. When a landmass was later discovered around the South Pole, Antarctica was identified as the true Terra Australis Incognita. The vast amount of scientific, botanical, and navigational information Cook brought back from the South Seas was equally important. As a result of his work, exploration turned from adventure into scientific discovery.

Artist records plant information

Sorting animal skins and specimens

▶ THE *ENDEAVOUR*
When he was in the merchant navy, Cook sailed colliers, or coal ships, out of his home port of Whitby, Yorkshire. He therefore chose a converted collier, the Endeavour, *to sail around the world in. The ship was slow but tough and spacious, with enough room for the 94 crew and their supplies.*

▼ COOK'S VOYAGES
Over the course of three voyages, between 1768 and 1779, Cook explored much of the Pacific Ocean, including eastern Australia, which he named New South Wales. He also discovered many islands, including Hawaii, where he was eventually murdered.

Voyages of James Cook
◄····· 1st journey 1768–71
◄····· 2nd journey 1772–75
◄····· 3rd journey 1776–79

0   Kilometers   3200
0   Miles   2000

EUROPE
ASIA
AFRICA
EAST INDIES
Torres Strait
Hawaiian Islands
Pacific   Ocean
NORTH AMERICA
Atlantic Ocean
Fiji
Tahiti
SOUTH AMERICA
Indian Ocean
Kerguelen Islands
AUSTRALIA
Tierra Del Fuego
Cape of Good Hope
New Zealand
Cape Horn
ANTARCTICA

Key Dates

- 1755 Cook joins the Royal Navy and rises in rank to captain.

- 1768–71 On his first voyage, Cook sails round New Zealand and explores the east coast of Australia, claiming it for Britain.

- 1769 Cook discovers the island of Tahiti

- 1772–75 Cook's second voyage takes him south toward Antarctica.

- 1776–79 His third voyage heads north into the Arctic Ocean, and he discovers Hawaii on the way.

- 1779 Cook is killed in a violent skirmish on a beach in Hawaii

Trekking across Australia

Aborigines believe that their Ancestral Beings shaped the land and created life in a period known as Dreamtime. These Beings live on in spirit form and are represented through paintings at sacred sites, such as caves and rocks.

AFTER COOK LANDED in Botany Bay, Europeans began to settle in Australia. But ninety years later they still knew little about their new country. The first settlers were convicts sent out from Britain to serve their prison sentences in Fort Jackson, now the city of Sydney. They were soon joined by farmers looking for a new start in a foreign land. There was plenty of land for everyone, so few ventured far inland from the coast.

Some intrepid explorers did investigate further, following the coastline or river valleys. In 1828 Charles Sturt (1795–1869) discovered the Darling River and then followed the Murray River to the sea. In 1844 he headed up the Murray inland. In 1840–41 Edward Eyre (1815–1901) walked along the southern coast from the town of Adelaide to find a route to the Western Australian settlement of Albany. Even by the late 1850s,

the settlers still did not know what lay in the interior of their enormous country. Some thought there was a huge inland sea, while others feared it was nothing but desert. In 1859 the South Australian government offered a prize to the first person who crossed the continent from south to north.

Two expeditions set out to claim the prize. The first was led by Robert O'Hara Burke (1820–61), who was more of an adventurer than an explorer, and his young companion William Wills (1834–61). This was the biggest and most expensive expedition

▶ CAMELS
Camels were imported from India for Burke and Wills's expedition. They proved unsuitable and most eventually ended up as food for the explorers. Descendants of those that survived still live in the outback.

EARLY AUSTRALIA

The Aborigines, or Native Australians, arrived on the continent more than 40,000 years ago. They lived in isolation from the rest of the world, existing by hunting and gathering their food, catching kangaroos and other animals and harvesting wild plants, nuts, and berries to eat. They were pushed off their native lands when the Europeans started colonizing Australia.

▼ ULURU
The name Uluru means "great pebble." It is a vast sandstone rock in central Australia which is more than 1.5 miles long and is sacred to the local Aranda Aborigines. It is also known as Ayers Rock.

▲ BOOMERANG
Aborigines hunted wild animals by throwing a boomerang at them. It returned to the thrower if it did not hit the target. Boomerangs were often patterned like this one.

◀ MODERN ABORIGINES
After the arrival of Europeans in 1788, Aborigines were reduced to second-class citizens in their own country. About 250,000 Aborigines live in Australia today.

▶ INTO AUSTRALIA

Despite their extensive knowledge of the coastline of Australia, few of the early settlers knew what lay inland. Over the course of 30 years a number of expeditions set out to explore and map the interior. By 1862 the continent had been successfully crossed from south to north by Burke and Wills, although they died on the way back.

Stuart 1828–30
1844-45
Eyre
1840–41
Stuart
1862
Burke and Wills
1860–61

Aborigines set fire to the bush to stop Stuart's advance into their land

Darwin

Daly Waters

Tennant Creek

Flinders

Stuart reaches the center of Australia

Cooper's Creek

Ashburton

Gascoyne

Murchison

Alice Springs

AUSTRALIA

Eyre digs to find water

Kangaroo

Oodnadatta

Burke and Wills find a note from the support party

Perth

Ceduna

Menindee

Darling

Adelaide

Burke and Wills set out

Sydney

Albany

Melbourne

ever organized in Australia. It consisted of 15 men, accompanied by camels and horses. It went north from Melbourne to the Gulf of Carpentaria. But the expedition was badly organized and both Burke and Wills died on the long journey back south.

John Stuart (1815–66) was more successful. He was an experienced explorer who knew how to survive in the outback. He set out from Adelaide to try to cross the continent but was turned back by Aborigines. He set out again but was blocked by long stretches of thorny bushes. Finally, in July 1862, he succeeded in reaching Darwin. Stuart proved that the interior of Australia was indeed desert, but his journey opened up the interior for settlement and farming.

▲ PROSPECTING
The discovery of gold in Australia in 1851 brought a rush of prospectors from Europe and America, but few people struck it rich.

▼ NED KELLY
Many bushrangers, or outlaws, lived in the Australian outback. The most famous of these was Ned Kelly (1855–80), whose gang of robbers killed three policemen and robbed several banks before Kelly was finally caught and hanged in Melbourne. Kelly, who wore a tin hat to protect himself, soon became a national hero for many people.

Key Dates

- 1770 Cook lands in Botany Bay.

- 1788 First convicts to Australia.

- 1828–30 Charles Sturt crosses the Blue Mountains and reaches the Darling River.

- 1840–41 Edward Eyre walks along the south Australian coast from Adelaide to Albany in Western Australia.

- 1844–45 Sturt travels into central Australia.

- 1860–61 Burke and Wills cross Australia from south to north.

- 1862 On his third attempt, John Stuart crosses Australia from Adelaide to Darwin.

The Amazon

DURING THE 1700S A NEW TYPE of explorer emerged. While most explorers set out to make their fortune, either by finding gold or by opening up new and profitable trade routes, this new breed of explorer wanted to expand the scope of scientific knowledge.

This was a period of great scientific and intellectual debate across Europe. Scientists such as Galileo and Newton had already worked out the laws of the natural world—the movement of the planets and how motion and gravity worked. Now philosophers began to challenge existing religious beliefs with `the power of human reason, or rationality. In France a

▶ UNKNOWN TRIBES
Explorers of the Amazon jungle discovered many tribes of people unknown to Europeans. But the arrival of settlers, and exposure to their diseases, soon killed off many of these native South American tribes.

group of intellectuals compiled a 35-volume *Encyclopédie* of all knowledge. This new thinking was called "The Enlightenment." It influenced explorers, who now searched for knowledge, not for gold or glory.

South America had barely been explored since the Spanish and Portuguese conquered it in the 1500s. Two hundred years later scientists started to examine this rich and varied continent. In 1735 the French mathematician Charles-Marie de la Condamine (1701–74) went to Ecuador to record the shape and size of the Earth—the science of geodesy—by calculating its width at the equator. He was so enthralled by the wildlife there that he stayed for another ten years.

At the end of the century, the German naturalist Alexander von Humboldt (1769–1859) and the French naturalist Aimé Bonpland (1773–1858) trekked up the River Orinoco and along the Andes mountains to study plant life. Over the course of five years they recorded more than 3,000 previously unknown plant species and gathered many samples. Fifty years later two pioneering English naturalists, Henry Bates (1825–92) and Alfred Wallace (1823–1913), ventured into the

THE AMAZON RAINFOREST
Even now, scientists have no idea how many different plants and animals live in the Amazon rainforest, as new species are constantly being discovered. Two hundred years ago the first European travelers were amazed at the sheer variety of wildlife they found and fascinated by the tribes of people they met living deep in the jungle.

▲ ALEXANDER VON HUMBOLDT
German naturalist Alexander von Humboldt traveled extensively throughout South America, examining plants and wildlife as well as the landscape and climate. The cold sea current that flows up the west coast of South America is named in his honor.

▲ RECORDING NATURE
In the days before photography, explorers recorded what they saw by drawing it. In his sketchbooks, Henry Bates drew hundreds of the butterflies and other insects he saw on his travels.

◀ CINCHONA
Among the many new plants discovered by Aimé Bonpland was the cinchona tree. Its bark was used to make quinine, a natural cure for malaria, one of the most deadly tropical diseases.

Amazon rainforest. When Bates returned to England in 1859, he took with him more than 14,000 insects and other specimens. Another scientist, Richard Spruce (1817–93), went back to England in 1864 with more than 30,000 plant specimens.

As a result of this scientific activity people became far more aware of the variety of life on Earth. New animals and plants were discovered, and medicines developed from some of the plants. The age of the scientific explorer was now well under way.

▶ TOUCAN ATTACK
Although toucans are normally shy and nervous, they can be aggressive. When naturalist Henry Bates attempted to capture one, he was attacked by a flock of its fellow birds.

▲ RIVER AMAZON
The Amazon in South America is the second-longest river in the world and runs east from the Andes Mountains, through Brazil to the Atlantic Ocean. It flows through the world's largest rainforest, which is home to many exotic animals and plants.

◀ COLLECTING RUBBER
Rubber is made from latex, a sticky white liquid drained from the trunk of the rubber tree and collected in pots. Columbus saw locals playing with a rubber ball, but la Condamine was the first European to take rubber back home, in 1744.

▲ TREE FROG
Tree frogs were among the many new and exciting species that European naturalists encountered for the first time in the rainforest.

Key Dates

- 1735–44 La Condamine studies the shape of the Earth at the Equator. He stays there to watch the wildlife.

- 1799–1804 Alexander von Humboldt and Aimé Bonpland study botany along the River Orinoco and in the Andes.

- 1848–59 Amazon explored by Alfred Wallace and Henry Bates.

- 1849–64 Richard Spruce travels up the Amazon, collecting 30,000 plant specimens.

- 1852 Wallace returns to England, but all his specimens are lost in a fire on board ship.

Deep inside Africa

THE ONLY PART OF AFRICA known to Europeans was its coastline, which for most of its length was an inhospitable place. There were few natural harbors, and much of the coast was either dry desert or wet jungle. Many of the rivers flowed out into the sea through swampy deltas. As a result, the interior of Africa was too difficult for European travelers to get into.

During the late 1700s Europeans began to venture inland, exploring both the major rivers and the vast Sahara Desert. In 1770 James Bruce (1730–94) discovered Lake Tana in the east, in what is now Ethiopia. He realized that it was the source of the Blue Nile, one of the main tributaries of the great River Nile. In the west, Mungo Park (1771–1806) set out in 1795 to explore the mysterious, little-known River Niger, which flowed inland and never seemed to reach the sea. He discovered that the river actually flowed east, not west as had always been thought, and that it turned south near Timbuktu. However, he was not clear what happened to it after that. He drowned when his canoe was ambushed by tribesmen.

Over the next fifty years attention turned to the Sahara Desert. In 1828 a French explorer named René Caillié (1799–1838) became the first European to survive a secret visit to the legendary and forbidden city of Timbuktu,

◀ TIMBUKTU
During the 1300s the city of Timbuktu became a prosperous center for trade across the Sahara Desert. Over the centuries, the city became famous for its wealth and learning, although no European had ever visited it.

THE SLAVE TRADE
The first black slaves were shipped out of Africa by the Arabs more than 1,000 years ago. Local rulers grew rich by selling captured enemies into slavery. In 1482 the Portuguese opened a trading post for exporting slaves to the New World. Other European nations joined in. From 1701 to 1810 more than seven million Africans were sent to the Americas. In the early 1800s slavery was abolished in Europe, but the Arabs continued the trade until 1873, when the main slave market in Zanzibar was closed.

▼ LIFE OF A SLAVE
Slaves worked very long hours, six days a week on the plantations of the New World. If a slave tried to escape, they were made to wear a heavy iron collar with long spikes, which made it difficult for them, if they tried again, to escape to freedom through the undergrowth.

▼ SLAVE SHIPS
Slaves were packed into the holds of ships for transportation across the Atlantic. Conditions were bad and more than one million people died on the way.

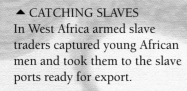

▲ CATCHING SLAVES
In West Africa armed slave traders captured young African men and took them to the slave ports ready for export.

▶ INTO AFRICA
From the 1760s onward, Europeans made determined attempts to explore the interior of Africa. The major rivers of the Niger and Nile were mapped and the great Sahara Desert was thoroughly explored. The south of the continent, however, remained largely unknown.

which as a Muslim city was closed to Christians. He was very disappointed to find that it was full of mud huts, not rich buildings, and few people believed him when he returned to France. His story was confirmed, however, by the German explorer Heinrich Barth (1821–65), who explored the entire region thoroughly for the British government during the 1850s.

In 1857 two hardy British explorers, Richard Burton (1821–90) and his friend John Speke (1827–64), set out to solve one of the great African mysteries—the source of the river Nile. They explored the great lakes in East Africa, but Burton fell ill and Speke continued alone. After two attempts, he discovered that the Nile flowed out of the northern end of Lake Victoria (which Speke named after the reigning British queen) and over the mighty Ripon Falls. The interior of Africa was slowly giving up its secrets.

Tangier
Rabat
Fez
Tripoli
Alexandria
Cairo
Barth crosses the Sahara
AFRICA
Jedda
Timbuktu
Segu
Agadez
Khartoum
Massawa
Kano
Burton and Speke search for the source of the Nile
Gondokoro
Lake Victoria
Park arrives at Segu but turns back
Congo
Bruce 1768–73
Lake Tanganyika
Tabora
Park 1795–1806
Caillié 1827–28
Victoria Falls
Barth 1844–55
Zulu warrior
Burton and Speke 1857-63
N
W
E
S
Cape Town

▲ TRANSPORTATION
The slave traders rarely traveled into the interior of Africa. Slaves would be brought to the coast for sale by tribal leaders who had enslaved their enemies. The slaves would either have been forced to walk to the coast or taken in canoes such as this one.

▼ SAHARA DESERT
Even the vast Sahara Desert was not a barrier to slave traders who would take caravans of slaves across the desert, empty but for occasional rock formations like this one.

Key Dates

- 1768–73 James Bruce searches for the source of the Nile.

- 1795–1806 Mungo Park explores the River Niger.

- 1827–28 René Caillié becomes the first European to visit the city of Timbuktu.

- 1844–55 Heinrich Barth travels across the Sahara Desert.

- 1857–58 Richard Burton and John Speke explore the great lakes of East Africa.

- 1858–63 John Speke investigates the Nile and eventually discovers its source.

Livingstone and Stanley

▲ LION ATTACK
In 1844 Livingstone was attacked by a lion, which mauled his left shoulder. Although he eventually got better, he never regained the full use of his left arm.

ONE MAN MORE THAN any other transformed European knowledge about Africa—David Livingstone (1813–73). He started out as a missionary and doctor, and went to Africa to convert the local people to Christianity and to improve their lives through medicine and education. Once in Africa, however, Livingstone became curious about everything he saw and began to travel extensively. He recorded it all in three large books, totaling more than 750,000 words, which made him and his journeys world-famous. But today some people think that his travels were not such a good thing, because he paved the way for the European colonization and exploitation of Africa.

Livingstone was born in Scotland and arrived in Cape Town on the Cape of Good Hope in 1841. From there he traveled to the mission station of Kuruman, on the edge of the Kalahari Desert. Here he met his future wife, Mary, and had a family. Together they established more missions, but Livingstone soon got restless and sent his wife and children back to England so that he could continue to explore by himself.

In 1851 he discovered the river Zambezi, which was previously unknown to people in Europe. Between 1852 and 1856 he became the first European to cross the continent from east to west, exploring the length of the Zambezi as he went. He then investigated the eastern coast and in 1865 set out to find the source of the river Nile. For a while, nothing was heard of him. An American newspaper, *The New York Herald*, sent a reporter, Welsh-born Henry Stanley (1841–1904), to find Livingstone.

◀ RIVER SCARES
Livingstone made many of his journeys by boat, braving rapids, waterfalls, and even hippopotamuses. On one occasion, his boat crashed into a hippo and overturned it, causing him to lose much of his equipment.

THE INTERIOR OF AFRICA

John Speke, who discovered the source of the river Nile, described Africa as an upside-down soup plate—a rim of flat land around the edge with a sharp rise up to a central plateau. Rivers flowing from the interior often crashed over rapids or waterfalls, and explorers had to carry their boats around them. Wild animals and hostile locals added to the problems.

◀ VICTORIA FALLS
On November 17, 1855, Livingstone came up against a huge waterfall on the river Zambezi. Clouds of water vapor gave it its local name of Mosi-oa-tunya, or "the smoke that roars." Livingstone named the falls after Queen Victoria of Britain, the only English name he gave to any discovery.

▲ STANLEY'S HAT
Stanley wore a hat like this one, and Livingstone a flat cap, at their famous meeting at Ujiji.

▲ ZULU WOMEN
The Zulus of southern Africa were a warlike people. Under their leader, Shaka, they built a powerful nation in the region in the early 1800s. Today there are more than seven million Zulu people living in South Africa.

◄ "DR. LIVINGSTONE, I PRESUME?" *In March 1871 Henry Stanley set out from Zanzibar to find Dr. Livingstone. Stanley was an adventurer, who was probably motivated by fame and fortune. Eight months later he heard from local people that Livingstone had recently returned to Ujiji, on the shores of Lake Tanganyika. Stanley rushed to meet the ailing Livingstone, greeting him on November 10 with the now famous words "Dr. Livingstone, I presume?" "Yes," replied the explorer.*

He managed to track him down eight months later. Stanley returned twice to Africa, once to explore the Great Lakes region and sail down the last great unknown river in Africa, the river Congo (now Zaïre). Then, after working for the Belgian king in the Congo, he went to rescue Emin Pasha, the British governor of Equatoria (north of the Great Lakes), who was besieged by enemy tribespeople. Stanley's expeditions helped both Britain and Belgium establish colonies in central Africa, and by the time he died in 1904, almost all of Africa was under European control.

▶ DR. LIVINGSTONE AND MR. STANLEY Between them Livingstone and Stanley explored much of central and southern Africa. They also navigated the two great and previously unknown African rivers—the Zambezi and Congo (now Zaïre)— although neither proved very easy to navigate. They also explored the Great Lakes region, confirming the source of the river Nile and settling disputes about how the different lakes drained into each other.

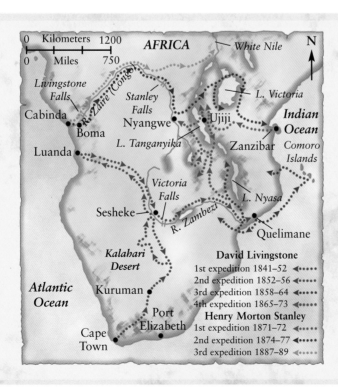

David Livingstone
1st expedition 1841–52 ◄••••
2nd expedition 1852–56 ◄••••
3rd expedition 1858–64 ◄••••
4th expedition 1865–73 ◄••••
Henry Morton Stanley
1st expedition 1871–72 ◄••••
2nd expedition 1874–77 ◄••••
3rd expedition 1887–89 ◄••••

Key Dates

- 1841–52 Livingstone explores southern Africa.

- 1852–56 Livingstone goes down the river Zambezi. Discovers Victoria Falls.

- 1858–64 Livingstone explores Lake Nyasa and eastern coast.

- 1865–73 Livingstone goes to the Great Lakes and disappears.

- 1871–72 Stanley looks for Livingstone. Finds him in Ujiji.

- 1874–77 Stanley goes down the river Congo to Cabinda in west.

- 1887–89 Stanley rescues besieged Emin Pasha.

The North Pole

▲ ROBERT PEARY
The American explorer Robert Peary made eight journeys to the Arctic, finally reaching his goal, the North Pole, in 1909.

IN 1881 A SHIP, the *Jeannette*, sank off the coast of Siberia. Three years later the wreckage turned up 3,000 miles away on the coast of Greenland, right on the other side of the Arctic Ocean. This extraordinary event caused great confusion, because everybody knew that the Arctic Ocean consisted of a thick layer of pack ice. How had the wreckage managed to travel such a great distance? And how had it moved through the ice?

The Norwegian explorer Fridtjof Nansen (1861–1930) decided to find out. He calculated that the wreckage could have been moved only by a powerful ocean current which had pushed it along in the ice. Nansen designed a boat, the *Fram*, which he intended to steer into the ice and allow the currents to move, just as they had the *Jeannette*. He worked out that the currents would carry

him close to the North Pole, in the middle of the Arctic Ocean. For three years, the *Fram* drifted in the ice from Siberia to the Spitsbergen islands to the east of Greenland. Although he failed to reach the North Pole, Nansen did prove that there was no land under the North Pole—it was just ice.

Nansen was not the first explorer to try to reach the North Pole. Between 1861 and 1871 an American, Charles Hall (1821–71), made three attempts on foot, dying after his last journey. But it was Nansen's voyage that raised huge international interest in the North Pole and a race to get there first began.

In 1897 the Swedish engineer Salomon Andrée tried to fly to the North Pole in a balloon, but he perished soon after taking off from Spitsbergen. Robert Peary (1856–1920) was more successful. He was an American explorer who made his first visit to the Arctic in 1886. For the next 22 years he devoted

◀ HUSKIES
Husky dogs have a thick, double coat of fur which helps to keep them warm in the extreme cold and snowy conditions of the Arctic. They can be trained to pull sledges of equipment over the ice.

WHAT'S IT LIKE AT THE NORTH POLE?
The North Pole is located in the middle of the Arctic Ocean, which is covered with pack ice all year round. Because the ice floats on top of the ocean currents, it is broken up and jagged, often rising to ridges 33 feet or more high.

▲ REFUELING AT THE NORTH POLE
Airplanes play a vital role in bringing in supplies to the North Pole. American explorers Richard Byrd and Floyd Bennett reached the North Pole by airplane in 1926.

▲ SEALSKIN
The first European travelers in the Arctic wore layers of woolen clothes, which failed to protect them from the cold. Later, they learned to wear Inuit-style animal-skin clothes, such as this sealskin hood.

▼ PEMMICAN
An ideal food for a long Arctic expedition is pemmican. It is made from dried, shredded meat mixed with melted fat. It is full of calories and lasts for years.

Icebergs and frozen pack ice pile up on either side of the Fram

◀ THE *FRAM*
Nansen needed a very strong ship for his plan. The Fram *was specially designed to be frozen into the Arctic ice so that it could then float with the currents across the Arctic Ocean without being damaged. Nansen hoped that the ice-bound ship would drift toward the North Pole. The ship went right across the Ocean, but it didn't get as near to the Pole as Nansen had hoped.*

Hull built to withstand the huge pressure of the ice

himself to polar exploration, returning year after year, each time getting closer to his goal of reaching the North Pole. In 1908 he set off up the west coast of Greenland and established a base camp at Cape Columbia on Ellesmere Island. His six-strong team set off from there, making a mad dash and reaching the North Pole on April 6, 1909. They then hurried back to base camp. The top of the world had been conquered.

Some people doubted that Peary had reached the North Pole, since he made the return journey in record time, covering 70 miles in one day. Nowadays most people think that Peary did indeed reach the Pole.

▼ USS *NAUTILUS*
In 1958 a U.S. nuclear-powered submarine, the U.S.S. *Nautilus*, sailed under the polar ice cap. It left Point Barrow in Alaska and sailed the 1,820 miles to Spitsbergen in the North Atlantic Ocean in four days. The submarine, which was 300 feet long and had a crew of 116, passed directly under the North Pole.

Key Dates

- 1871 Charles Hall sails up the west coast of Greenland and gets nearer to the North Pole than anyone before him.

- 1893–96 Fridtjof Nansen sails the *Fram* into the polar ice and drifts toward the North Pole, but fails to reach it.

- 1897 Salomon Andrée attempts to reach the Pole by balloon, but dies in the attempt.

- 1908–09 Robert Peary reaches the North Pole.

- 1958 U.S.S. *Nautilus* sails under the polar ice cap.

Race to the South Pole

AFTER ROBERT PEARY MADE his successful attempt on the North Pole in 1909, all eyes turned toward the South Pole. Because it was the last unconquered place on Earth, the South Pole held a huge attraction for explorers, but it was a daunting place to visit.

Unlike the North Pole, the South Pole is covered by land. The vast, frozen continent of Antarctica is the coldest place on Earth, with ridges of mountains and large glaciers, making traveling extremely difficult. In addition, the land is surrounded by pack ice and icebergs that stretch far into the Southern Ocean. Two people prepared themselves to conquer this icy wilderness. The first was Robert Scott, a British explorer who had visited the region in 1901–4 and came to think of the continent as his to conquer. As his intention to

▶ ROALD AMUNDSEN

Norwegian polar adventurer Roald Amundsen (1872–1928) was a skilled explorer and had three impressive records to his name. He was the first person to sail through the Northwest Passage, in 1903–6, the first person to reach the South Pole, in 1911, and the first person to fly an airship across the North Pole, in 1926.

lead an expedition to the South Pole became known, a second explorer, the Norwegian Roald Amundsen, joined the race. He kept his plans secret to prevent Scott from speeding up his preparations. Amundsen, too, was an experienced polar explorer, and far better equipped and prepared than Scott.

Both expeditions arrived in Antarctica in January 1911 and spent the winter on either side of the Ross Ice Shelf. Amundsen, however, had left two weeks before Scott and was 68 miles closer to the Pole. He was also better prepared, having already made several journeys to leave food stores at stages along the route. His five-strong party made fast progress, climbing the steep Axel Heiberg glacier onto the plateau surrounding the

◀ PENGUINS
The Antarctic is home to several different species of penguin. Penguins cannot fly, but use their wings as flippers to swim.

SCOTT'S JOURNEY

In 1910 Robert Scott set out for Antarctica on board the ship *Terra Nova*. After spending the winter at Cape Evans, he set out for the South Pole in November 1911. Unlike his rival Amundsen, Scott used ponies as well as dogs to haul the sledges, but the ponies died in the cold. As a result, the party of five made slow progress and were devastated to discover, when they reached the South Pole on January 17, 1912, that Amundsen had beaten them to it. All five died on the return journey.

▲ ROBERT SCOTT
The naval officer Robert Scott (1869–1912) led a scientific expedition to Antarctica in 1901. His ill-fated expedition to the Pole in 1910–12 captured the imagination of the world.

◀ CHEMISTRY SET
Scott's expeditions were scientific as well as exploratory. His team carried this chemistry set with them when they set off in 1910.

▶ SCOTT'S BASE CAMP
Scott established his base camp at Cape Evans, on the east side of the Ross Ice Shelf. Here he and his team spent the winter of 1911, planning their route to the Pole, studying maps, and also writing letters and reports.

▶ BATTLING ACROSS A FROZEN LAND
Amundsen and his party were well equipped to endure the cold conditions and were all expert skiers. They used husky dogs to pull their sledges. As food and other provisions were used up and the sledges got lighter, unwanted dogs were shot and eaten, reducing the amount of food required for the expedition. As a result, Amundsen and his team traveled far faster than Scott's team.

South Pole. They arrived at the Pole on December 14, 1911. Scott set out on November 1, 1911, but encountered far worse weather and made slow progress, finally getting to the Pole a month after Amundsen, on January 17, 1912.

Amundsen's expedition skills and equipment ensured that all his party returned home safely. Sadly, Scott and his team all perished, three of them within 11 miles of a supply depot equipped with food and other life-saving provisions. The race to the South Pole was over, but although Amundsen claimed the prize, Scott has continued to hold a special fascination for people, because of the tragic ending to his expedition.

▼ RESEARCH STATION, ANTARCTICA
In 1959 an agreement was made to reserve Antarctica for scientific research. Today, 18 nations have scientific bases there to conduct research into the environment, wildlife, and weather. In 1987 scientists found a hole in the ozone layer above Antarctica. The ozone layer protects the earth from the harmful rays of the sun.

Key Dates

- 1840 Antarctic coastline visited by James Wilkes and Jules Dumont d'Urville.

- 1841 James Ross from Britain explores the Ross Sea and its vast ice shelf.

- 1901–04 Scott explores the Antarctic coast and Ross Sea.

- 1908 Ernest Shackleton gets within 112 miles of the Pole.

- 1911 Roald Amundsen reaches the South Pole.

- 1912 Scott gets to the Pole but the team dies on return journey.

Seas, Summits, and Skies

▲ CHARLES LINDBERGH
The first solo flight across the Atlantic was made by 25-year-old Charles Lindbergh in 1927, when he flew the Spirit of St. Louis *from New York to Paris in 33 hours.*

WITH THE CONQUEST of the South Pole in 1911, an age of exploration came to an end. All the major undiscovered parts of the world had now been explored. But eight years earlier, in 1903, a new method of transportation had made its début. Orville and Wilbur Wright took to the skies over North Carolina in the airplane they had built, called the *Flyer*. Powered aircraft created new opportunities for exploration and discovery, and in the first 30 years of the 20th century a series of epic flights took place.

Louis Blériot made the first crossing of the English Channel in 1909. The first non-stop journey across the North Atlantic, from Newfoundland to Ireland, followed a decade later. It was made by John Alcock and Arthur Brown. Charles Lindbergh flew solo over the Atlantic in 1927, and Amy Johnson made the first solo flight by a woman, from Britain to Australia in 1930. These and other historic flights opened up the skies to commercial travel, and airlines began regular

▲ BALLOONING AROUND THE WORLD
In 1999 Brian James and Bertrand Piccard became the first people to circumnavigate the world non-stop in their balloon, the Breitling Orbiter 3. *The pair set off from Switzerland and used the jet streams in the upper atmosphere to glide eastward around the world.*

flights between the major cities of the world. People were now able to travel to faraway places without spending months at sea in order to get there.

As a result, more and more people decided to travel to other countries and explore the world for themselves. The growth in foreign travel led to a change in the nature of exploration. Now explorers took to the

HIGHS AND LOWS
Although nearly three-quarters of the world's surface is covered by sea, we still know very little about what lies beneath the ocean's surface. The development of underwater craft enabled explorers to study the seas in greater detail. At the other extreme, the highest places on the earth's surface have similarly fascinated explorers.

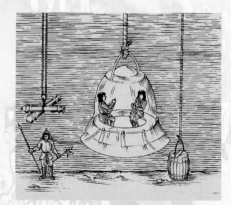

▲ THE *TRIESTE*
The *Trieste* bathyscaphe was designed to withstand the great pressure under the sea. In 1960 Jacques Piccard descended nearly 7 miles into the Marianas Trench in the western Pacific Ocean, setting a world record that survives today.

▶ JACQUES COUSTEAU
One of the world's most famous ocean explorers, Jacques Cousteau (1910–97) invented the aqualung in 1943 to help divers breathe underwater. It was an air tank connected to a face mask.

▲ DIVING BELL
Edmund Halley invented the diving bell in 1690. It consisted of a watertight barrel anchored to the sea floor by heavy weights. Barrels of air were lowered and connected to the bell to supply the divers with fresh air.

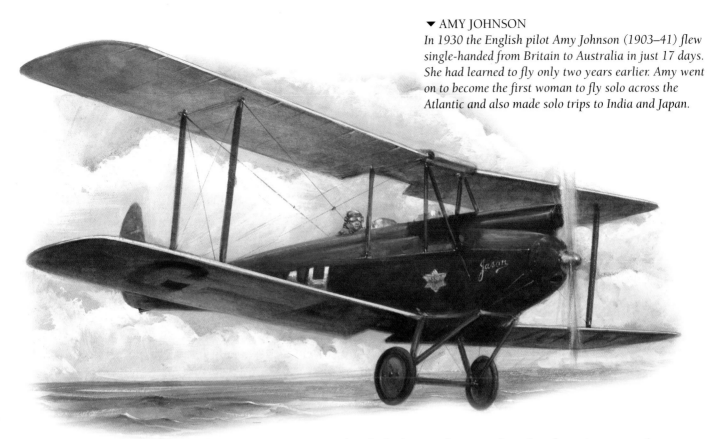

▼ AMY JOHNSON
In 1930 the English pilot Amy Johnson (1903–41) flew single-handed from Britain to Australia in just 17 days. She had learned to fly only two years earlier. Amy went on to become the first woman to fly solo across the Atlantic and also made solo trips to India and Japan.

air, surveying lands by airplane and producing detailed maps by aerial reconnaissance. For those expeditions still on foot, supplies and reinforcements could now be airlifted in, and any casualties flown out for medical treatment. As a result, explorers face less physical danger than they used to, and their emphasis has shifted away from exploration from its own sake toward exploration for scientific reasons. Today, teams of scientists investigate the impact of global warming in Antarctica, for example, or the effects of the climate change in the Pacific Ocean. They use highly complex scientific instruments and techniques, and have a support team ready to fly them out of danger at a moment's notice.

▶ MOUNT EVEREST
Climbing to the summit of the highest peak on Earth has always fascinated mountaineers. Mount Everest (29,000 feet) lies between Nepal and Tibet, and mountaineers found it a very difficult challenge. Thirteen expeditions tried to reach the summit before the New Zealander Sir Edmund Hillary (born 1919) and the Nepalese Tenzing Norgay (1914–86) succeeded on May 29, 1953. Within a year, most of the other major Himalayan peaks were also conquered by European mountaineers.

Key Dates

- 1903 Wright brothers' flight.

- 1909 Louis Blériot flies nonstop across the English Channel.

- 1919 Alcock and Brown cross the Atlantic.

- 1927 Charles Lindbergh crosses the Atlantic.

- 1930 Amy Johnson flies single-handed from Britain to Australia.

- 1953 Everest conquered.

- 1954 Italians climb K2—world's second-highest mountain.

- 1960 Jacques Piccard descends to record depths below the sea

Blasting into Space

ON OCTOBER 4, 1957 an aluminum sphere no bigger than a large beachball was launched into space by the USSR. It measured 23 inches across and had four antennae trailing behind it. It orbited the Earth once every 96 minutes. This was *Sputnik I*, the world's first artificial satellite, and it began a period of intense space exploration and discovery that continues to this day.

Modern rocket technology had made it possible to travel out of the Earth's atmosphere and into space. It then became easier to fly to the Moon and to examine our closest planet neighbors in the solar system. Scientists wanted to find out the answer to some of the oldest questions on Earth—is there life elsewhere in the universe?

▲ FLOATING IN SPACE
Astronauts are able to venture outside their spacecraft to do repairs or to help it dock with another craft. They must be tethered to their own craft to stop them from drifting off into space.

▲ LAUNCH SITE
A rocket needs huge power to lift it and its load off the launch pad. Once in space, the rocket is no longer needed and falls away, leaving the spacecraft or satellite to continue on its own.

▶ MOON LIVING
Astronauts lived in this lunar module when they landed on the Moon. When they were ready to leave, the module blasted off to rejoin the orbiting main spacecraft.

THE SPACE RACE
The former USSR launched the world's first satellite in 1957, beginning a space race with the U.S. that lasted until 1969. The Americans feared that the USSR would use space for military purposes, and wanted to prove that the U.S. was the world's leading superpower. The race ended when the U.S. landed a man on the Moon. Today the two countries cooperate on missions.

▲ DOG IN SPACE
The first living creature in space—a Russian dog named Laika—was launched into space on board *Sputnik 2* in November 1957 and remained in orbit for two days. Many other creatures, such as monkeys and jellyfish, have made the trip.

▶ SPACE FOOD
Prepackaged, specially prepared food is taken on space missions. It requires heat or water to make it edible. Fresh foods are rarely taken because they do not keep well.

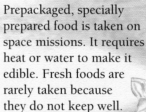

◀ YURI GAGARIN
The first human to go into space was the Russian cosmonaut Yuri Gagarin (1934–68). On April 12, 1961 he orbited the Earth once while on board *Vostok I*, returning to Earth after 108 minutes in space. Gagarin became a hero throughout the USSR and was given many national honors.

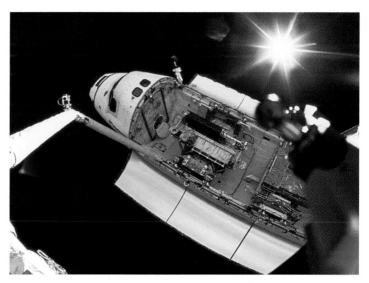

◀ MOON WALK

Neil Armstrong became the first person to walk on the Moon on July 24, 1969 . He said, "That's one small step for man, one giant leap for mankind." Today, only 12 astronauts, including Buzz Aldrin, pictured, have been there.

▼ WORKING IN SPACE

The space shuttle is launched like a rocket, but returns to Earth like a plane. It can then be used again. In space the shuttle is used for launching, repairing, and recovering satellites and for further scientific research.

How and when were the Earth, and the universe itself, formed? They also wanted to explore the nearest planets and find out more about them.

This combination of technology and curiosity has sent men to the Moon and unmanned spacecraft to examine every planet in the solar system. Weather, communication and spy satellites now orbit the Earth in huge numbers. At least two new satellites are launched each week. Orbiting telescopes send back detailed information about distant stars, and permanent space stations enable astronauts to spend many months in space. Gradually a more complete picture is being built up about our solar system and its place in the universe, and new discoveries are made every year.

▼ THE HUBBLE TELESCOPE

In 1990 the *Hubble* space telescope was launched into orbit high above the Earth. It sends back X-ray and other photographs free from interference or distortion by the Earth's atmosphere.

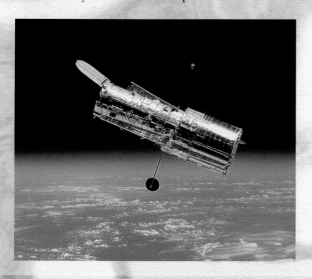

▲ THE GALAXY

The exploration of space has told scientists more about our own galaxy (the Milky Way) and the millions of stars it contains. By observing how these stars are born and die, scientists have begun to understand how the universe itself was formed.

Key Dates

- 1957 Russians launch *Sputnik I*, the first satellite, into space.

- 1960 First weather, navigation, communication satellites (U.S.).

- 1961 Soviet cosmonaut Yuri Gagarin is first person in space.

- 1966 *Luna IX* lands on Moon.

- 1969 Neil Armstrong is first person to walk on the Moon.

- 1970 USSR launches *Salyut I*, the world's first space station.

- 1981 *Columbia* space shuttle.

- 1983 *Pioneer 10* is first space probe to leave solar system.

GAZETEER OF

PEOPLE
AND
PLACES

———

GLOSSARY

People & Places

Agincourt, site of the battle in France where the English inflict a decisive defeat on the French in A.D. 1415

Alexander the Great, king of Macedonia 336–323 B.C., creates a huge empire in the Middle East, Near East and northwestern India

Amundsen, Roald, Norwegian explorer, becomes the first man to reach the South Pole in A.D. 1911

Angkor Wat, site of the temple city in Cambodia that was built from A.D. 1113 as the core of the Khmer empire

Arbela, site of the battle in Middle East where the army of Alexander the Great in 331 B.C. inflicts a decisive defeat on the Persians

Armstrong, Neil, American astronaut, becomes the first human to set foot on the Moon in A.D. 1969

Asoka, ruler of the Mauryan empire 269–232 B.C., establishes Buddhism as the state religion of the Mauryan empire

Athens, site in eastern Greece that is the core of the city-state generally considered to have been the most advanced of the Classical period

Augustus, emperor of Rome 27 B.C.–A.D. 14, establishes the Roman Empire as successor to the Roman republic

Babylon, city on the Euphrates River in Mesopotamia that is the capital of a great empire from about 1700 B.C.

Balboa, Vasco de, Spanish soldier, becomes the first European to see the Pacific Ocean after crossing central America in A.D. 1513

Barents, Willem, Dutch explorer, seeks to find the northeast passage around northern Russia to the Pacific Ocean, in several voyages between A.D. 1594 and A.D. 1597, but dies in the process

Bering, Vitus, Danish explorer, crosses to Siberia by land and then explores the northeastern and northwestern coasts of the Pacific Ocean in Siberia and Alaska in voyages between A.D. 1725 and A.D. 1741

Bruce, James, British explorer, seeks the source of the Nile River and discovers Lake Tana, source of the Blue Nile, between A.D. 1768 and A.D. 1773

Burke, Robert O'Hara, Australian explorer, collaborates with William Wills in the first crossing of Australia from south to north in A.D. 1860–1861

Burton, Richard, British explorer, collaborates with John Speke in an exploration of The Great Lakes of central Africa, between A.D. 1857 and A.D. 1858

Cabot, John, English explorer, discovers the island of Newfoundland off Canada and claims it for England in A.D. 1497

Carthage, site of the most important Phoenician colony in North Africa

Cartier, Jacques, French explorer, reaches the estuary of the St. Lawrence River in eastern Canada and surveys the area in A.D. 1534 before moving up the river to reach in A.D. 1536 the point where Montreal was established

Champlain, Jacques de, French explorer, between A.D. 1603 and A.D. 1615 explores along the rivers and lakes of eastern Canada as far as Lakes Huron and Ontario, and also establishes Quebec

Chandragupta, ruler of the Mauryan empire 322–301 B.C., creates a great empire extending over much of modern India and Pakistan

Charlemagne, Frankish leader, starts the process of European reunification (after the fall of Rome) during A.D. 768 and in A.D. 800 and is crowned as the first emperor of the Holy Roman Empire

Clark, William, American soldier explorer, collaborated with Meriwether Lewis in the exploration of the northeastern United States between A.D. 1804 and A.D. 1806 to find a route from the upper reaches of the Missouri River to the Pacific Ocean at the mouth of the Columbia River

Columbus, Christopher, Spanish explorer of Italian birth, in A.D. 1492 becomes the first man of the modern era to sail across the Atlantic Ocean and reach the islands of the Caribbean Sea's northeastern edge

Constantinople, capital of the Byzantine Empire until its capture by the Turks in A.D. 1453

Cook, James, British naval officer and explorer, sails around New Zealand and maps the eastern coast of Australia in the course of his first voyage of exploration in A.D. 1768–1777. The second voyage in A.D. 1772–1775 explores Antarctica and the third in A.D. 1776–1779 results in the discovery of the Hawaiian Islands

Cortes, Hernan, Spanish soldier, conquers and destroys the Aztec empire in Mexico by his victory at Tenochtitlán in A.D. 1521

Crécy, site of the battle in France where the English in A.D. 1346 inflict a decisive defeat on the French

Damascus, major Moslem city in Syria celebrated for the manufacture of high-grade steel for use in the construction of weapons

Darius I, king of the Persians 522–486 B.C., extends the Persian Empire to include parts of Egypt and India to the west and east, but fails to conquer Greece

Dias, Bartolemeu, Portuguese explorer, becomes the first European to round the Cape of Good Hope at the southern tip of Africa in A.D. 1487–1488, and so reach the Indian Ocean

Dordogne, region in southwest France where important Cro-Magnon (prehistoric people) remains are discovered

Drake, Francis, English explorer, completes the second voyage around the world between A.D. 1577 and A.D. 1580

Eric the Red, Viking explorer, sails from Norway in A.D. 982 and reaches Greenland off the northeast coast of North America

Eyre, Edward, Australian explorer, walks along the south coast of Australia from Adelaide to Albany in A.D. 1840–1841

Fa Hsien, Buddhist monk A.D. 399, travels from China to India and Sri Lanka for the study of Buddhism

Franklin, John, English explorer, makes the first major effort to find the northwest passage around the north of Canada, starting in A.D. 1845 but dies in the ice during A.D. 1847

Frobisher, Martin, English explorer, reaches Baffin Island off the northwestern coast of Canada in A.D. 1576 as he seeks the entrance to a northwestern passage to the Pacific Ocean

Gagarin, Yuri, Soviet air force officer and cosmonaut, becomes the first human to enter space in A.D. 1961

Gama, Vasco da, Portuguese explorer, becomes the first European of the modern era to reach India by ship in A.D. 1497–1498

Genghis Khan, ruler of the Mongols, starts the conquest of northern China that is complete by A.D. 1234

Great Zimbabwe, site of the city in Zimbabwe that is the capital of one of the first civilizations of southern Africa

Hall, Charles, American explorer, makes three voyages to try to reach the North Pole on foot, and dies on the last in A.D. 1871 after coming closer than any man before him

Hammurabi, king of Babylon 1792–1750 B.C., creator of a major law code and conqueror of Mesopotamia

Han Wu Di, emperor of China 140–87 B.C., extends the empire of the Han dynasty to its greatest extent after defeating the northern nomads

Hanno, Carthaginian of about 500 B.C., sails round the coast of West Africa on a voyage of discovery

Hartog, Dirk, Dutch explorer, sails too far south on his way to the East Indies in A.D. 1615 and discovers the western coast of Australia

Henry the Navigator, prince of Portugal, spurs the pace of maritime exploration by establishing a school of navigation in A.D. 1419

Hillary, Edmund, New Zealand explorer and mountaineer, becomes the first person, with the Nepalese Tenzing Norgay, to reach the summit of Mount Everest in A.D. 1953

Hudson, Henry, English explorer, in A.D. 1610 sails into the vast bay in northern Canada now named after him, but his crew later mutinies and return home without him

Ibn Battuta, Islamic traveler, explores the limits of the Islamic world in voyages between A.D. 1325 and A.D. 1353, reaching western and eastern limits at Mali in West Africa and Xiamen in China

Jansz, Willem, Dutch explorer, sails south from the East Indies in A.D. 1605 and discovers the northeast coast of Australia

Jayavarman II, king of the Khmer A.D. 802–850, creates the Khmer empire that comes to rule much of the southeast Asian area now known as Cambodia (Kampuchea)

Jericho, site in the Levant where the first known domesticated grains are grown

Jolliet, Louis, French explorer, collaborates with Marquette in the exploration of the upper parts of the Mississippi River area in A.D. 1672

Julius Caesar, killed 44 B.C., is the last great leader of the Roman republic and also a great soldier who conquers Gaul and launches raids into Germany and Britain

Khusrau Parviz, king of Sassanian Persia A.D. 614–628, conquers Syria and Egypt and is the last of the major Sassanian rulers

Knossos, site of the city in Crete that is the capital of the Minoan Empire that ended in about 1450 B.C.

Lascaux, site in France for important cave paintings

Leif Eriksson, Viking explorer, sails from Greenland in A.D. 992 and establishes a small settlement at Vinland on the North American continent

Lepanto, site in the Mediterranean off which, in A.D. 1571, an Austrian fleet inflicts a decisive defeat on a Turkish fleet

Lewis, Meriwether, American administrator and explorer, collaborates with William Clark in the exploration of the northeastern United States between A.D. 1804 and A.D. 1806 to find a route from the upper reaches of the Missouri River to the Pacific Ocean at the mouth of the Columbia River

Lindbergh, Charles, American aviator, becomes the first man to make a nonstop solo flight between two cities on opposite sides of the North Atlantic Ocean in A.D. 1927

Livingstone, David, British explorer and missionary, explores southern Africa and travels down the Zambesi River during A.D. 1841–1856, in the process discovering the Victoria Falls. Between A.D. 1858 and A.D. 1864 he explores Lake Nyasa and the east coast of Africa

Magellan, Ferdinand, Spanish explorer, departs in A.D. 1519 for the first voyage around the world, completed in A.D. 1522 by Juan de Elcano after Magellan's death in A.D. 1521

Marathon, site in eastern Greece where the Greeks in 490 B.C. check a Persian invasion

Marquette, Father Jacques, French explorer and missionary, explores the upper part of the Mississippi River area in A.D. 1672 and discovers a route linking the Great Lakes and the river

Meadowcroft Rock Shelter, site in Pennsylvania of the first known settlement in North America

Mecca, city in Arabia and birthplace of Mohammed, founder of the Islamic religion

Mohammed, dies A.D. 632, creator of Islam as the major religion of the peoples of Arabia, who expand in a torrent of conquest

Nebuchadnezzar, king of Babylon 605–562 B.C., creates the fabled hanging gardens of Babylon and reigns over the most sophisticated city of the Near East

Nineveh, city near the Tigris River in Mesopotamia that is the capital of the Assyrian Empire from about 880 B.C.

Nordenskjold, Nils, Finnish explorer, completes the first passage around the northeast passage into the Pacific (1878–1879)

Offa, king of Mercia in the 8th century A.D., creates one of the strongest countries in England and builds Offa's Dyke to protect his kingdom from Welsh raids

Olduvai Gorge, site in northern Tanzania where many prehistoric remains are found.

Park, Mungo, British explorer, explores the Niger River in West Africa between A.D. 1795 and A.D. 1806

Peary, Robert, American explorer, becomes the first man to reach the North Pole, A.D. 1909

Pericles, ruler of Athens 443–429 B.C., lifts the city-state to its peak of political and economic power, and is also responsible for the modernization of the city into a place of exceptional beauty

Persepolis, city in southeast Iran that is the capital of the Persian Empire from about 835 B.C.

Pizarro, Francisco, Spanish soldier, conquers and destroys the Inca Empire of Peru in A.D. 1532

Polo, Marco, Italian explorer and trader, travels overland to China and undertakes extensive travels in the Chinese Empire between A.D. 1271–1295

Puritjarra Rock Shelter, early site in the Northern Territory for inhabitation of Australia

Pytheas, Greek astronomer of Massilia (Marseilles), in 330 B.C. sails on a voyage of discovery to the north, rounding the British Isles and possibly reaching southern Norway or Iceland

Rome, site of the city in the western part of central Italy that was the capital of the Roman Empire

Ross, James, British explorer, surveys much of the coast of Antarctica in a voyage in A.D. 1841

Saladin, Muslim leader in the Middle East, in A.D. 1187 retakes Jerusalem from the Crusaders and overruns most of their conquests in the Middle East

Salle, Robert de La, French explorer, explores the Great Lakes from A.D. 1678 to A.D. 1680 and becomes the first European to travel down the Mississippi River to the sea

Sargon, king of Assyria in the late 8th century B.C., builds Khorsabad as the capital of the Assyrian Empire at its peak

Scott, Captain Robert, British naval officer and explorer, is the leader of the second expedition to reach the South Pole in A.D. 1912, but dies on the way back to the coast

Soto, Hernando de, Spanish explorer, surveys Florida and the northern edge of the Gulf of Mexico in A.D. 1541, and in the process becomes the first European to see the Mississippi River

Speke, John, British explorer, collaborates with Richard Burton in an exploration of The Great Lakes of central Africa, between A.D. 1857 and A.D. 1858, and discovers that Lake Victoria is the source of the White Nile

Stanley, Henry Morton, Welsh-born American newspaper reporter and explorer, finds Livingstone in A.D. 1872, and in A.D. 1874–1877 travels down the Congo River to the sea

Stonehenge, site in England of the world's largest monolith structure

Stuart, John, Australian explorer, makes the first crossing of Australia from north to south on his third attempt in A.D. 1862, setting off from Darwin and arriving in Adelaide

Sturt, Charles, Australian explorer, crosses the Blue mountains in A.D. 1828–1830 and finds the upper reaches of the Darling River before moving down the Murray River to the sea. He later explored central Australia in A.D. 1844–1845

Sumeria, region in Mesopotamia that sees the rise of one of the world's first civilizations

Tasman, Abel, Dutch explorer, sails from the Indian Ocean into the Pacific Ocean in A.D. 1642–1643, in the process discovering Tasmania and seeing New Zealand and the Fiji Islands. In the following year he maps the northern coast of Australia

Thule, name of what the ancients regarded as the northernmost land of the world, probably Iceland

Torres, Luis, Spanish explorer, proves that Australia is a vast island in A.D. 1607 by finding the sea passage between northern Australia and New Guinea

Troy, site of a city in eastern Turkey that the Greeks besiege for 10 years in the Trojan War of about 1200 B.C.

Willoughby, Hugh, English explorer, reaches Novaya Zemlya off the northern coast of Russia in A.D. 1554

Wills, William, Australian explorer, collaborates with Robert Burke in the first crossing of Australia from south to north in A.D. 1860–1861

Yamato, ruling clan of Japan about A.D. 350, create the first unified control of the Japanese islands

Yangtze Delta, region at the mouth of the Yangtze River in which rice is first grown

Glossary

Amphitheater
A circular or oval open-air theater, with seats arranged around a central area.

Aqueduct
A bridge carrying a canal for transporting water.

Archaeology
The study of the remains of past societies.

Artillery
Large weapons that need transport to move them around the battlefield and a crew of soldiers to use them.

Astrolabe
Navigation instrument used by sailors to measure the height of the sun at noon, thus giving the ship's latitude.

Bayonet
A blade attached to the end of a musket, named after the French town of Bayonne.

Bronze Age
Period in which the use of bronze for making tools and weapons is well established.

Burial mound
Artificial earth mound containing graves.

Celts
People who lived in central and western Europe during the Iron Age, just before these areas were occupied by the Romans.

Civilization
A settled society that has developed writing, organized religion, trade, grand buildings and a form of government.

Crusade
A military expedition launched from Christian Europe to attempt to recover the Holy Land from Muslim rule.

Cuirass
Armor for the front and back of the upper body, originally made from leather.

Cuneiform
A type of writing that uses wedge-shaped figures, carved with a special tool. It developed in Mesopotamia from about 3000 B.C.

Earthwork
Bank or rampart made of earth. They were usually for defensive purposes.

Emplacement
The position of an artillery gun on the battlefield or outside a besieged castle.

Halstatt
The first stage of the Iron Age in Europe, named after an Iron Age site in Austria.

Hieroglyphics
A type of picture writing used in ancient Egypt.

Hoplite
A heavily armed infantry soldier from ancient Greece.

Hunter-gatherers
People who live on meat that they hunt and plants that they gather.

Ice Age

Period during which the temperature was much lower than today, and when large parts of Earth's surface were covered in ice and snow.

Infantry

The soldiers who fight on foot with handheld weapons.

Iron Age

Period during which iron became the main metal used for producing tools and weapons.

Irrigation

Using canals or watercourses to bring water to dry land so that crops can grow.

Jousting

Sporting combat between two knights on horseback. Jousts were often social gatherings.

Kiln

A furnace or an oven in which pottery is fired or baked.

La Tène

Style of art produced by the Celtic peoples of Europe, known for its use of beautiful curved and abstract designs.

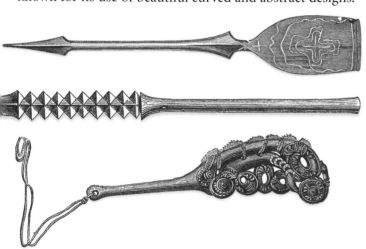

Legion

The main unit of the Roman army. Roman soldiers were called legionaries because they belonged to a legion.

Medieval

Term describing people, events and objects from the time known as the Middle Ages.

Megalith

Large stone, standing alone or used as part of a tomb, stone circle or other monument.

Mesopotamia

The fertile area of land between the Tigris and Euphrates Rivers in the Middle East.

Middle Ages

Period in history that lasted from around A.D. 800 to 1400.

Mummy

A mummified or dead body like those of ancient Egypt.

Neolithic

The New Stone Age. The period when people began to farm but were still using stone tools.

Nomads

A group of people who move around in search of food, water and land for grazing animals.

Obelisk

A tall, four-sided tapering pillar, usually made of stone, and with a pyramid-shaped top.

Obsidian

A naturally occurring glass-like substance formed in volcanoes. Used in the same way as flint for making tools of the prehistoric period. It varies in different places around the world depending on when people began to develop writing.

Oracle

A means by which ancient peoples could contact the gods to ask for advice or questions about the future. An oracle could be a place or a person.

Pack ice

Ice floating on a sea or ocean which has become packed together in huge sheets.

Papyrus

A kind of paper made from layers of papyrus reeds.

Pharaoh

A title for the later kings of ancient Egypt. The word pharaoh means "great house."

Pommel

The weighted end of the handle of a broad sword, used to deliver a hammer blow in battle.

Quadrant

Navigation instrument, consisting of a quarter-circle marked in degrees. This was used by sailors to calculate the angle of the sun and thus figure out the ship's latitude.

Samurai

A word first used to describe the imperial guard of ancient Japan. Later it was used to describe the warrior class in general. Warriors could only be Samurai by birth.

Seal

An engraved disk used to leave an impression on soft wax. Government documents are sealed to show that they are official.

Shrine

A sacred place or container where religious objects or images may be kept.

Silk Road

The ancient overland route between China and Europe, used mainly by merchants traveling on camels.

Spanish Armada

An armada is a fleet of battle ships. The Spanish Armada was a fleet sent by Philip of Spain that tried to invade England in 1588 but was not successful. The fight was about Spain's rich territories in southern America.

Spartan

Word describing people, events and objects from Sparta, a city-state of ancient Greece.

Squire

A trainee knight about 14 years old. He carried the shield and equipment of his instructor, attended to his horse and defended him in battle. He was taught courtly as well as military skills.

Stone Age

Period of prehistoric human culture when stones and flints were used to make tools and weapons.

Swiss Guard

Group of Swiss soldiers chosen to guard the Pope. The tradition was begun in the early 1500s. Today, a Papal Swiss Guard is still used to guard the Pope.

Tournament

Armed contest between knights, fought for honor and ceremony.

Tribe

A group of people descended from the same family or sharing the same language and culture, with a recognized leader.

Trireme

Warship used by ancient Greeks. Its name comes from the Greek word for "three" and "oar" because it was powered by men rowing in three ranks.

Ziggurat

A pyramid-shaped temple built by the ancient Babylonians.

Index

A

Africa 7, 200
  civilizations 67, 92–3
  European exploration 204–5,
    230–3
  hominids 12, 16–17, 18–19, 25
  hunter-gatherers 18–19, 56, 57
  post-Ice Age 38–9, 56
  rock art 40–1, 44
Alaska 218, 219
Alexander the Great 71, 79, 80,
  104, 105, 151, 168, 190
America 8, 9, 34–5, 44–5, 54–5
  Central 8, 54, 55, 123, 124–5,
    207, 208
  North 34–6, 38, 54, 120–1, 194,
    212–13, 220–1, 240
  South 8, 34–5, 40, 55, 122, 196,
    207–11, 228–9

Amundsen, Roald 215, 236–7
Antarctica 225, 236–7
Arabs 198–9, 230
Arctic Ocean 214, 216, 217, 225,
  234, 235
armies
  Assyrian 76, 77
  Chinese 112
  Greek 102, 104
  Hittite 76
  Islamic 82

  Mayan 124, 125
  Mycenaean 96
  Persian 78, 80
  Roman 108
armor 144–6, 148–9, 150, 153
art 32, 33, 40–1, 44, 57, 66
Asia 52–3, 190–1, 199, 200–1,
  216–7, 218–9
Assyrians 76, 77
Atlantic Ocean 206–7, 212
Australia 32–3, 41, 56–7,
  222–7, 238
Australopithecines 16–17
Aztecs 208–9, 211

B

Babylon 74–5
battering ram 77, 166, 167, 172
battles
  Agincourt 129, 134, 135, 149
  Arbela 151
  Crécy 134
  Flodden 139
  Hastings 130, 144
  Hydaspes 151
  Issus 105
  Lepanto 177, 179
  Maiden Castle 171
  Marathon 183
  Mylae 180
  Poitiers 134
  Salamis 176–7
  Sluys 177
  Waterloo 132–3
bone carvings 24, 28, 29, 30
bone tools 26, 28, 38, 62
bone weapons 28, 30, 34, 38

bow 134–5, 153, 156, 162, 165
Britain 9, 36, 38, 60, 149, 189
bronze 8, 13, 58–9, 64
Buddhism 86, 87, 191, 218, 219
burial 14–15, 22–3, 47, 53, 60
Burton, Richard 230–1

C

Caesar, Julius 108, 164
Canada 212–3, 214–5, 220
cannon 162, 174–5, 181
carving 13, 24, 28, 30, 36, 47
castles 158–63, 166–73

catapult 170, 171
cavalry 141, 152–3, 154–5, 156–7
cave paintings 26–7, 30–1, 33
chain mail 144, 145, 156
Chandragupta Maurya 86, 87
chariot 72, 76, 77, 98, 154–5
chauffron 153, 156
China 9, 20–1, 48–9, 52–3, 65, 71, 110–15, 190–1, 200–1, 218
Christianity 187, 195, 209, 218
civilization 7, 66–7
Clovis culture 13, 34, 35
coinage 103, 104, 112

colonization
  in Africa 232–3
  in America 209, 213, 220
  in Australia 226
  by Phoenicians/Greeks 188
  by Polynesians 196
  by Vikings 195
Columbus, Christopher 206–7
Cook, James 224–5
copper 8, 13, 58–9
Crete 94–5, 96
crossbow 134–5, 162, 165
"crow" 168–9, 180, 181
Crusades 202, 203

D

Darius I 78, 79, 151, 183
De Balboa, Vasco 208, 209
Dezhnev, Semyon 216, 217, 219
Drake, Francis 211, 222

E

education
  Babylon 74
  China 114
  Greece 100, 102
  Islam 82

Egypt 7, 71, 76, 88–91, 104, 188
Etruscans 98–9, 141
Euphrates River 7, 66
Europe 50–1, 189, 190–1, 192, 202–3
  Bronze Age 59
  civilization 67
  Cro-Magnons 23, 26
  farming 44, 45, 50–1
  hominids 19, 20, 21, 25, 27
  Ice Age 28, 29, 30–1, 37
  Iron Age 64–5
  lake villages 62–3
  megaliths 60–1
  Neanderthals 22, 23, 27
Everest, Mount 9, 239

F

farming 6, 7, 8, 70–1

Fertile Crescent 42–3, 46, 66

fire 12, 18–19, 28

fish 13, 28, 36, 57, 62, 94, 116

fossils 16, 17, 19, 34

France 9, 20, 22, 26, 30, 31, 37, 60, 220

funeral customs, 71, 72, 88, 90, 102, 117, 120, 121

G

Gama, Vasco da 204, 205

Genghis Khan 129, 156–7, 200–1

goddess figures 30, 31, 47

gold 92, 208, 210, 211, 227

Great Lakes 213, 220, 221

Great Wall of China 112–3, 164, 165

Greeks 7, 8, 79, 96–7, 98, 100–5, 128, 172, 189

gunpowder 142–3, 174–5

H

Hadrian's Wall 164–5

Han China 114–15

Hannibal 150, 151, 152, 182

Henry VIII 134, 163, 178, 179

Hinduism 86, 118

Hittites 74, 76, 77

Hominids 6, 12, 16–17, 18–19, 20–7

horse 145, 152–7, 182

hunter-gatherers 6, 18–19, 24–5, 29, 36, 50, 56–7

hunting 7, 9, 17–21, 24, 28–9, 36–7, 77, 85, 90, 106

I

Ibn Battuta 198, 199

Ice Age 12, 13, 28–9, 30–1, 34, 36–7

Iceland 189, 194, 195

Incas 208, 209

India 41, 52, 53, 67, 86–7, 191, 199, 205, 218

Indian Ocean 199, 201, 205, 222

Indus Valley 67, 70, 84–5, 104

Iraq 23, 66–7

Iron 8, 13

Iron Age 64–5

Islam 82–3, 198–9

Israel 23, 24, 29, 39

J

Japan 116–17, 218, 219

Jesuits 218, 219, 220

jewelry 14, 32, 52, 57, 58–9, 63, 64, 66

K

Khmers 118–19

Knossos 94, 95

Kon-Tiki 196, 197

Kublai Khan 200, 201

L

La Salle, Robert de 220, 221

Lewis, Meriwether 220–1

Lindisfarne Priory 192, 195

Livingstone, David 232–3

M

Magellan, Ferdinand 210–11, 222

mammoth 13, 26, 28, 30, 34, 38

Maya 124

Mediterranean 188, 192, 195

Mesopotamia 7, 12, 13, 66–7, 72, 73, 74, 76
metalworking 8, 58–9, 64–5
Mexico 13, 208, 209, 211, 220
Middle East 38–9, 45, 47, 64, 188, 195, 198, 199, 202
Minoan civilization 94–5, 132
Mohammed 82, 198, 199

N
Native Americans 212, 220
navigation 187, 194, 196, 199, 204–5
Neanderthals 12, 22–3, 24

O
Olmecs 13, 70, 123

P
Pacific Ocean 9, 196–7, 211, 216, 217, 218, 222–5
Persians 75, 78–81, 104, 105, 128, 190
Peru 196, 208–9
pharaohs 88, 89, 90–1
Phoenicians 188–9
pilgrimage 198, 199, 202, 230
Pizarro, Francisco 208–9

Polo, Marco 201
Polynesians 9, 196–7
Portugal 9, 192, 204–5, 210, 230
pottery 6, 42, 47, 48–9, 50, 51, 52, 62, 66

Q
Qin China 112–13

R
rock art 32, 33, 35, 40–41, 57
Romans 8, 71, 99, 100, 106–9, 190, 192–3
Russia 195, 216–17, 218–19, 240

S
Scott, Robert 236, 237
sculpture 26, 30, 66
shelters 13, 16, 20, 26, 29, 32, 35, 36, 39
shield 146–7, 167, 168
ships and boats 32, 33, 36, 55, 66, 186–7
Siberia 34, 35, 36, 39, 216–7, 218, 219
siege weapons 166–9, 180

slavery 176, 178, 179, 230–1
South Pole 224, 236–7
Spain 192, 199, 206–7, 210, 220
Sparta 100, 102, 103
Sumerians 67, 70, 72–3
sword 136, 137, 138–9, 153, 157

T
Tibet 218, 219, 239
Tigris River 7, 66, 81
tools 16, 17, 19, 20, 21, 22, 26, 36, 39, 62
trade 6–7, 8, 46–7, 66, 70–1, 98–9, 186–8, 190–1, 194–5, 198–9, 202–5, 212

V
Vandals 192, 193
Vespucci, Amerigo 207
Vikings 8, 146, 177, 179, 183, 194–5

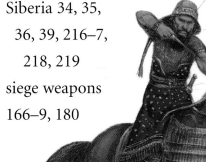

This edition is published by Southwater

Distributed in the UK by
The Manning Partnership
251–253 London Road East
Batheaston
Bath BA1 7RL
tel. 01225 852 727
fax 01225 852 852

Published in the USA by
Anness Publishing Inc.
27 West 20th Street
Suite 504
New York
NY 10011
fax 212 807 6813

Distributed in Canada by
General Publishing
895 Don Mills Road
400–402 Park Centre
Toronto, Ontario M3C 1W3
tel. 416 445 3333
fax 416 445 5991

Distributed in Australia by
Sandstone Publishing
Unit 1, 360 Norton Street
Leichhardt
New South Wales 2040
tel. 02 9560 7888
fax 02 9560 7488

Southwater is an imprint of Anness Publishing Limited
Hermes House, 88–89 Blackfriars Road, London SE1 8HA
tel. 020 7401 2077; fax 020 7633 9499

© Anness Publishing Limited 2000, 2001

Publisher: Joanna Lorenz
Managing Editor: Gilly Cameron Cooper
Editor: Nicole Pearson
Designer: Joyce Mason

Previously published in four separate volumes, *Prehistoric Peoples; Ancient Civilizations; Ancient
Weapons;* and *Exploration and Discovery.* These single volumes were produced by Miles Kelly
Publishing Limited.

10 9 8 7 6 5 4 3 2 1

PHOTOGRAPHIC ACKNOWLEDGMENTS
Page 14 (B/L) AKG Photo; 15 (B) Erich Lessing/ AKG London; 17 (B) Mary
Jelliffe/ Hutchison Library; 22 (B/R) E.T. Archive; 24 (B/R) E.T. Archive; 32 (B/L)
The Stock Market; 34 (B/R) The Stock Market; 41 (B) Mary Jelliffe/ Hutchison
Library; 44 (T/R) Erich Lessing/ AKG London; 47 (B) Ancient Art & Architecture
Collection; 50 (T/R) English Heritage Photo Library; 58 (M) English Heritage
Photo Library; 61 (T) English Heritage Photo Library; 64 (T/R) English Heritage
Photo Library; 67 (B/L) Southwell/ Hutchison Library; page 77 (B/L) Erich
Lessing/AKG London; 83 (T/L) Paul Almasy/AKG London; 86 (B/R) Jean-Louis
Nou/AKG Berlin; 104 (T/R) Mary Evans Picture Library; 117 (T/L) AKG London;
131 (T/L) Erich Lessing/AKG London; 138 (B/L) E.T. Archive; 24 (T/R) AKG
London; 154 (B/R) British Museum/E.T. Archive; 156 (T/R) E.T. Archive; 47 (B/L)
Mary Evans Picture Library; 175 (T/R) E.T. Archive; 57 (T/R) Mary Evans Picture
Library; 179 (B/L) Mary Evans Picture Library; 181 (B/L) E.T. Archive; 61 (T/R)
Mary Evans Picture Library; 218 (C/R) A. Zvoznikov/Hutchison Library; 220
(B/R); R. Francis/Hutchison Library; 222 (T/R) N.Haslam/Hutchison Library; 222
(B/L) E. Parker/ Hutchison Library; 222 (B/R) Hutchison Library; 224 (M/R)
Hutchison Library; 226 (T/L) The Stock Market; 226 (B/L) A. Singer/ Hutchison
Library; 228 (M) C. Pasini/ Hutchison Library; 229 (B/L) N. Smith/Hutchison
Library; 234 (B/L) Corbis; 235 (B) Popperfoto; 236 (B/R) Popperfoto; 238 (B/L)
Popperfoto; 238 (T/R) Popperfoto/ Reuter. All other pictures from Dover
Publications and Miles Kelly archives.